New Guide to

;

General Editor:
Daniel Meyer-Dinkgräfe

# New Guide to Poetry and Poetics

James Aitchison

Amsterdam - New York, NY 2013

Cover image: www.dreamstime.com

Cover design by Aart Jan Bergshoeff.

The paper on which this book is printed meets the requirements of "ISO 9706:1994, Information and documentation - Paper for documents - Requirements for permanence".

ISBN: 978-90-420-3763-2
ISSN: 1573-2193
E-Book ISBN: 978-94-012-1013-3
E-book ISSN: 1879-6044
© Editions Rodopi B.V., Amsterdam - New York, NY 2013
Printed in the Netherlands

*In Memory of My Guides*

*Edwin Morgan*
*Alastair Dunnett*
*I. F. Clarke*
*Keith Wright*

# Preface

For a period of ten years I taught English language and linguistics in a Scottish university and reviewed poetry for a national Scottish newspaper. In the same period I continued to write poems. My reading of works on psycholinguistics led me to works on neuroscience. After a few years I found that these works began to inform my reading of the poems I reviewed, and as I grew more aware of the language functions of the brain I found that the newly acquired knowledge, however limited, was relevant to my making of poems. I found, too, that this knowledge, along with my experience of writing poems, gave me new insights as a reader and reviewer of poetry and as an essayist on creativity and poetics.

I grew increasingly aware that this complex set of interactions – assimilating the findings of psycholinguists and neuroscientists, reading and reviewing poetry, writing poems and articles – was influencing my modes of thought and allowing me to make independent discoveries about the working of the poet's mind in the making of poems. I found that I was reading and reviewing poetry not as the academician I was when I published *The Golden Harvester: The Vision of Edwin Muir* in 1988 but as a writer of poems and a student of language. I regard these differing approaches not as opposites but alternates; I differ from the more traditional critic – the kind of critic I once was – in that I take account of the creative process and the findings of linguists and neuroscientists; I differ from literary theorists in that I reject ideologies, methodologies and orthodoxies.

Although neuroscience has not and will not transform the study of poetry and poetics as it has transformed psychology, psychiatry and some branches of philosophy, the subject is of interest to poets, critics and readers because it allows a new understanding of poetry and the making of poems.

These modes of thought and the language in which they are expressed superseded the works of Sigmund Freud and Carl Gustav Jung decades ago but in a study such as this Freud and Jung must be refuted yet again. Freud influenced the thinking of some twentieth-century poets and critics. Ted Hughes, a British Poet Laureate, applies a Freudian method of analysis in his major critical study, *Shakespeare and the Goddess of Complete Being* and in some of his collected essays in *Winter Pollen*. The eminent and otherwise liberal-minded critic, Lionel Trilling, uses Freudian concepts explicitly in his essay, 'Freud and Literature' in *The Liberal Imagination*. Some literary theorists still pay tribute to Freud. Even T. S. Eliot has Freudian moments, notably in his essay on Matthew Arnold in *The Use of Poetry and the Use of Criticism* when he writes of "sinking to the most primitive and forgotten, returning to the origins and bringing something back, seeking the beginning and end".

Jung still deserves attention because some of his writings, for example, 'On the Relation of Analytical Psychology to Poetry', 'On the Relation of Analytical Psychology to Literature', in 'The Problem of Types in Poetry' in *Psychological Types*, and in 'Psychology and Literature' in *Modern Man in Search of a Soul*, still have relevance today. In these works Jung is as sympathetic to the creative writer as Freud is hostile. Jung had an extended influence in Britain where his benign doctrines influenced the works of the psychiatrist and writer, Anthony Storr.

*New Guide to Poetry and Poetics* opens with discussions of the great motive forces in poetry and the arts: the creative impulse, the creative imagination and the sacred impulse. These discussions reveal the true nature of features of poetry and the creative mind that are often referred to but seldom adequately explained: voice, vision, the poetic self and, most importantly, the vital interactions of the poetic imagination with memory and the creative impulse. Without the creative impulse there can be no sincere expression of creativity. The creative imagination, like the creative impulse, cannot readily be induced through a course in creative writing. The impulse, which is largely nonconscious, cannot be expressed until it has been transduced and transmuted by the creative imagination, which is a largely conscious mental state or set of states. The starting points for my discussion of imagination are Coleridge's comments in *Biographia Literaria*, in his *Essays and Lectures*

on *Shakespeare*, his notebooks and his letters. The concept of the fluidity of the imagination is elegantly expressed by Shelley in *A Defence of Poetry* and by Kant in his statement, 'On the faculties of Mind that Constitute Genius' in the Second Book of *Critique of Judgment*.

The sacred impulse might once have been fused with the creative impulse in a single prehistoric mental state. Poetry is never wholly secular; it is often an expression of joy, sorrow, reverence and wonder. The sacred impulse might also be an expression of an allegiance to a particular faith or doctrine, but agnostic poets, too, are aware of a spiritual element in the creative process and the finished work of art. *New Guide to Poetry and Poetics* shows how poets' minds actually work in the making of poems and how, in the making of successive poems, poets form their voice and vision, extend the limits of their imagination and create a poetic self.

Chapters on rhythm and music in poetry illustrate ways in which the poet creates rhythmic and musical effects that influence the form, the structure and the meaning of a poem. In the course of these discussions, I dispel some long-held false assumptions about rhythm and music in poetry. *New Guide to Poetry and Poetics* also explores the nature of mysticism, myth, reality and meaning in poetry, and challenges the persistent widespread misconception that language is corruptible, and that from the middle of the twentieth century it has been corrupted by journalism and advertising.

My central argument is that the creative impulse and the creative imagination, like our capacity for language, are innate, and that poetry is a natural and inevitable outcome of language and mind. A parallel argument in *New Guide to Poetry and Poetics* is that poetics is a way of reading poems in order to discover some of the properties of poetry and the extent to which recurring features in poems reveal underlying principles of poetry. In discussing poetics, I show some ways in which concepts of what poetry is and what it does change over time.

Underlying these theses is my belief that language and mind are irreducible mysteries. They remain mysterious because we shall never know the origins of consciousness, mind and language, or the full extent of conscious and nonconscious minds. *New Guide to Poetry and Poetics* shows that, for the poet and the reader of poetry, mystery is not a problem to be solved but is a faculty of mind.

## Acknowledgements

I thank Daniel Meyer-Dinkgräfe, Robert Nye and Susan Marriott for their wise counsel on the content of this book. I acknowledge the kind permission of New Directions Publishing Corporation to quote from the work of Denise Levertov. I am grateful to the editors of *Acumen*, *Agenda*, *Chanticleer Magazine*, *The Dark Horse*, *The David Jones Journal*, *Equinox*, *The London Magazine*, *The Montreal Review* and *The Reader*. I am, as ever, indebted to my wife for creating and furnishing places where I can write.

A note on the text: All words in italic type are the original authors'.

# New Guide to Poetry and Poetics

## Contents

# 1

# The Creative Impulse

## How Poems Begin

A MONG POETS WRITING IN ENGLISH in the late twentieth century
there is general agreement about the first stage of the creative proc-
ess. Ted Hughes writes in 'Sylvia Plath: The Evolution of "Sheep in
Fog"' in *Winter Pollen*: (Hughes 1994: 207) "The first 'inspiration' of a
poem can be, and often is, without words, without images, without any
clear 'idea' of any sort. It need be no more than a dimly sensed mood or
tone". Hughes' use of inverted commas for "inspiration" and "idea" is
an acknowledgement of the ambiguity of these words. One of the aims
of this book is to make sense of these and other ambiguities. The first
stirring might be inspiration or it might be a false alarm; ideas, if they
exist at this stage of the creative process, are usually vague. Hughes'
contemporary, Thom Gunn, in an interview with John Haffenden in
*Viewpoints* says: (Gunn 1981: 35-6)

> I'm often asked about the genesis of my poems, and my answer is that
> I might begin just with an idea, really rather a general one [...] The
> thing you want to write about – whether a specific scene, incident, or
> idea – gestates, and the process of writing becomes an exploration. [...]
> But my point is that the subject of a poem can only gestate if you are
> obsessed by it in the first place.

That is, parts of the poet's conscious and nonconscious minds must be
possessed by the undifferentiated creative impulse; the impulse then
follows a period of development from conception to the act of writ-
ing, or from conception to the finished poem. In the same collection of
interviews, *Viewpoints*, Geoffrey Hill says this about the emergence of
a poem: (Hill 1981: 82) "It would be too fanciful to call it a Platonic
shape, but I can't think of any other way of describing that strange mix-

ture of nagging and calming allurement – sometimes clear, sometimes hazy but definitely unattainable for the time being". The first stirring reminds Hill of the metaphysical world of original, ideal forms that Plato says are the sources of all reality. Hill's mixture of nagging and calming allurement is similar to Gunn's period of possession and gestation. Hill continues: "Then, if I'm lucky, various germinal phrases or a hint of rhythm or something as minutely technical as the cadence of an enjambment will begin to stir, and for a time I have to be content to let the work grow by this process of accretion". The process is discontinuous, incoherent and partly nonconscious. In his next sentence Hill states: "Again, if I'm lucky, there will come a point when things begin to click into shape, and I can push ahead at a somewhat faster rate, but never very fast". When things click into shape the process becomes conscious as well as nonconscious; the largely nonconscious creative impulse continues, but it is now part of the conscious process of actual composition.

A poet with a different background, Iain Crichton Smith, who spent his boyhood on the Isle of Lewis, describes a similar experience in 'Structure in My Poetry' in *The Poet's Voice and Craft*. Smith describes the stirrings of the creative impulse: (Smith 1981: 106)

> I would feel first of all an urgency, a sense of lack, a stirring, an inchoate thing moving towards expression. At that stage there were no words, only a restlessness, a dynamic impulse seeking form, needing privacy. The words would come and from then only was it a case of trying to contain the inspiration by metre.

Poets who are aware of their mental states in the making of poems will recognize Crichton Smith's feeling of the need for privacy: until a poet feels that the poem is complete, creativity is a solitary and secret process; in its embryonic form the poem-in-the-making must be protected from the distractions of other mental processes and from external interests.

Seamus Heaney in 'Feeling into Words' in *Finders Keepers* describes the preliminary stage of the creative process in similar terms: (Heaney 2002: 21) "The crucial action is preverbal, to be able to allow the first alertness or come-hither, sensed in a blurred or incomplete way, to dilate and approach as a thought or a theme or a phrase". All five poets – American, English, Irish and Scottish – discuss the experience in remarkably similar terms: they are aware of an innate creative faculty that functions consciously and nonconsciously.

## Innateness: Conscious and Nonconscious

The innateness of our capacity for speech was reported by the French surgeon, Paul Pierre Broca, in the 1860s when he discovered that a patient's ability to speak was impaired after damage to a particular part of the cerebral cortex. In the 1870s the German neurologist, Carl Wernicke, discovered that a patient's ability to understand speech was impaired after damage to an area of the cortex adjacent to but different from the area identified by Broca. The terms, "Broca's area" and "Wernicke's area", are still sometimes used today.

Charles Darwin deduced the innateness of the language faculty after decades of observation and reflection. In the *Descent of Man and Selection in Relation to Sex* he writes: (Darwin 1981: 106) "The half-art and half-instinct of language still bears the stamp of its gradual evolution". Later he observes: (Darwin 1981: 390) "A great stride in the development of the intellect will have followed, as soon as, through a previous considerable advance, the half-art and half-instinct of language came into use". And in the *Expression of the Emotions in Man and Animals* Darwin states: (Darwin 1998: 63) "man has invented articulate language; if, indeed, the word *invented* can be applied to a process completed by innumerable steps, half-consciously made".

In the twentieth century the innateness of the language faculty began to be explored by neurosurgeons, notably Wilder Penfield, who sometimes practised open-skull surgery at the Montreal Neurological Institute from 1934 to 1960. And from the late twentieth century innateness has been recorded by successive generations of increasingly sensitive non-invasive scanning techniques, including electroencephalography (EEC), an adaptation of EEC known as transcranial magnetic stimulation, Positron Emission Tomography (PET), and Functional Magnetic Resonance Imaging (fMRI).

The linguist, Noam Chomsky, must have known of these machines when he was writing his Whidden Lecture, 'On Cognitive Capacity', published in *Reflections on Language*, but his viewpoint is theoretical, or psycho-philosophical, when he writes of language and mind: (Chomsky 1976: 23) "I want to consider mind (in the narrower or broader sense) as an innate capacity to form cognitive structures". And in 'Problems and Mysteries in the Study of Human Language' in *Reflections on Language* he writes: (Chomsky 1976: 137) "we may say that humans are innately endowed with a system of intellectual organization". In his later work, the Third Edition of *Language and Mind*, Chomsky states: (Chomsky 2006: 83) "Particularly in the case of language, it is natural to expect a close relation between innate properties of the mind and features of linguistic structure". In the final chapter of *Language and Mind* he expresses the concept, and biological fact, of innateness in fundamental terms. He writes of the acquisition and use of language and states: (Chomsky 2006: 175) "Call it the 'faculty of language' [...] This component is more or less on a par with the system of mammalian vision, insect navigation, or others".

Most poets know, if only intuitively, that the innate faculty is partly nonconscious. I use the term, "nonconscious", because "unconscious" is still associated with the work of Sigmund Freud and Carl Gustav Jung. The great achievement of Freud and Jung was to make us aware of hidden dimensions of our humanity; that is, they made us conscious of our nonconscious. Freud defied a prohibition of the prevailing culture: by discussing our sexuality he partly liberated us from sexual guilt while at the same time making his patients, and then his readers, accept personal responsibility for his and our breaching of taboos. But Freud reduced the complexity of the nonconscious to a rigid doctrine, as the next chapter, 'Jung, Freud and Creativity', will show.

Jung, by contrast, was concerned to discover the vastness of nonconsciousness and its natural, often peaceable, interaction with consciousness; his writings reconcile the two. More than half a century before the development of palaeontological dating techniques Jung deduced the millennial origin of humanity. Some poets find the mythogenic nature of some of Jung's work congenial, but poets today may find it difficult to follow Jung into his fields of alchemy, astrology and occultism. Jung's major work on the occult is *Psychology and Alchemy*, first published in 1944. Some of his letters to Freud in *The Freud/Jung Letters* reveal how he was drawn to the subject. In his letter of 8 May 1911 to Freud he writes: (Freud 1979: 223) "Occultism is another field we shall have to conquer [...] At the moment I am looking into astrology, which seems indispensable for a proper understanding of mythology. There are strange and wondrous things in these lands of darkness". And in his letter of 12 June 1911 to Freud he writes: (Freud 1979: 226) "My evenings are taken up very largely with astrology. I made horoscopic calculations in order to find a clue to the core of psychological truth". And in the next sentence he adds: "I dare say that we shall one day discover in astrology a good deal of knowledge that has been intuitively projected into the heavens". My later chapter, 'Visionary Poetry', will show that W. B. Yeats and Ted Hughes also cast horoscopes.

The human brain is the subject of intensive study in universities, hospitals and research institutes throughout the world. In the United Kingdom alone there are now, in the year 2013, departments of neurology in twenty-four universities and thirty hospitals. In addition, some departments of psychology in British universities conduct research in neurology and most departments take account of neuroscientists' findings. A problem for the lay person, and even for the specialist, is that there are more findings – research papers, conference lectures, books – than any one person can read. What makes it less difficult to keep pace with the torrents of information is that some of it is confirmation of the results of earlier experiments and some of it an extension of existing knowledge.

In academic and medical communities there is general agreement that there are different but interactive systems of mind, the conscious and the nonconscious, and that the conscious mind emerged from its nonconscious substrate, the brain. The psychologist, Guy Claxton, writes in *The Wayward Mind*: (Claxton 2005: 227) "Creative ideas, especially, explode into consciousness as insights, or sidle in as glimmerings and hunches, yet their 'feeling of rightness' cannot be justified by any conscious process". The psychologist, Merlin Donald, in *A Mind So Rare: The Evolution of Human Consciousness* states: (Donald 2001: 286-7) "The deep cultural unconscious exists in a representational limbo that is temporarily uncaptured. The cognitive unconscious, on the other hand, is the golem, the automaton world of instincts and zombies". The word, "zombies", is part of the argot used by some neuroscientists. The term, "cognitive unconscious", suggests a level of nonconsciousness that is available for cognition, that is, for consciousness.

Poets who are interested in how the mind works during the creative process can make independent observations. Two of our main faculties in the making of poems are, of course, perception and memory. We know that some acts of perception are nonconscious: in writing a poem we sometimes find that we recall things we did not know we knew because we were not conscious of perceiving them at the time. Robert Frost expresses the experience neatly in that statement in 'The Figure a Poem Makes', the preface to *The Complete Poems of Robert Frost*: (Frost 1951: 18) "For me the initial delight is the surprise of remembering something I didn't know I knew". And he adds: "The impressions most useful to my purpose seem always those I was unaware of and so made no note of at the time". A memory, too, is nonconscious until it is recalled, and we know that our vast store of memories, like our store of knowledge, is unactivated until the moment of recall. The term, "unactivated", seems more appropriate than "inactive". We know that our nonconscious memories change over time and come back to us with a semantic, emotional or moral charge that is different from the original experience. As poets we also know that we misremember, sometimes wilfully, in shaping memories into poems.

Unless an experience is wholly unprecedented, perception and cognition seem simultaneous. In making poems we sometimes experience two or more feelings, thoughts, words or half-formed words at the same time. Our linear writing system requires us to treat items of ideation serially: a single word, a single line at a time; but we feel a plurality. A commonplace example of the simultaneity of perception and cognition is the sight and sound of a fast-moving police car: we see the colour of the bodywork and the colour of the flashing light; we hear the sound of the engine and the wailing of the siren. But the neurosurgeon, V. S. Ramachandran, says in 'The Artful Brain', the third in his series of BBC Reith Lectures in 2003, updated in November 2009: (Ramachandran 2009: 6 in transcript) "It's a well known fact that you can't have two overlapping patterns of neural activity simultaneously. Even though you've got one hundred billion nerve cells, you can't have two overlapping patterns".

Merlin Donald makes an even more drastic assertion of neural nescience than Ramachandran. In *A Mind So Rare* Donald states: (Don-

ald 2001: 178) "The conscious brain can never become aware of itself
– [...] There is simply *no* direct awareness of the brain's activity and
no possibility of achieving it." Perhaps poets misunderstand. Perhaps
we delude ourselves when we become acutely aware of a voice that is
not the same as our everyday voice, and aware of a self – a self without
personality – with whom we commune in the making of a poem. We are
acutely aware of being aware of our search for a missing word, aware
of a change of mood or feeling or thought between one line of a poem
and another.

We are aware, too, of prelinguistic and protolinguistic processes that
precede the arrival of words in our minds. The word, "prelingual", was
coined in the late nineteenth century, and "prelinguistic" in the mid-
twentieth century to refer to cognition and ideation – feelings, images,
ideas, fleeting thoughts – that have not been formulated into words.
The two terms are also used to refer to the stage in human evolution
just before the emergence of language, and the stage in a child's de-
velopment that immediately precedes his or her use of language. In the
creative process, the prelingual state is an initial stirring followed by a
period of inchoate, fragmentary neuronal activity, an experience that is
partly nonconscious. Another coinage of the mid-twentieth century is
"proto-language", a hypothetical first or parent language, now lost in
time, from which actual languages have evolved. The coinages, "pro-
tolingual" and "protolinguistic", are here applied to the conscious and
semi-conscious mental activity that is incipiently linguistic but has not
reached that stage in the processing of language at which words assume
their forms or meanings.

If poets ignore the creative impulse at this initial stage, or if they
stifle it by engaging in some other activity, especially a semi-creative
activity like gardening or a vicariously creative activity like listening
to music or reading, then the neural network might cease to transmit its
signal and the electrochemical conductivity in the brain might return
to its normal level. If, on the other hand, poets make a positive, con-
scious response to the signal, then they initiate an interaction of mind
and brain, consciousness and nonconsciousness. As the interaction de-
velops, it seems to increase the rate of flow or the chemical concentra-
tion of neurotransmitters, which further increases the electrochemical
conductivity to the extent that it influences mind as well as brain and

induces the states and processes of mind that are the creative imagination at work, and at play. It is this fluidity of mind and brain that allows the interaction, indeed, the interpenetration, of functions of mind and brain. As the essentially conscious creative imagination interacts with the essentially nonconscious creative impulse, so unactivated memory networks are activated and lost memories are found; memories of disparate experiences are harmonized; thoughts and emotions are unified.

Although the increased conductivity allows the interaction and sometimes the interpenetration of consciousness and nonconsciousness, the neural activity of the brain is not subject to direct conscious control by the mind. Some poets find that, after the initial stage that Hughes describes as being no more than a dimly sensed mood or tone and Heaney as a pre-verbal first alertness, then words, images, and ideas begin to flit spontaneously in and out of consciousness, as if these flickering fragments were associated with the creative impulse. And if, in their flitting in and out of the poet's mind, ideas become identifiable, if the images grow clear enough to see or hear or touch, if a key word begins to gather other words around it, words with their sounds and some of their connotations as well as their lexical meanings, and if the ideas, images and words begin to cohere, then the poet knows that a poem has begun. When it begins, existing neural networks are extended, two or more networks might combine in a new configuration, and entirely new networks might be formed.

The science writer, Jonah Lehrer, is aware of this process. In *Imagine: How Creativity Works*, he comments on the imagination at work and states: (Lehrer 2012: 62) "This excess of ideas allows the neurons to form connections that have never existed before, wiring themselves into novel networks". A more technical interpretation is offered by Robert Winston in *The Human Mind* where he writes: (Winston 2003: p 274) "When a neuron receives an intense signal due to incoming information, its interior floods with calcium. [...] The calcium also encourages the neuron to make growth changes, developing new connections to other neurons".

As a result of these changes, the poet sometimes finds that what emerges from the nonconscious networks into consciousness can be so trivial or strange or grotesque that, in a discussion other than this, the emerging information might be described as unimaginable. Irrelevant neural connections are sometimes made; irrelevant information is released from the networks but its irrelevance can go unrecognized until it has been transduced from the prelinguistic to the fully linguistic stage, a process that can take hours, days or even years. In some instances it is only when a sequence of neural firing exhausts the supply of neurotransmitters that the conscious, editorial function of the imagination recognizes that the information is not suitable for the poem in progress.

Writing a poem is a conscious exercise in linguistic problem-solving as well as a nonconscious or semi-conscious process. Linguistic problem-solving begins only when the mind begins to transduce primary neural activity into language, either through the prelinguistic and proto-linguistic stages or through the more rapid process of inspiration. How the brain and the mind make that series of transductions is a mystery, but it is certain that no words can be written without these processes; and it is the failure to transduce, especially from the purely neurophysiological stage to the prelinguistic, that is the poet's biggest and most frequent problem. Poets commonly experience a sense of frustration or even despair when the failure occurs; some poets have the sensation of a gap between the non-linguistic and the prelinguistic stages, a gap, that is, between brain and mind.

One way of bridging the gap and solving the linguistic problem is innate and commonplace: when our conscious efforts to solve the problem fail, and when we abandon the attempt for an hour or a day or a longer period, we sometimes become aware, perhaps suddenly and unexpectedly, that the problem has solved itself and left the solution in our conscious mind. A possible interpretation of this kind of occurrence is that the energy discharged by the active and conscious neural networks creates a chain reaction, or a radial reaction, that activates adjoining networks, or extends an existing network, or in exceptional cases creates a new network. And when networks are activated, their information can sometimes be transduced to language. Popular awareness of this process is reflected in the colloquial expression, "Sleep on it", which does not, of course, mean that the solution will appear in the sleeper's dreams, although that is possible, but that the problem will be solved by the sleeping, nonconscious mind.

Some poets make deliberate use of this conscious-to-nonconscious and nonconscious-to-conscious process of problem-solving. Poets

sometimes feel that they have solved the creative and linguistic prob-
lem before the final version of the poem is written. In the mind of
the poet, the intimation can be the feeling that neural activity is being
transduced into language and, at a later stage in the creative process,
the feeling that a rough, incoherent draft is assuming the coherence of
a poem.

## Jung, Freud and Creativity

One of the factors that put an end to the friendship between Sigmund
Freud and Carl Gustav Jung was their irreconcilable views on the im-
portance of the creative writer. Another difference was that for Jung,
but not for Freud, the concept of the psyche included its original con-
cept: soul, or breath of life. Our present understanding of the creative
impulse and the initial stages of the creative process is consistent with
Jung's account in 'On the Relation of Analytical Psychology to Poet-
ry', first published in 1922 and reprinted in *Critical Theory since Plato*
where Jung states: (Jung 1971a: 814-5)

> We would do well, therefore, to think of the creative process as a liv-
> ing thing implanted in the human psyche. In the language of analytical
> psychology this living thing is an autonomous complex. It is a split-off
> portion of the psyche, which leads a life of its own outside the hierarchy
> of consciousness.

The autonomy that Jung attributes to the creative complex is consistent
with the fact that neural networks can activate spontaneously.

Jung states that the creative autonomous complex, that is, the com-
plex sets of neural networks encoded for creativity, is split off from the
rest of the mind and is outside the hierarchy of consciousness; but the
fact that artists are sometimes aware of the activity of the networks,
and must be aware of that activity if they are to create a work of art,
shows that the networks are not, as Jung claims, "outside the hierarchy
of consciousness". Even when the networks are not activated and we
are not conscious of their activity, they are still part of the intercon-
nected hierarchy of brain and mind. And although the creative impulse

might seem to lead a life of its own in the sense that it changes without our being conscious of the process of change and can activate itself spontaneously, it is not, of course, a truly independent life, because that life is lived within the hierarchy of brain and mind.

This nonconscious activity, which is also a feature of the religious impulse, of memories, values, beliefs, and attitudes, is a normal feature of our mental life. We know that these functions of mind are active even when they seem to be inert because memories sometimes return to consciousness with a different emotional or moral charge. We also know that our moral and social values, our taste in music, in painting, and in poetry can change without our having made a conscious reassessment. Indeed, these involuntary changes can be so great that we are sometimes embarrassed to think of the values, tastes, and attitudes we held in the past. Clearly, neural networks can be active without being activated for consciousness. At any given moment the conscious mind can control few items of information; several items may exist concurrently in the mind but consciousness, and spoken and written language, must deal with these items consecutively. We are not conscious of the vast majority of our neural networks, but those networks, and thus a nonconscious dimension of mind, certainly exist.

In the same paragraph of 'On the Relations of Analytical Psychology to Poetry', Jung writes of the creative autonomous complex: "Depending on its energy-charge, it may appear either as a mere disturbance of conscious activities or as a superordinate activity which can harness the ego to its purpose". That is, a weak or brief firing of neurons and discharge of neurotransmitters can be ignored; a more powerful and sustained episode can, as Jung states, take possession of our mind. Other intense experiences, love, for example, or grief or hate or jealousy, can also possess us. Jung's paragraph ends with the words: (Jung 1971a: 815)

> Accordingly, the poet who identifies with the creative process would be one who acquiesces from the start when the unconscious imperative begins to function. But the other poet, who feels the creative force as something alien, is one who for various reasons cannot acquiesce and is thus caught unawares.

The poet who acquiesces is likely to be interested in the life of the mind and the interplay of mind and language in the making of a poem. With that approach, the poet might find that although writing is a demanding, frustrating, exhausting activity, it is nevertheless a deeply satisfying and sometimes revealing activity. Poets who cannot acquiesce are not, as Jung claims, likely to be caught unawares; they might be unprepared and reluctant, in which case they might find writing to be an ordeal, but they will probably be aware of the stirring of the creative impulse and recognize it for what it is.

Jung's work has not been undermined by the neurosciences to the same extent as Freud's. In 'On the Relation of Analytical Psychology to Literature', in 'The Problem of Types in Poetry' in *Psychological Types*, first published in 1923, and in 'Psychology and Literature' in *Modern Man in Search of a Soul*, first published in 1933, Jung gives the impression that his understanding of the creative process and the mind of the creative writer is a result of his, Jung's, imaginative involvement as well as observation and analysis. He described himself as an analytical psychologist but he sees the mind as a mythogenic force at work in a mythological context; indeed, some of Jung's work is mythopoeic, creative rather than analytical or descriptive.

By contrast, Freud's writings on the subject are not only lacking in insight and understanding but also in observation. In his best-known statement on the subject, 'Creative Writers and Day-Dreaming', first published in 1908 and reprinted in *Critical Theory since Plato*, Freud's thesis is that the creative writer, just like the child at play, creates a fantasy world. The small child between the ages of two and five engages in serious play with sand, water, modelling clay, crayons and other materials; that kind of activity is an exploration of reality. One of Freud's main arguments in support of his thesis is disingenuous. He writes: (Freud 1971: 752)

> for the purpose of our comparison, we will choose not the writers most highly esteemed by the critics, but the less pretentious authors of novels, romances and short stories, who nevertheless have the widest and most eager circle of readers of both sexes.

That is, to support his case that the creative writer produces fantasy, Freud focuses on writers of popular fiction, whose main subject is fantasy. And in saying that these writers are less pretentious, he implies that the work of the creative writer is pretence. Later in his argument he seems to make a concession: "We are perfectly aware that very many imaginative writings are far removed from the model of the naive day-dream". The work of the imaginative, or creative, writer differs from that of the more popular writer. But in the same sentence he withdraws the concession: "and yet I cannot suppress the suspicion that even the most extreme deviation from that model could be linked with it through an uninterrupted series of transitional cases". Even the most creative work, or "extreme deviation", is, according to Freud's unsuppressed suspicion, related to escapist literature.

Towards the end of 'Creative Writers and Day-Dreaming' Freud makes the kind of dogmatic, reductive assertion that now reads like self-parody. Of his view of the creative writer he states: (Freud 1971: 752-3)

> You will not forget that the stress it lays on childhood memories in the writer's life – a stress which may perhaps seem puzzling – is ultimately derived from the assumption that a piece of creative writing, like a day-dream, is a continuation of, and a substitute for, what was once the play of childhood.

The creative writer does, indeed, engage in play, but it is the play of artistry, craft and sometimes technical virtuosity, accomplishments that are beyond the ability of all but the most prodigiously gifted children. The adult writer's skills could be developments of a talent exhibited in childhood, and they could be the realization of childhood promise, but they cannot be substitutes for childhood play, because the fully developed adult brain with its countless millions of networks and its adult hormones and neurotransmitters is different from the brain of a child.

'Creative Writers and Day-Dreaming' is a fairly early work. Freud could have listened to creative writers or read some of their work with a more open mind; he could even have taken some account of Jung's writings on the subject, but he persists in denigrating the artist. In 1920, in the chapter, 'General Theory of the Neuroses: Development of the Symptoms' in *A General Introduction to Psychoanalysis* Freud writes these frequently quoted words about the creative artist: (Freud 1920: 251)

He is impelled by too powerful instinctive needs. He wants to achieve
honour, power, riches, fame and the love of women. But he lacks the
means of achieving these satisfactions. So like any other unsatisfied
person, he turns away from reality, and transfers all his interests, his li-
bido, too, to the elaboration of his imaginary wishes, all of which might
easily point the way to neurosis.

The two phrases, "too powerful instinctive needs" and "imaginary
wishes", are inconsistent. The creative impulse is not the same as an in-
stinct, and the list of wishes – honour, power, riches, fame and the love
of women – could be ascribed to all manner of men, including psycho-
analysts. If a male writer is homosexual, he is unlikely to seek the love
of women; if a female writer is heterosexual, she, too, will not seek the
love of women. The unsatisfied creative artist, as artist and not "any
other unsatisfied person", seeks satisfaction by putting an end, tempo-
rarily, to his or her creative discontent through the realization of the
creative impulse in their next work of art, and the next, and the one
after that. What the creative artist really wants is to write a better son-
net, paint a better still life, compose a better string quartet than the one
before. In pursuit of these aims, artists must to some extent turn away
from external physical reality in order to explore the inner reality of
mind. In a later work, *Civilization and its Discontents*, first published in
1930, Freud states that the artist's delight in creating consists in "giv-
ing his phantasies body" (Freud 1961: 26), that art is a "mild narcosis"
and a "Sublimation of instinct" (Freud 1961: 44). And even in his com-
paratively late work, *New Introductory Lectures on Psychoanalysis* in
1937, he states in the lecture, 'Anxiety and Instinctual Life': "poets are
irresponsible beings; they enjoy the privilege of poetic license". (Freud
1937: 137)

Freud's concept of substitution is related to his concept of sublima-
tion: since the work produced by the creative writer is a substitute for
something else – and Freud says that the something else is childhood
play – so the force that prompts the writing of the work, the creative
impulse, must also be a substitute for something else. In Freudian doc-
trine, the second kind of substitution is sublimation, that is, the modi-
fication of an instinctual drive, especially the sexual urge, in order to
produce thoughts and feelings that are socially acceptable. But the mind
evolved in such a way that many of its functions, including artistic cre-

ativity, were freed from instincts; the creative impulse and the work of art are not substitutes for other things but exist in their own right. Why would an instinct change in such a way that it had to be gratified by writing *King Lear*, or *Prometheus Unbound*, or *In Memoriam* or *The Dream Songs*? The fact is that the instincts did not evolve; they remain instinctual, different in kind from the impulse that prompts a person to create a work of art.

After several decades of credulity, readers began to see that Freud's claims – art is an escape from reality, or art is a substitute and compensation for childhood, or the adult life of the creative writer is a re-enactment of childhood – are too sweeping to have any value. And yet literary theorists continue to promote his ideas. Peter Barry in *Beginning Theory*, Terry Eagleton in *Literary Theory: An Introduction* and Raman Selden, Peter Widdowson and Peter Brooker in *A Reader's Guide to Contemporary Literary Theory* all pay tribute to Freud. The French psychoanalyst, Jacques Lacan, in 'Sign, Symbol, Imaginary' in *On Signs* edited by Marshall Blonsky, notes the influence of Freud. (Lacan 1986: 204) In "The insistence of the letter in the unconscious" in *Modern Criticism and Theory* edited by David Lodge, Lacan writes this of Freud and Freudianism: (Lacan 1988: 104)

> No need to collect witnesses to the fact: everything involving not just the human sciences, but the destiny of man, politics, metaphysics, literature, art, advertising, propaganda, and through these even the economy, everything has been affected.

My reading of Freud is influenced by his metaphysics and his mode of reasoning. The elaborate intellectual structure of his system of psychoanalysis is metaphysical in the fundamental sense: it is not related to physical reality. In his extended essay, *The Unconscious,* first published in 1915, he writes of unconscious forces: (Freud 2005: 51) "As far as their physical characteristics are concerned, they are totally inaccessible to us; no physiological concept, no chemical process can give us any notion of their essential nature".

Physiological concepts and processes are discussed in detail by Freud's contemporary, William James, in *The Principles of Psychology*, first published in 1890. In the section, 'The Ambiguity of the Term "Unconscious" and the Topographical Perspective' from the same extended essay, Freud writes: (Freud 2005: 57)

> But every attempt to go on and hypothesize a localization of psychic processes, every endeavor to conceive of ideas as something stored in nerve cells, or excitations as something travelling along nerve fibres, has been a complete failure.

Did Freud not know that the French surgeon and anthropologist, Paul Broca, located a speech area of the brain around the year 1861 or that the German neurologist, Carl Wernicke, identified language areas of the brain? Had he not heard that nerve cells and cerebral patterns of transmission had been discussed by James in *The Principles of Psychology*? Even in that fascinating, unfinished late work in 1939, *Moses and Monotheism*, Freud makes the same dissociation: (Freud 1939: 97) "the psychical topography that I have developed here has nothing to do with the anatomy of the brain". A psychical topography that is divorced from the reality of its physical substrate is a metaphysical system, or a form of mythology.

Freud's mode of reasoning is clearly outlined in 'Negation' in *The Unconscious*: (Freud 2005: 89)

> Occasionally we can get sought-after information about unconscious repressed material by a very easy method. We ask: "so what would you say is absolutely least likely in this situation? What do you think was furthest from your mind at that point?" If the patient walks into the trap and tells us what he would find most incredible, he almost always gives the truth away.

The method is that of the grand inquisitor: denial is proof of guilt. The method is also part of a catechism, a set of questions that demand fixed, prescribed answers; and a catechism in turn, is part of an ideology, a rigid unquestioning and unquestionable set of beliefs.

## Creativity and Chaos

Poets must go beyond the previous limits of their imagination in order to create new and original work. But the poem is more than a venture into that unknown: the poet must first risk the danger of creating the unknown. Poets cannot explore new areas of the imagination until they have made them, and they make them through the interaction of the largely nonconscious creative impulse and the largely conscious creative imagination. Through this interplay, which is seldom subject to our will, we can activate nonconscious neural networks in the brain, link two or more networks to form new combinations containing new information, and occasionally we can form entirely new networks.

Some of this neural agitation is partly conscious; the poet can actually feel the mental stirrings as they occur. Without them the poem might not be completely original, because an important source of originality in a poem is the information released by the new and original neural configurations. But poets cannot know in advance which networks will be extended or recombined, or what new networks will be formed; they cannot predict if the networks can be decoded and transduced into words; nor can poets predict what the words will be.

Because the neural activity of the inchoate creative impulse is amorphous and nonconscious or semi-conscious, some poets have difficulty in transducing that energy into consciousness in the forms of identifiable images, feelings, thoughts, or words. The creative impulse is inarticulate without the creative imagination. The stirring of the impulse acts as a trigger for the imagination, but if the imagination falters – appropriate neurons may fail to fire or the flow of neurotransmitters may be too slow or weak – the brain's electrochemical conductivity might not be powerful enough to release the latent energy of the creative impulse and bring about the vital interaction between the poet's conscious and nonconscious areas of mind.

The idling mind or the mind involved in steady, sustained activity is a homeostatic system, that is, a dynamically stable state that is maintained by means of neural, largely nonconscious, regulatory processes. But when the creative impulse and the creative imagination are in a state of agitation but are not fully activated, or when one is activated and the other is not, then the mind is dynamically unstable. Homeostasis is temporarily destroyed, and the result of the destruction can be a sense of vacuity, bewilderment, or chaos. Indeed, these states of mind are so commonly experienced in the process of creating a work of art that the states could, for some poets, be integral, essential features of the creative process.

Chaos can be experienced as a void, the opposite of creation: the poet goes to the edge of his or her imagination, and finds nothing. Poets needs a special kind of persistence if they are to continue to look into the void while fearing that they might be sucked into it; and they need a determination that is a kind of courage if they are to do this many times over many years. For the poet who composes by inspiration – the creative impulse and the creative imagination interacting smoothly and their interplay being transduced almost effortlessly into words – this account will seem absurd, perhaps grotesque. For the poet in the grip of chaos, the gap may seem unbridgeable.

It is this kind of experience that makes writing an ordeal for some poets. Samuel Taylor Coleridge, for example, in his letter of 19 November 1796 to the political radical and poet, John Thelwall, writes: (Coleridge 1988: 32) "I compose very little – & I absolutely hate composition. Such is my dislike, that even a sense of Duty is sometimes too weak to overpower it". Coleridge's fear of the act of creating probably has the same basis as his fear of sleep and dreams; in their different ways, these conditions of mind release nonconscious forces that might overwhelm consciousness for a time.

Several entries in Stephen Spender's *Journals 1939-83*, from November 1939 (Spender 1992: 54-5) to July and October 1979, (Spender 1992: 363) show that he, too, found writing an ordeal. And in 1955 in the title essay in *The Making of a Poem* he states: (Spender 1955b: 61)

> I dread writing poetry, for, I suppose, the following reasons: a poem is a terrible journey, a painful effort of concentrating the imagination; words are an extremely difficult medium to use, and sometimes when one has spent days trying to say a thing clearly one finds that one has only said it dully; above all, the writing of a poem brings one face to face with one's own personality with all its familiar and clumsy limitations.

The kind of ordeal Spender describes is probably experienced by many artists, especially those whose mode of creating is not inspirational.

Painters and musicians as well as poets sometimes feel that their media are intractable; the intractability lies not in the artists' media but in an unresolved interaction between the imagination and the creative impulse, or in the need to extend the existing limits of the imagination in order to make a completely new work or art. These mental conditions are what Spender calls "a terrible journey". And what he feels as the "familiar and clumsy limitations" of personality are the kinds of metaconsciousness in which the artist is aware of the inadequacies of his artistic self, or in which the artistic self confronts but cannot quite displace the everyday self in a stasis that, in Spender's case, could last for days.

But the nature of the poetic imagination is such that chaos can be made imaginable and thus comprehensible. If poets in the grip of chaos can accept that through persistence or preoccupation over hours or days or weeks, the incomprehensible can be made comprehensible by the imagination, then poets sometimes find that chaos begins to take the form of disorientation; they are lost, not in a territory that is featureless or whose features are meaningless, but in what they gradually recognize as an extension of existing territory, that is, an extension of the creative imagination. Such experiences are variations on the universal religious paradox of having to lose one's way in order to find a new way.

At a later stage in the creative process poets sometimes experience a different kind of chaos if they cannot see the sequence of ideation that will give the poem its overall semantic structure. There are occasions when poets know that they have all the words and lines they need for the complete poem, but they cannot see the order in which the lines should appear in the final version. In her Introduction to *The Letters of T. S. Eliot: Volume I 1898-1922* (Eliot V.1988: xxvi) Valerie Eliot notes the influence of Ezra Pound in shaping the final version of *The Waste Land*. And Hugh MacDiarmid notes the assistance of the composer, Francis George Scott, in shaping the final version of his visionary comedy, *A Drunk Man Looks at the Thistle,* first published in 1926. (MacDiarmid 1985: 82)

Chaos is not, of course, the exclusive experience of poets and other creative artists. Anyone who loses that everyday, often unquestioning relationship with his or her familiar self – the loss can follow illness, rejection, or bereavement, or it can be spontaneous – might also experience chaos. And anyone who cannot make a tolerable pattern of the various aspects of life: home and family, work and colleagues, and the expression of a talent or preoccupation other than home or work, might also suffer chaos. But poets deliberately take this risk, the impairment or loss of their sense of identity, when they give themselves, or give the various selves that make up their compound self, to the service of the inchoate, amorphous, semiconscious creative impulse. They commit their creative imagination, which is an intensified form of consciousness, to the decoding of information from the neural networks as these networks change from their nonconscious to their activated, conscious state; but the poet cannot know what forms the new information will take, or whether it will take any recognisable form at all.

It is this crisis that Anthony Storr refers to in 'Is Art Adaptive?' in *The Dynamics of Creation*: (Storr 1976: 187) "Toleration of the anxiety caused by chaos is [...] one characteristic of the creative person, who must be prepared to see his grasp of the world broken, before he can renew it". Each time they embark on a new work, creative artists risk failure, and some artists feel the failed attempt as a failure of self. The conflict between creative order and chaos is discussed by C. Day Lewis in 'The Pattern of Images' in *The Poetic Image*, where he refers to the Holy Ghost and associates the creative and the religious impulses: (Day Lewis 1947: 68) "We may speak of the poetic imagination as the Holy Ghost brooding over chaos, but it is still chaos over which it broods, and will remain so unless the poet's concentration is intense enough to elicit what is latent there".

Another, metaphysical, form of chaos pleases those artists who think of their work of art as a microcosmic re-enactment of Creation out of Chaos. In some astrophysical as in Biblical mythology there is the chaos of the void before there is creation and order. Creation did not eliminate chaos but assimilated it within the order of creation. Chaos, then, is an integral part of creation and an integral part of the work of art. Some modern artists, especially painters and musicians, feel that in order to express the truth of their experience they must represent both sets of forces, chaos and order, in their work. The view is entirely valid and yet it presents an artistic problem, because the natural tendency of the creative imagination is to bring the disparate into unity, the discordant into harmony, or to bring the constituent elements of a work of art into structures of colour or sound or language that suggest completeness. It is also the natural tendency of the creative impulse to continue to stir until it has been realized and its force temporarily exhausted. Artists who wish to include chaos in the finished work must resist this natural tendency or else control it in such a way as to produce a paradoxical work of orderly chaos or chaotic order.

# 2

# Imagination

## The Poetic Imagination

IMAGINATION IS PART OF THE MIND'S design, and anyone who is born with a normal brain has the capacity for imagination. Why some imaginations are closed to artistic experience while others remain open, and why some imaginations are devoted to the creation of works of art while others are unable to create but find pleasure as observers – these things remain unknown.

The structure and growth of the human brain is biologically predetermined, but the development of human mental faculties varies widely and, as a result, everyone has a uniquely individual mind. If reading poetry is a normal activity in a child's family home, in the school, and a network of acquaintances, then poetry will be a familiar element in the child's mind and will be represented by sets of neural networks in the child's brain. But there is no guarantee that poetry will remain an essential element in the person's life. Even if children are fascinated by poetry to the extent that they read and write poems when they are six or eight or ten years old, the fascination might not survive beyond adolescence, because on either side of puberty children have a different identity. In late adolescence, when a young person's physical development is complete, the overall physical structure of his or her brain is also complete, but the brain as a neurophysiological structure grows rapidly as it forms new neural networks. And when adult hormones begin to be released into the young person's blood stream and brain, then the chemistry of neurotransmitters and the electrochemical flow across synapses are changed. The rapid growth of networks in the brain is often followed by new ways of thinking and feeling and by new patterns of behaviour.

There are critical periods for the development of mental faculties, including creative imagination, and if development does not occur during these periods then the faculty might be impaired. More fundamentally, there are critical periods for the acquisition of language.

In *Words and Rules: The Ingredients of Language* Steven Pinker writes: (Pinker 1999: 190) "At around eighteen months children start to utter two-word microsentences like *See Baby* and *More cereal*". In *The Stuff of Thought* Pinker states (Pinker 2008: 28) that by the age of three, most children will have "a vocabulary of thousands of words, a command of the grammar of the spoken vernacular, and a proficiency with sound patterns". The linguist, David Crystal, discusses research studies in language acquisition in the chapter, 'How Children Learn Speech Sounds', in *How Language Works*. These studies, he states: (Crystal 2005: 80) "have shown how babies turn their heads towards the source of a sound within the first few days of life, and prefer human voices to non-human sounds as early as two weeks. Abilities of this kind are so apparent that researchers have concluded that some auditory training must begin within the womb".

If the language areas of the brain are not activated by around the age of seven the young person will find it difficult, perhaps impossible, to acquire language, because the neural areas for language will have been taken over by different mental functions. Atrophy of the capacity for language was confirmed by the frequently quoted case of Genie in S. Curtiss' *Genie: a psycholinguistic study of a modern-day wild child* in 1977. Other cases of children who in their first seven years were deprived of interaction with speakers are recorded in the two-in-one volume, *Wolf Children* by Lucien Malson and *The Wild Boy of Aveyron* by Jean Itard. In *Musicophilia: Tales of Music and the Brain*, Oliver Sacks, the physician and author of several works on the brain, contrasts the critical stage for language acquisition with the longer or later stage for music appreciation. He states: (Sacks 2011: 103) "To be language-less at the age of six or seven is a catastrophe [...] but to be musicless at the same age does not necessarily predict a musicless future".

The creative imagination, too, has critical periods for its development. If the neural networks for imagination are part of the rapid development in childhood and then in adolescence, imagination will be a feature of the adolescent mind; and if adolescents are responsive to the needs of the imagination, then it will continue to develop in adult life. But if the child grows up in a home and neighbourhood in which all signs of creative imagination and artistry are ignored or discouraged, then that faculty might be weakened. And if the neural networks that form the substrate of imagination are not part of the rapid neurophysiological growth in the brain of the seven-year-old child, and if the child around the age of puberty decides, either independently or through peer pressure, to suppress his or her creative imagination, then the adolescent who succeeds the child, and the adult who succeeds the adolescent, might have only a rudimentary imagination.

A few forms of art might be still acceptable: paintings in which the subjects are treated in representational and idealized ways, music with easily recognized melodies and rhythms that make a direct appeal to emotion, and poems that use regular rhyme and metre to tell stories or paint vivid word-pictures. Such minds may be open to sentimentality in the arts, because sentimentality simplifies experience and offers consolation. They might also be open to the style of art that has its origins in Greek and Roman sculpture and is sometimes known as heroic realism; the style was widely used in political posters in the twentieth century to portray ideal warriors and workers with whom the mass of the population might identify. Artistic expression beyond that limited range of subjects and styles is likely to be ignored or rejected by the undeveloped imagination, partly because in art as in life the closed imagination categorizes experience as right or wrong, good or bad. Individuals with closed imaginations might feel that if they were to open their mind to different kinds of art, not only new works but works that will always seem different – visionary poetry, music with no recognizable melodies or rhythms, abstract expressionism, cubism, surrealism – different because these works play with pre-existing concepts of art, of physical reality and thus with concepts of mind, then individuals' existing views on art and life would be challenged, perhaps overwhelmed. People with closed imaginations might feel that some forms of artistic expression are so far outside their safe circle that they must be products of deviant minds; they are deviant in the sense that the creative imagination deviates from the non-creative.

There are other people who are not artists but remain open to varieties of artistic experience throughout their lives. Perhaps they have found that it can take several years to develop the talent needed to create works of art, or that years might be spent before they discover, or before they can admit to themselves, that they do not have a talent to be developed. And then, knowing these things, they satisfy their creative imagination vicariously through the imaginations of creative artists and performers in the creative arts.

Coleridge remains one of the great authorities on the nature and function of the poetic imagination, and it is worth considering his illuminating, sometimes startling insights in detail. In Chapter XIII of *Biographia Literaria*, first published in 1817, he notes the fluid, recombinative functions of imagination, its tendency towards harmony and wholeness, and its animating power: (Coleridge 1956: 167) "It dissolves, diffuses, dissipates, in order to re-create; or when this process is rendered impossible, yet still, at all events, it struggles to idealize and unify. It is essentially vital, even as all objects (as objects) are essentially fixed and dead". These features describe the action of what Coleridge calls the secondary imagination; earlier in the same paragraph he describes the primary imagination: "The primary imagination I hold to be the living power and prime agent of all human perception, and as a repetition in the finite mind of the eternal act of creation in the infinite I AM". That is, the primary imagination is consciousness, which is designed in its microcosmic way to re-enact each day the original mystery of the Creation.

Coleridge was also aware of the difference between the conscious and the nonconscious, and in Lecture XIII in *A Course of Lectures* he stresses the importance of the nonconscious in the making of a work of art: (Coleridge 1951: 315)

> In every work of art there is a reconcilement of the external with the internal; the conscious is so impressed on the unconscious as to appear in it; [...] He who combines the two is the man of genius; and for that reason he must partake of both. Hence there is in genius itself an unconscious activity; nay, that is the genius in the man of genius.

In the statement, "that is the genius in the man of genius", the second "genius" has its modern meaning of exceptional imaginative or creative power, while the first "genius" expresses older meanings: a person's prevailing disposition and character, and his innate or attendant and partly divine, spirit. Coleridge is saying that the prevailing characteristic or spirit of the artist lies in his nonconscious mind. Perhaps his own experience of the creative process – in 'Christabel', 'The Rime of the Ancient Mariner', and 'Kubla Khan' – leads him to attach so much importance to the nonconscious. The creative impulse is, indeed, a largely nonconscious force, but the poet's decision to respond to the impulse, and the working of the poetic imagination, are largely conscious processes.

A more detailed account of the reconciling power of poetry appears in Chapter XIV of *Biographia Literaria*, where Coleridge writes: (Coleridge 956: 173-4) "'What is poetry?' is so nearly the same question with, what is a poet? that the answer to the one is involved in the solution of the other". His subsequent discussion of the powers of the poet is, in effect, a discussion of the poetic imagination:

> The poet, described in ideal perfection, brings the whole soul of man into activity, with the subordination of its faculties to each other, according to their relative worth and dignity. He diffuses a tone and spirit of writing that blends and (as it were) fuses, each into each, by that synthetic and magical power to which we have exclusively appropriated the name of imagination.

Imagination synthesizes the faculties of thought and feeling; it conjures up memories so that the past comes alive in the present; it allows the interpenetration of consciousness and the nonconscious so that the poet has access to his most secret self. Coleridge counterbalances the emphasis he puts on the nonconscious in *A Course of Lectures* by stating that imagination is activated and sustained by conscious will. In a remarkably revealing and comprehensive sentence, he writes: (Coleridge 1951: 174)

> This power, first put into action by the will and understanding and retained under their irremissive, though gentle and unnoticed, control (laxis effertur habenis) [carried onwards with loose reins] reveals itself in the balance or reconciliation of opposite or discordant qualities: of sameness, with difference; of the general, with the concrete; the idea, with the image; the individual, with the representative; the sense of novelty and freshness, with old and familiar objects.

Coleridge stresses the need for complementarities of emotion and thought: "a more than usual state of emotion, with more than usual order; judgement ever awake and steady self-possession, with enthusiasm and feeling profound or vehement".

The poet, says Coleridge, is responsible for activating his imagination and for sustaining the activity until the poem is complete. We can add that poets are also responsible for developing and enlarging their imagination. In the act of writing, and in intervals between writing one poem and another, poets are aware of some of the ways in which the creative mind works: how the creative impulse announces itself and how it can be realized; how memories with their emotional and moral charges change over time; how memory and imagination engage in serious play with language. Poets should be aware of the naturally occurring changes in their values and beliefs, their modes of thought and feeling, and aware that these, along with a changing vision of life, can lead to new subjects and perhaps new themes. These changes could be expressed in a changing use of language that reflects a changing – ideally, a maturing – voice; and expressed, perhaps, in different forms. The poet's everyday imagination and everyday vision of life change naturally and inevitably over time; what makes it increasingly difficult for some poets to reflect these changes in their poetry is that the creative imagination and creative vision, unlike their everyday counterparts, do not change in the same automatic way but must be developed through conscious artistry. And what makes that kind of development increasingly difficult for some poets is that, with age, as the brain begins to lose some of its plasticity, that is, its capacity to form new neural networks, so the mind might begin to lose some of its creative energy and creative stamina. The stark fact is that eventually brain and mind begin to close down.

The problem for some older poets is that, if they cannot change, then they cease to be original, as Eliot writes in his essay of 1940, 'The Poetry of W. B. Yeats': (Eliot 1955: 203)

> For a man who is capable of experience finds himself in a different world in every decade of his life; as he sees it with different eyes, the material of his art is continually renewed. But in fact, very few poets have shown this capacity for adaptation to the years. It requires, indeed,

an exceptional honesty and courage to face the change. Most men ei-
ther cling to the experiences of youth, so that their writing becomes
an insincere mimicry of their earlier work, or they leave their passion
behind, and write only from the head, with a hollow and wasted virtu-
osity. There is another and even worse temptation: that of becoming
dignified, of becoming public figures with only a public existence.

Some poets, and not only older poets, are genuinely unaware of their
loss of originality; each new poem strikes them as a new departure
when it is, in fact, merely a minor variation on an otherwise exhausted
theme. Responsibility for the extension and revitalizing of the creative
imagination is a responsibility that some poets are unable to accept and
might be unable to understand. The problem is so common – in their
strikingly different ways, Yeats, Siegfried Sassoon, Eliot, MacDiarmid,
William Carlos Williams, W. H. Auden, David Gascoyne, and Edwin
Morgan are exceptions in twentieth-century poetry – that is worth con-
sidering in more detail.

The idea that poets are responsible for the renewal or extension of
their imagination is not new. In Immanuel Kant's 'Of the Faculties of
Mind that Constitute Genius' in the Second Book of *Critique of Judge-
ment*, first published in 1790 and included in *Critical Theory Since
Plato*, Kant writes: (Kant 1971: 397)

> The poet ventures to realize to sense, rational ideas of invisible beings,
> the kingdom of the blessed, hell, eternity, creation, etc.; or even if he
> deals with things of which there are examples in experience – death,
> envy and all vices, also love, fame, and the like – he tries, by means
> of imagination, which emulates the play of reason in its quest after a
> maximum, to go beyond the limits of experience and to present them to
> sense with a completeness of which there is no example in nature. This
> properly speaking is the art of the poet.

Imagination is not, of course, the same as reason; but the working of
the poet's imagination, says Kant, is similar to the working of the rea-
soning mind in its attempt to bring to consciousness a maximum, a
condition of ultimate knowledge or understanding. The poet must, "by
means of imagination", "go beyond the limits of experience" to achieve
a completeness of vision that, contrary to a view of poetry current at

that time, is not an imitation of nature but an interpretation, sometimes a transcendental interpretation, of nature. That is, poets can go beyond the limits of experience and beyond the bounds of their imagination only by enlarging the imagination.

Percy Bysshe Shelley makes a similar claim in *A Defence of Poetry*, written in 1821and published in 1840. Shelley writes: (Shelley 1956: 112)

> Poetry enlarges the circumference of the imagination by replenishing it with thoughts of ever new delight, which have the power of attracting and assimilating to their own nature all other thoughts, and which form new intervals and interstices whose void forever craves fresh food.

His concept of new interstices is consistent with the formation of new neural networks. But the process of enlargement is not entirely one of delight, and Shelley adds: (Shelley 1956: 116) "The imagination is enlarged by a sympathy with pains and passions so mighty, that they distend in their conception the capacity of that by which they are conceived".

*A Defence of Poetry* is said to have been written as a response to Thomas Love Peacock's *The Four Ages of Poetry* published in 1820. Peacock's premise is this: (Peacock 1951: 843) "A poet in our times is a semi-barbarian in a civilized community. He lives in the days that are past. His ideas, thoughts, feelings, associations, are all with barbarous manners, obsolete customs, and exploded superstitions". Peacock's denunciation of poets and poetry is so obviously excessive that *The Four Ages of Poetry* should be read as boisterous comedy. And yet one of Peacock's observations has proved partly prophetic: (Peacock 1951: 845) "the poetical audience will not only continually diminish in the proportion of its number to that of the rest of the reading public, but will also sink lower and lower in the comparison of intellectual acquirement". The accuracy of the prophecy of a diminishing readership for poetry is accidental; in Peacock's day, poems by Byron and Scott were best-sellers.

Neuroscientists have confirmed what Kant deduced. In *A User's Guide to the Brain* the psychiatrist John Ratey writes: (Ratey 2001: 364) "New mental tasks increase neural connections and help the brain become more adaptive to future events". He adds: "You have the best chance of growing connections [...] by tackling activities that are unfamiliar to you". Writing poems, and reading unfamiliar poems, are two such ways.

## Poetry and Inspiration

For some poets, composition is a comparatively rapid and continuous process in which line after line appears spontaneously in the mind so that the poems seem to write themselves; poets might even feel that the poems are being created by another self and that their own conscious selves merely make a written record of the dictation. Poets who compose in that way can complete a poem of, say, twenty to thirty lines, in an hour or less; others struggle for a week or more before they are satisfied that the poem is complete. What makes such rapid composition possible is inspiration, a function of the creative imagination by which nonconscious as well as conscious neural information is transduced almost effortlessly from electrochemical energy into words; the words are then edited, if editing is necessary, almost instantaneously. The experience is so mysterious that one can understand why some poets and critics in the past regarded inspiration as the working of a divine or supernatural agency.

Shelley, for example, writes in *A Defence of Poetry*: (Shelley1956: 133) "It [poetry] is as it were the interpenetration of a diviner nature through our own". Shelley, an atheist, is repeating received Platonic opinion about the divine source of poetry; but in attributing poetic inspiration and the resulting poems to God, Plato is knowingly denying the achievement of the poet. In the Socratic dialogue, *Ion*, written around 390 BC, Plato writes: (Plato 2001: 3-24) "For all good poets, epic as well as lyric, compose their beautiful poems not by art, but because they are inspired and possessed". And he adds: "God would seem to demonstrate to us and not allow us to doubt that these beautiful poems are not human, nor the work of man, but divine and the work of God". If poets in the past believed that inspiration, or the imagination working at a slower and more deliberate pace than inspiration, was divine, then they also believed that whatever truths the poems contained were divine truths. But inspiration is a function of imagination, imagination is a function of mind, and the mind is a natural feature of our humanity. Alexander Pope is closer to a modern, agnostic concept of inspiration when he writes in *An Essay on Criticism*, first published in 1711: (Pope 1930: 53)

> And snatch a grace beyond the reach of art,
> Which without passing thro' the judgment, gains
> The heart, and all its end at once attains. (lines 153-5)

Keats comments indirectly on the subject of inspiration in his letter of 27 February 1818 to John Taylor in his much-quoted axiom: (Keats 1952: 107) "That if Poetry comes not as naturally as the Leaves to a tree it had better not come at all".

For the American poet, Richard Eberhart, composition was just such a spontaneous foliation. In 'How I Write Poetry' in *Poets on Poetry* edited by Howard Nemerov, Eberhart explains: (Eberhart 1966: 23)

> When a poem is ready to be born it will be born whole, without the need to change a word, or perhaps with the need to change only a word or two. I thus go back to an ancient theory of inspiration. It must suggest strong, active memory and an instantaneous synthesizing power when the whole being, not the mind alone, or the sense of the will alone, can come to bear on life with significance.

In the same paragraph Eberhart adds:

> Probably more than half of my best-known poems have come to me in this way, when the being was a seemingly passive vehicle for the overwhelming dominance of the poem, which was then put down with ease, immediacy, fluency and comprehensive order.

Spender, by contrast, sometimes found composition an ordeal and yet, paradoxically, he was acutely aware of the nearness of the condition of mind that makes inspiration possible. In an entry for November 1939 in his *Journals 1939-1983* he writes: (Spender 1992: 55) "Somewhere there's a fountain of words waiting to say the things I can say, only directly I set myself to will them out of me, the fears, ambitions, habits of thought, prejudices, demands of style form a barrier between me and what is perfectly clear". Perhaps the barrier was, and is, that mysterious boundary between mind and brain, consciousness and non-consciousness, linguistic and prelinguistic kinds of information. The inspirational mode of composition seems alluring and yet alien to the poet who composes in slower, more painstaking ways, just as the slower mode of composition seems laborious to the inspirational composer. But there are as many ways of writing poems as there are poets; what matters is the final version of the poem.

When the poetic imagination is steadily at work, poets sometimes experience a trance-like state. The creative trance is an active, precisely focused condition that occurs when poets are so completely absorbed in the act of creating that they are unaware of their physical surroundings, of body, of time and the passing of time. They are freed not only from time and place but from their particular personalities. Wordsworth re-creates the experience of the poetic trance in that moment of perfection in 'Lines Composed a Few Miles above Tintern Abbey': (Wordsworth 1956: 164)

> that serene and blessed mood
> In which the affections gently lead us on,
> Until, the breath of this corporeal frame
> And even the motion of our human blood
> Almost suspended, we are laid asleep
> In body, and become a living Soul:
> While with an eye made quiet by the power
> Of Harmony, and the deep power of joy,
> We see into the life of things.

W. B. Yeats in 'The Symbolism of Poetry', first published in 1900, suggests that the poetic trance is induced by the rhythm of a poem: (Yeats 1971: 724)

> The purpose of rhythm, it has always seemed to me, is to prolong the moment of contemplation, the moment when we are both asleep and awake, which is the one moment of creation, by hushing us with an alluring monotony, while it holds us waking by variety, to keep us in

that state of perhaps real trance, in which the mind liberated from the
pressure of the will is unfolded into symbols.

Yeats' concept of the mind being unfolded into symbols is consistent
with the concept of nonconscious neural networks releasing their infor-
mation to the conscious mind. Writing of Yeats, Seamus Heaney links
the deliberate and the inspired in a way that seems at first to be para-
doxical. In 'Yeats as an Example?' in *Finders Keepers*: Heaney writes:
(Heaney 2002: 107) "He proves that deliberation can be so intensified
that it becomes synonymous with inspiration". Deliberation and inspi-
ration are different modes of composition, but an act of deliberation is
an act of reflection on a subject matter, of considering the significance
of an experience or of a word. Deliberation can be a process of interior
counselling, or interior conjuring, with words and images and ideas. It
can be a way of approaching and activating the imagination, a tuning in
to the beginning of a poem. Through deliberation the poet can achieve
the intensification of consciousness, the state of mind that allows the
creative imagination to come into play. And even when the mind is
functioning at a lesser intensity, the poet through craft and artistry can
invest the poem with qualities of spontaneity, immediacy and inevitabil-
ity that are indistinguishable from the same qualities in a poem created
through inspiration. The science journalist, Jonah Lehrer, recognizes
the effectiveness of deliberation. In the chapter, 'The Unconcealed', in
*Imagine: How Creativity Works*, he writes: (Lehrer 2012: 56) "The real-
ity of the creative process is that it often requires persistence, the ability
to stare at a problem until it makes sense".

Heaney returns to the question of inspiration in his interviews with
Dennis O'Driscoll in *Stepping Stones: Interviews with Seamus Heaney*,
where he expresses the experience of inspiration more explicitly than
he does in his poems. He recalls a period of inspiration in May 1969 and
says: (Heaney 2008: 147) "It was a visitation". During a later, extended
experience of inspiration from September 1988 to the end of 1989 he
wrote the *Squarings* sequence, published in *Seeing Things* in 1991 and
in *Opened Ground: Poems 1966-1996* in 1998. Of the first poem in
the sequence Heaney says: (Heaney 2008: 318) "I may exaggerate if I
say that, in general, I was subject to the poems and not the other way
round". And he adds: "I learned what inspiration feels like but not how
to summon it". For Heaney the experience of visitation is similar to in-

spiration. He says: (Heaney 2008: 197) "Poetry had come into my life suddenly [...] So that the old-fashioned understanding of poetry as a visitation has been a determining one for me". Of some of his poems he says: (Heaney 2008: 366) "They leave you with a sense of having been visited". Heaney's visitations are sacred experiences.

Robert Graves' belief in poetic magic and a pantheon of poetic goddesses and gods is similar to Yeats' belief in a Celtic mythological pantheon. In 'Harp, Anvil, Oar' in *The Crowning Privilege,* Graves insists that the trance experience is magical. He explains: (Graves 1955: 99) "I say magic, since the act of composition occurs in a sort of trance, distinguishable from dream only because the critical faculties are not dormant, but on the contrary, more acute than normally". And then, in a remark that is part-dogma and part-mischief, Graves adds that those poets who have experienced the poetic magic of the trance: "know that to work out a line by exercise of reason, rather than a deep-seated belief in miracle, is highly unprofessional conduct". There is, of course, no necessary division between reason and the miracle of creativity, or between reason and emotion. One faculty without the other would lead to a lesser poetry if, that is, the two could be divorced; but reason and creativity, reason and emotion, are equal components in the creative imagination.

When Spender returns to the subjects of inspiration and trance in the title essay of *The Making of a Poem,* he writes: (Spender 1955b: 47) "the concentrated effort of writing poetry is a spiritual activity which makes one completely forget, for the time being, that one has a body". Spender's sense of disembodiment is similar to that of Ralph Waldo Emerson, who finds phantasmagoric elements in the trance experience. In 'Poetry and Imagination' in *Letters and Social Aims* he writes of the poet entranced: (Emerson n.d.: 577) "His own body is a fleeing apparition, his personality as fugitive as the trope he employs. In certain hours we can almost pass our hand through our own body".

In the act of making, poets suspend most of the conscious functions of the mind and live only in the imaginative function; indeed, they are so completely involved in the working of the imagination that they forgets that it is, in fact, their own imagination at work in their own mind. The imaginative function fills the mind to the extent that the poet sometimes has the sensation of the mind being contained within the imagination rather than imagination being contained by mind. The creative trance is a condition similar to mysticism in which poets feel that they are in communion with another dimension of self, the true poetic self.

Practitioners in other arts experience the same kind of creative trance. The British painter, Frank Auerbach, is one of the persons interviewed by John Tusa in *On Creativity*. Tusa asks Auerbach how he behaves when he is painting a portrait, and Auerbach replies: (Tusa 2004: 46)

> If things are going really well and I feel that it's almost as though some-
> thing arose on the canvas of its own accord [...] and an image seems to
> call to you from out of the paint – when I'm actually in pursuit of this,
> I really haven't the faintest idea what I'm doing.

Tusa then asks if he talks to the canvas, and Auerbach says: "Yes, yes I may do but I'm really not aware of it [...] I no longer quite know what I'm doing because all my conscious energies are engaged in this pursuit of the possibility that's arisen on the canvas". The moment when – or rather, the state of mind in which – the image seems to rise spontane-ously from the canvas and call out is the moment when the creative im-agination fills, or takes over, normal consciousness. Auerbach no longer quite knows what he is doing, not only because his conscious mind is wholly engaged in the pursuit, but also because the conscious dimen-sion of the creative imagination is interacting with the nonconscious.

Ted Hughes questions the existence of the poetic trance. In 'The Poetic Self: a Centenary Tribute to T. S. Eliot' in *Winter Pollen* Hughes states (Hughes 1994: 275) that a "well-worked law, fundamental to psy-choanalysis and to the modern secular outlook has brought about a new poetic self who is not affected by the power of trance". Hughes adds: "It has changed things for the poet by removing his susceptibility to the trance condition, the mood in which the poetic self could overpower the whole mind in a more unhindered fashion. That this susceptibility has gone is a fact". By contrast, Heaney is wholly susceptible to the power of trance. In his interview with John Haffenden published in *Viewpoints* Heaney is asked if he has a problem of self-consciousness in writing. He replies: (Heaney 1981: 64) "That is never a problem, because I only write when I'm in the trance. It is a mystery of sorts". In using the article, "the" – "the trance" and not "a trance" – Heaney implies that the trance is not only his personal mode of composition but one that is widely known and practised.

The power of trance has not been, and cannot be, eliminated. A trance or trance-like condition is a normal and necessary state of mind for the artist in the act of creating, and for many people who are absorbed in a task. In order to focus more intently on the work in progress, artists must shut out distractions; and when they do this effectively, the neural networks associated with the creative imagination become more active, while other networks in the mind remain unactivated. The outlook of the modern poet is, as Hughes states, more secular. But the religious impulse, and with it a sense of the sacred, are so closely related to the creative impulse that the making of poems will never be an entirely secular activity.

## The Poet's Muse

The muse that once existed in the mind of the male poet as an elusive part of his poetic identity took the form, not of one of the nine or more daughters of Mnemosyne and Zeus, but of a female spirit who controlled the poet's creativity. The fact that the spirit was not always present in his mind and, even when present, often ignored the poet's attempts to invoke or seduce her, made her more mysterious and more desirable.

I write of the muse uncertainly and in the past tense because her myth seems finally to have expired. In effect, the myth had lost some of its force by the second decade of the nineteenth century, when poets' references to the muse became merely conventional or fanciful, and when writing poems had come to be seen by most poets as a natural, not a supernatural activity.

Milton refers sincerely to his muse when, in that confessional aside at the beginning of Book IX of *Paradise Lost*, first published in 1667, he writes of his mode of composition: (Milton 1862: 209)

> If answerable style I can obtain
> Of my celestial patroness, who deigns
> Her nightly visitation unimplored,
> And dictates to me slumbering, or inspires
> Easy my unpremeditated verse:
> Since first this subject for heroic song
> Pleased me, long choosing, and beginning late (lines 20-6)

The "celestial patroness" is Calliope, the muse of epic poetry. A reader may find it surprising that so monumental a work was dictated nightly to Milton in his sleep, and that its composition was "easy" and "unpremeditated"; but the phrase, "long choosing", suggest that the subject of *Paradise Lost* had been in his thoughts, and in his nonconscious mind, for many years.

Byron by contrast is dismissive when he writes in the first stanza of the first Canto of *Childe Harold's Pilgrimage*, which was published in sections between 1812 and 1818: (Byron s.d.: 17)

> Muse, form'd or fabled at the minstrel's will!
> Since shamed full oft by later lyres on earth.

The word, "lyres", is, of course, a pun. Eliot makes a rare reference to the muse when he discusses Coleridge in 'Wordsworth And Coleridge' in *The Use of Poetry and the Use of Criticism*: (Eliot 1933: 69) "But for a few years he had been visited by the Muse (I know of no poet to whom this hackneyed metaphor is better applicable) and thenceforth was a haunted man". He calls the muse a "hackneyed metaphor" and yet he is obviously sincere in the reference to Coleridge's muse. In the same sentence, Eliot adds: "for anyone who has ever been visited by the Muse is thenceforth haunted". 'The Rime of the Ancient Mariner' and 'Kubla Khan' were probably written in 1797 and 1798, which could have been when the haunting began. However hackneyed the metaphor, Eliot takes the muse, or the concept of the muse, seriously.

In 'Writing' in *The Dyer's Hand* Auden is often sceptical, sometimes dismissive, of received opinions on poetry but he, like Eliot, takes the muse seriously, and he seems sure of her existence as a natural rather than supernatural agency when he writes: (Auden 1963: 16)

> It is true that, when he is writing a poem, it seems to the poet as if there were two people involved, his conscious self and a Muse whom he has to woo or an Angel with whom he has to wrestle, but, as in an ordinary wooing or wrestling match, his role is as important as Hers.

Auden clearly implies that the poet's conscious self regards the muse as a feminine element in the nonconscious mind, and that the element can be brought to consciousness through the constancy of the poet's adoration, or the intensity of his struggle. In neurophysiological terms the muse could have been – and could, perhaps, still be – a set of neural networks encoded for an aspect of self and identity but difficult to activate because the natural domain of that set of networks was the nonconscious mind. And it would seem that, even when the networks were activated, they were particularly difficult to decode into language. It was only when the networks were decoded that the poet could conjure up and commune with that mysterious dimension of self that he called his muse and then, in a transformation that resolved and yet compounded the mystery, the muse disappeared and was replaced by words.

In the theistic past the muse was thought to be divine, just as other poetic material that was transduced only with difficulty from the nonconscious to consciousness was thought to be divine. Auden wrestling with his Angel is similar to Spender's observation, (Spender 1955b: 61) "In poetry one is wrestling with a god", in the title essay in *The Making of a Poem*. The origin of the concept is probably the ambiguous sequence in *Genesis*, Chapter 32 verses 24 to 30. At first Jacob's opponent is human: "And Jacob was left alone; and there wrestled a man with him until the breaking of the day". But at the end of the combat the opponent is divine, and Jacob says: "I have seen God face to face, and my life is preserved". The ambiguity is not only the doubt about the nature of Jacob's opponent, human or divine, but also the doubt that Yahweh, the invisible God of the Old Testament, should allow himself to be seen. What is not in doubt is that the poet's wrestling with the sometimes intractable and partly nonconscious creative impulse is a spiritual quest in which the poet must engage.

The poet's conscious role, Auden adds in the quotation above, is as important as the usually nonconscious role of the muse; and he makes the same point in different words in a later paragraph in 'Writing': (Auden 1963: 22) "A poet has to woo, not only his own Muse but also Dame Philology, and, for the beginner, the latter is the more important. [...] It is only later, when he has wooed and won Dame Philology, that he can give his entire attention to his Muse". Auden's word, "philology", literally the love language and learning, has been displaced by the word, 'linguistics'. Philologists regarded their study as a branch of the arts within the wider realm of the humanities; linguists regard the study of language as a science and refer to the subject as linguistic science. Auden is saying that the poet cannot woo his muse effectively until he has gained some knowledge and understanding of the language of poetry and has learned the art and a craft of poetry. And although Auden regards philology as a less alluring creature than the muse, philology, too, has to be courted.

Some of Auden's comments on the muse are similar to those of Robert Graves, but there is this difference: Graves' prose works, *The White Goddess: A historical grammar of poetic myth*, first published in 1948, *The Crowning Privilege* in 1955, and many of his poems, make it clear that his belief in the myth of the muse is a form of religious faith. Indeed, his belief is expressed with such consistency that it seems not only a conviction but a mode of thinking and feeling; almost, at times, a mode of being. In the Chapter, 'These Be Your Gods, O Israel!' in *The Crowning Privilege* Graves writes: (Graves 1959: 137) "'Grace' is the presence of the Muse Goddess; but she does not appear unless the poet has something urgent to say and to win her consent a poet must have something urgent to say". Graves is using the word, "Grace", in its religious sense of a divine blessing or divine inspiriting power. But the urgency lies not in any statement the poet might already have in mind but in the urging of the creative impulse; that is, what the poet feels is not the need to make a specific utterance but the need to search for the words that will prove to be the right utterance, and then to utter them.

In 'The War in Heaven' in *The White Goddess*, Graves writes: Graves 1948; 390)

> The Muse is a deity, but she is also a woman, and if her celebrant makes love to her with the second-hand phrases and ingenious verbal tricks that he uses to flatter her son Apollo, she rejects him more decisively even than she rejects the tongue-tied and cowardly bungler.

It is clear from their context that the words, "makes love", have the older meaning of woo or pay court to as well as physical sexual love. The muse, says Graves, is both divine and human, both a spirit and a person, or a personification. As a deity, she is mysterious and often inaccessible, an unrealized self in the poet's nonconscious mind; as a woman, or as a personification of the feminine, she can be approached more directly by the poet. But she must not be addressed in terms that he has previously used; and because the poet's originality must be more than linguistic, more than mere invention, the originality must have its source in new information released through the interaction of imagination and the creative impulse. Graves' disparaging reference to Apollo follows his earlier reference to what he calls Apollonian poetry: the "ability to express time-proved sentiments in time-honoured forms"; that is, a conventional poetry that is produced by custom rather than imagination.

Later in 'War in Heaven' Graves relates the spiritual more closely and explicitly to the sexual. The spiritual element is expressed in the words: (Graves 1948: 393) "Constant illiterate use of the phrase 'to woo the Muse' has obscured its poetic sense: the poet's inner communion with the White Goddess, regarded as the source of truth". The fact that the sacramental union takes place in the poet's mind confirms the idea that it is a merging of the poet's conscious self with the sacred self that emerges from the nonconscious. The union, says Graves, is the poet's source of truth. In his next sentence he notes the physicality of the union: "Truth has been represented by poets as a naked woman: a woman divested of all garments or ornaments that will commit her to any particular position in time and space". Graves writes as if he actually experienced the muse as a visual image. It is as if the goddess, by emerging into the light of the poet's consciousness, assumes a mortal form through a process of personification that is also a mythical transformation from goddess to human.

Graves returns to the theme of the muse in his lectures as Oxford Chair of Poetry, published as *Poetic Craft and Principle* in 1967. In Lecture One he states that the Muse Goddess is the guardian of a love magic, and he adds: (Graves 1967: 97) "Only poets are convinced that a watchful trust in the undisciplined Muse Goddess will eventually teach them poetic wisdom and make them welcome to her secret paradise". In a later paragraph the love magic becomes poetic magic which, says Graves, "cannot be explained". The magic can be interpreted as the nonconscious and thus inexplicable ways in which the creative impulse activates the creative imagination, and the "secret paradise" can be seen as the poetic imagination at work.

The poet and novelist, Robert Nye, argues that the muse is more than an immanent element, more than an unrealized, perhaps unrealizable, aspect of the poet's self; she is also the representation of a real flesh-and-blood person. In a personal communication, Nye writes:

> Consider how poems by a particular poet, shall we say Graves, vary in accordance with the particular woman who inspired them, how his poems addressed to Laura Riding are quite different in tone and manner from the ones addressed to Beryl Pritchard who became his second wife.

Through his reading of Graves' poetry, Nye's understanding of the muse is at once as wide as and more precise than Graves'. The muse takes the identity of a real woman, and the reality of her presence in the poet's mind influences the poem. Nye continues:

> It is the nature of the woman in whom the poet finds the Muse incarnate that gives interest and variety to his verse. Donne's poems to and about Anne are quite different from those in which he expatiates cynically about womankind in general, or perhaps a series of fleeting loves in particular.

Graves' biographer, Martin Seymour-Smith, confirms Nye's views. In Chapter Seven '1919-25' of *Robert Graves: His Life and Work,* Seymour-Smith writes: (Seymour-Smith 1982: 94) "*The White Goddess* is not, as it has too often been called, simply a 'rationalization of Riding'". And in Chapter Twelve '1928-29' he states: (Seymour-Smith 1982: 153) "His real, and finest, love poems belong to the forties, and were addressed to his second wife, Beryl". Seymour-Smith identifies four other women with whom Graves fell in love or idealized at different times in his life, and Seymour-Smith shows that each woman prompted love poems.

A later biographer, Graves' nephew, Richard Perceval Graves, in *Robert Graves and the White Goddess 1940-1985* (Graves, R.P.1995: xx) identifies the four women as Judith Bledsoe, Margot Callas, Cindy Lee alias Aemilia Laracuen, and Julia (Juli) Simon. These biographers' observations confirm the centuries-old belief that, for some poets, the function of mind associated with falling in love is related to the function that produces the creative impulse that leads to the making of poems.

Not all poets' minds function in these ways, but for Graves and other poets the muse is a powerful force.

The similarities between Graves' myth of the muse and the White Goddess, or the muse as the White Goddess, and Jung's myth of the anima suggest that the myths are variations on a theme that is produced by the same or similar mental processes and conditions. In 'The Problem of Types in Poetry' in *Psychological Types*, Jung states, without any supporting argument: (Jung 1946: 272) "Individualism seems to have begun with the service of women, thereby effecting a most important reinforcement of man's soul as a psychological factor; since service of woman means service of the soul". Could it be that the poet, in searching for his muse, was searching for his soul, the essence of his being? In *Psychological Types* and elsewhere, Jung uses the term, "anima", to identify the soul of a man, and the equivalent term, "animus", for the soul of a woman. He defines the terms in his autobiography, *Memories, Dreams, Reflections*: (Jung 1971b: 114-5)

> Anima and Animus Personification of the feminine nature of a man's unconscious and masculine nature of a woman's. This psychological bisexuality is a reflection of the biological fact that it is the larger number of male (or female) genes which is the decisive factor in the determination of sex.

He continues: "The smaller number of contrasexual genes seems to produce a corresponding contrasexual character, which usually remains unconscious. As regulators of behavior they are two of the most influential archetypes".

The poet's mind necessarily diverges from other minds because part of the poetic task is to bring the usually nonconscious contrasexual character, or anima, into consciousness. Jung claims to find this kind of personification in *Paradiso* in Dante's *The Divine Comedy*, which was probably completed around the year 1320. In 'The Problem of Types in Poetry' Jung states that Dante is "the spiritual knight of his lady", and he adds: (Jung 1946: 273)

And in this heroic labour her image is exalted into that heavenly, mystical figure of the Mother of God – a figure which in its complete detachment from the object has become a personification of a purely psychological entity, i. e. that unconscious content whose personification I have termed the anima or soul.

Graves' White Goddess is produced by the same mental act of personification as Dante's Mother of God; and his concept of the muse is produced by the same process and state of mind as Jung's concept of the anima.

Jung, like Graves, sees the connection between the spiritual and the sexual. In 'Definitions' in *Psychological Types* he writes: (Jung 1946: 277) "That the complementary character of the soul [or anima] is also concerned with the sex-character is a fact which can no longer be seriously doubted". And in 'The Problem of Types in Poetry', in a discussion of *The Shepherd*, which was written around 140 AD, Jung suggests that, in the mind of a man, the erotic is not the opposite but the obverse of the sacred:

His mistress appears before him, not in an erotic phantasy, but in 'divine' form, seeming to him like a goddess in the heavens. [...] The erotic impression has evidently become united in the collective unconscious with those archaic residues which from primordial times have held the imprints of vivid impressions of women's nature: woman as mother, and woman as desirable maid.

Questions about the nature, and the very existence, of a collective unconscious have been partly answered by neuroscience. Since the anatomy of the human brain is universal, and since our brains have had the same anatomy for some thousands of years, it seems likely that those parts of the brain that function nonconsciously are also universal. But Jung's concept of a collective unconscious includes content as well as structure. The content could be Jung's "archaic residues", innate potentialities or susceptibilities bequeathed by successive generations. These innate potentialities could include a faculty for myth-making. Some myths have their origins in physical reality: if one generation suffered the cataclysm that followed an ice age, or the close threat of actual monsters such as sabre-toothed tigers, or the holocaust of bush fires and forest fires, or the tectonic convulsions of earthquakes – if one generation experienced these catastrophes, then the imprint on the brain could perhaps be transmitted to future generations as a folk memory. Anecdotal testimony suggests that younger children, under the age of seven, still dream of monsters; older children and adults do not; and yet the existence of monsters is a recurring subject in science fiction, illustrated novels and cinema.

Towards the end of his life, Freud, too, discusses the collective unconscious. In the chapter, 'Difficulties' in *Moses and Monotheism* he states: (Freud 1939: 94) "an impression of the past is retained in unconscious memory-traces"; he makes three references to "an archaic heritage"; he writes of "memory-traces of the experience of earlier generations". In the later chapter, 'The Historical Development', Freud states: (Freud 939: 132) "I do not think we gain anything by introducing the concept of a 'collective' unconscious"; but in his next sentence he states: "The content of the unconscious, indeed, is in any case a collective, universal property of mankind".

The poet's muse could be part of an archaic inheritance. Graves and Jung create two versions of the same essentially religious myth. But the muse and the anima seem to have been overtaken by agnosticism and neuroscience, and the myths of the muse and the anima, like other myths and like theistic religion, seem to have died. Modern poets in the act of composing still seek to activate the nonconscious networks that are mysteriously encoded for a spiritual self that is also a poetic self, but when they succeed in activating the networks and realizing that self, they do not regard the process as sexual or symbolically sexual, and they do not regard the self as feminine.

## Childhood, Memory and Imagination

The persistence of our memories of childhood events, and the strong emotional and moral charges of some of these memories, clearly suggests that our memories of these events remain important to us in our adult lives; but exactly what their importance is, and exactly what we remember of our childhood, is uncertain. Our memories not only select themselves automatically for encoding; they also edit themselves while they are in our nonconscious memory store. It follows, then, that the adult's memories of childhood events, and of the emotional or moral charges associated with these events, will differ from the originals. Some of our memories of childhood may not, in fact, be ours but part of family lore. When, as children, we hear a parent recall an incident from our earlier childhood, an incident of which we had been unaware because it had occurred before we had the power of memory or a developed consciousness, then the parent's memory of the incident is assimilated into our store of childhood memories as if that particular memory were independently ours.

Few children, and few adults looking back on their childhood, can recall their first two or three years of life because, as the previous paragraph suggests, the brain of the young child does not have the neural capacity to store and retrieve many memories. The geneticist, Robert Winston, offers a neurological interpretation in *The Human Mind*: (Winston 2004: 243) "As the hippocampus, site of the brain's long-term memory, does not reach maturity until we are three years old, it is very likely that most 'early memories' are false". In the same paragraph, Winston adds: "some parts of our brain do not reach maturity until we are in our late teens, even in our twenties". Another possible interpretation of our inability to remember our first two years is that, as we acquire language and begin to do some of our thinking, including thinking about the past, in words, so our way of decoding memories must change. Children do, in fact, encode and store memories before they begin to speak, but it might not be possible for them at a later stage in life to decode these prelinguistic memories into words. Small children can, of course, distinguish tone and loudness of adult voices, and the emotions expressed in these voices, before they, children, understand the meanings of the words being spoken. Clearly, the minds of young children are designed to remain unburdened by an independent memory until around the age of seven, when their autobiographical memory begins to develop and they can tell the difference between events in which they themselves participated and events they learned from family lore. And it is around the age of seven that children begin to lose the innocence of childhood by distinguishing fact from fantasy; they begin to accept that there is no Santa Claus. Even when we allow for these distortions and lacunae, we find that childhood memories can be so persistent and so emotionally intense that we are led to believe that the state of childhood is a particular mystery.

That line from the nursery song, "London Bridge is falling down, falling down, falling down", seems to sing itself spontaneously in the final stanza of Eliot's *The Waste Land* (Eliot 1958: 77), and there is the same kind of spontaneous irruption from childhood into adulthood, from innocence into experience, in the opening lines of section V of *The Hollow Men*, where the mulberry bush of the nursery rhyme becomes Eliot's prickly pear: (Eliot 1958: 89-90) "Here we go round the prickly pear", with its echo in the finality of "This the way the world ends [...] Not with a bang but a whimper". The possibility that the rhythmic and rhyming qualities of songs and slogans make them memorizable seems inadequate to explain the persistence of such worthless things. Memory seems to be telling us that these things are not trivial or peripheral, telling us that some memories are childish because parts of our memory and mind never grow up, and that the childishness somehow retains an importance in our adult life.

Childhood recalled can seem like a golden age. Thomas Traherne (1637-1674), in the second item of his *Third Century* in *Thomas Traherne: Poems, Centuries and Three Thanksgivings*, remembers his childhood in these terms: (Traherne 1966: 263) "All appeared New, and Strange at the first, inexpressibly rare, and Delightfull, and Beautifull. I was a little Stranger which at my Entrance into the World was Saluted and Surrounded with innumerable Joys". And in the poem, 'The Myth', Muir recalls his early childhood on the small island of Wyre in Orkney: (Muir 1991: 141)

> My childhood all a myth
> Enacted in a distant isle.

Muir's prose account of his early years is expressed even more hauntingly in the first chapter in *An Autobiography*. The mythological isle is the real island of Wyre in the Orkney archipelago; the myth is potent when set against Muir's experience of the squalor of Glasgow and west-central Scotland in the early decades of the twentieth century, and the wasteland of bombed European cities through which Muir travelled immediately after the Second World War. The childhood landscapes of

Traherne and Muir are partly real and partly allegorical: the child sees places, even the everyday places of the street, the home, the garden, with an unguarded detailed intensity that seems to magnify the places and make them legendary.

The Scottish poet and translator, Alastair Reid, grew up in Galloway in south-west Scotland and on the Isle of Arran off Scotland's west coast. In his essay, 'Borderlines', in *Memoirs of a Modern Scotland* Reid states that he is attached to these places: (Reid 1970: 154) "almost mystically, for it was there I experienced all the epiphanies of dawning consciousness". And as Reid continues, it becomes clear that for him the dawning of consciousness is a continuing experience. When an adult in that state of mind revisits the actual places of childhood, the places are not diminished. Reid observes: "I carry these two landscapes inside me like secrets, and I revisit them in awe and trepidation". Heaney, too, recalls childhood experiences of awe. In his extended series of interviews with Dennis O'Driscoll, published in *Stepping Stones*, Heaney speaks of standing alone outside his primary school and experiencing "a taste of yourself in all your own solitude and singularity". (Heaney 2008: 244) Later in *Stepping Stones* Heaney recalls similar boyhood experiences when he climbed trees: "I remember much of my childhood as a trance of loneliness, and in those places something in me was utterly at peace". (Heaney 2008: 264)

There is no allegory in Walt Whitman's 'There Was a Child Went Forth' but Whitman creates a legendary effect through the accumulation of precisely observed detail. The child is at one with the natural world: (Whitman 1987: 386-8) "The early lilacs became part of this child"; at one with the intimate social world of the family and the wider social world of the town with its "Vehicles, teams, the heavy-planked wharves"; at one with the seas and the skies. And in the end, Whitman's child –

> that child who went forth every day,
> And who now goes, and will always go forth every day

embodies Whitman's vision of unifying, imperishable innocence.

# 3

# The Sacred Impulse

## Poetry and Religion

IN HER INTRODUCTION TO LATER EDITIONS of *Collected Poems*, Laura Riding writes at first as if poetry, the realization of the creative impulse, is similar to the realization of the religious impulse except that poetry is non-spiritual: "Poetry made itself the secular twin of religion". And then, as she develops her theme, Riding begins to recognize explicitly what she must have known intuitively: writing poetry is itself a spiritual activity. She states: (Riding 1991: 2)

> But its secularity has not been of a 'worldly' cast. Rather than endeavoring to serve as a ritual of spirituality symbolic of the religiously serious, a process of metaphorical imitation of it, a 'mere' art, it has, except in vulgar conception and practice, endeavored to serve as an area for the exercise of spiritual consciousness as a directly, personally possessed human function, not just a derivative of a mysterious condition of spiritual blessedness.

That is, poetry is not a representation of some other kind of spirituality, and it is not derived from some other spiritual source. Poetry is the expression of its own spirituality, a spirituality that is not divine but innately human: "a directly, personally possessed human function". And in her next sentence, as if to clarify her view beyond all possible ambiguity, she states: "Poetry, that is, made itself a charter of the internal, personally independent spirituality of the human being".

Riding is then led to the view that theistic religion separates one part of the self from another and requires what she calls the soul to act as an intermediary between the parts of the divided self, whereas the spirituality expressed through poetry is an enlightening and unifying force: (Riding 1991: 2)

> Where religion dealt with the separation of a spiritual part from the
> mixed body-and-soul, or mixed body-and-mind, with the soul as inter-
> mediary factor, poetry gave the spiritual element the role of a teaching
> presence in the complex composition of the individual human being.

Poetry can achieve such unity more readily than religion, because po-
etry is often a fusion of the religious and creative impulses brought
about by the creative poetic imagination. Riding's view is similar to one
concept of Christianity: Christ's role is to act as intermediary between
humans and God, and to persuade humans that the God they once dared
not approach directly because he was so vengeful and irascible is now
a God of love. But if we accept that religion and spirituality are innate
human forces, and that these forces can be realized through poetry, then
there is no need for an intermediary because there is no God.

Riding states that, as expressions of spirituality, poetry and religion
have developed in different ways: (Riding 1991: 2)

> Poetry may be described as an institution devoted to the pursuit of spir-
> itual realism, in relation to religion as an institution devoted to the pur-
> suit of spiritual idealism. For those to whom the spiritual nature of the
> human being calls for literal expression, living fulfilment, there presses
> a sense of necessity of choice between poetry and religion – the quality
> of the urgency determines the choice.

Poetry or religion? Riding's phrase, "the quality of the urgency", sug-
gests that there are two kinds of spirituality: one emerges from the reli-
gious impulse alone and is expressed through theistic religion; the other
emerges from the creative impulse, and thus from the innate, non-the-
istic religious impulse, and is expressed through poetry. Riding clearly
implies that, in the mind of an individual, the two are unequal forces
and that the stronger, the one with the greater quality of urgency in
the individual mind, will prevail. One can readily picture someone in
whom only the religious and not the creative impulse is active; it is
more difficult to picture a creative artist in whose mind there is no re-
ligious impulse, no sense of the sacred, no need to celebrate mysteries.
By Riding's argument, poetry can be the "literal expression, living ful-
filment" of "the spiritual nature of the human being". In the act of writ-
ing a poem, the poet can express the creative and the religious impulses

in such a way that creativity and spirituality are one. And this raises the question: Can poetry be regarded as a form of religion?

In stanza VII of 'Resolution and Independence', which was probably completed in 1802, Wordsworth writes of Thomas Chatterton and poets generally: (Wordsworth 1956: 156) "By our own spirits are we deified". That is, poets, through their spiritual act of making poems, are god-like. In Book XIV, the Conclusion to *The Prelude*, which was probably completed in 1805, Wordsworth writes of love as a sacred element, "Bearing a tribute to the Almighty's Throne," and then he adds: (Wordsworth 1956: 585)

> This spiritual Love acts not nor can exist
> Without Imagination, which, in truth,
> Is but another name for absolute power
> And clearest insight, amplitude of mind,
> And Reason in her most exalted mood.

If imagination is another name for absolute power, then imagination rivals, or even displaces, the Almighty. In their devotional poems, none of Wordsworth's predecessors – John Donne, John Milton, George Herbert, Richard Crashaw, Henry Vaughan, Thomas Traherne – makes such a claim.

Matthew Arnold in 'The Study of Poetry' in *Essays in Criticism*, Second Series, makes the prediction: (Arnold 1888: 10) "More and more mankind will discover that we have to turn to poetry to interpret life for us, to console us, to sustain us". His prediction has proved wrong, of course. In his next sentence, he makes the further prediction: "Without poetry, our science will appear incomplete; and most of what now passes with us for religion and philosophy will be replaced by poetry". An exclusively scientific view of life is clearly incomplete, but Arnold states that religion, which claimed and still claims to offer a whole view of life, and perhaps of an afterlife, will be replaced by poetry. And in the same paragraph he says of religion and philosophy: "what are they but the shadows and dreams and false shows of knowledge?" Arnold is less than absolute in his claims; he states that he is speaking of religion as he sees it in the late nineteenth century, but he clearly believes that poetry would, and should, replace religion.

The contention – Poetry or religion? – continues. Stephen Spender sees the making of poems as a spiritual activity, but he does not claim that poetry is a religion. In the chapter, 'The New Orthodoxies' in *The Creative Element*, he reaches a conclusion similar to Matthew Arnold's when he writes: (Spender 1953: 176) "Although poetry cannot be a substitute for religion the poetic function tends to become a substitute for defective spiritual institutions". That is, poetry can replace what William James calls (James 1982: 334) "religion as an institutional, corporate, or tribal product" in 'The Value of Saintliness' in *The Varieties of Religious Experience*.

Four American poets, by contrast, make the equation: Poetry is religion. In his extended essay, 'Poetry and Imagination' in *Letters and Social Aims,* Emerson writes: (Emerson s.d.: 591) "Poetry is inestimable as a lonely faith, a lonely protest in the uproar of atheism". William Carlos Williams in 'Notes in Diary Form' in *Selected Essays*, writes: (Williams 1969: 71)

> The only human value of anything, writing included, is intense vision of the facts. God – sure if it mean sense. 'God' is poetic for the unobtainable. Sense is hard to get but it can be got. Certainly that destroys 'God', it destroys everything that interferes with simple clarity of apprehension.

The concept of God is acceptable if it makes sense, but God is unobtainable; and when sense, that is, meaning and understanding, is attained, it destroys God. Williams' words are chiastic but his point is clear: God is displaced by a human, and humanist, vision life.

In his credo, 'Poetry and the Mind of Modern Man', Conrad Aitken speaks of the power of poetry and concludes: (Aitken 1966: 7) "In the evolution of man's consciousness, ever widening and deepening and subtilizing his awareness, and in the dedication of himself to this supreme task, man possesses all that he could possibly require in the way of a religious credo". And in a conclusion that echoes Wordsworth's "By our own spirits are we deified" Aitken writes of the poet: "when the half-gods go, the gods arrive; he can, if he only will, become divine".

Wallace Stevens enters the debate in prose and in poetry. In 'Adagia' in *Opus Posthumous*, Stevens' aphorisms include these: (Stevens 1982: 158) "After one has abandoned a belief in god, poetry is that essence which takes its place as life's redemption". And (Stevens 1982: 167) "God is a symbol for something that can as well take other forms, as, for example, the form of high poetry". And again in (Stevens 1982: 172) "God is in me or not at all (does not exist.)" In Section V of his poem, 'The Man with the Blue Guitar' in his *Selected Poems* he writes: (Stevens 1965: 54)

> The earth, for us, is flat and bare.
> There are no shadows.  Poetry
>
> Exceeding music must take the place
> Of empty heaven and its hymns,
>
> Ourselves in poetry must take their place

In Stevens' 'Final Soliloquy of the Interior Paramour' there is the line that partly echoes Wordsworth's assertion of imagination as an absolute power: (Stevens 1965: 143) "We say God and the Imagination are one".

For Wordsworth, Arnold, Emerson, Williams, Aitken and Stevens, the sacred impulse that compels them to make poems is a more powerful force than a belief in God.


## Religion in some Twentieth-Century Poetry

Eliot's Anglo-Catholicism is implicit in *Ash-Wednesday*, in the Ariel poems, especially 'Journey of the Magi' and 'A Song for Simeon', and in some passages of *Four Quartets*, written between 1935 and 1942. His religious impulse is expressed more explicitly in some sections of *The Rock*, in *Murder in the Cathedral*, and in his Preface to the collection of essays, *For Lancelot Andrewes*, where Eliot makes this frequently quoted statement: (Eliot 1970: 7) "The general point of view may be described as classicist in literature, royalist in politics, and anglo-catholic in religion". And he reinforces his declaration by opening the collection with the essay, 'Lancelot Andrewes', and by using as the title of the book a form of words that is also a dedication. In fact, the dedication page reads, 'FOR MY MOTHER'.

Eliot's most sustained study of religion is *The Idea of a Christian Society*, where he makes some categorical claims. He writes: (Eliot 1939: 24) "the only hopeful course for a society which would thrive and continue its creative activity in the arts of civilization, is to become Christian". Others would argue that the only course is to become Buddhist, or Judaic, or Islamic, or to express one's innate, non-theistic spirituality. Eliot adds (Eliot 1939: 57) that Christianity is "permanent" and "absolute" whereas political and social systems are "transitory" and "contingent". But Christianity varies over time and place; it has sometimes been contingent in several senses of the word; it has been and might still be a political and social system: the British head of state is also head of the Church of England. Elsewhere in *The Idea of a Christian Society* Eliot is less categorical. He states: (Eliot 1939: 28-9) "For the great mass of humanity [...] their religious and social life should form for them a natural whole" and "The unitary community should be religious-social" but he concedes that these ideal states are unattainable. In some sections of *The Idea of a Christian Society* Eliot writes not as a conservative but as a conservationist with a strong sense of social justice. (Eliot 1939: 61) He attacks "the principle of private profit" as "leading both to the deformation of humanity by unregulated industrialism, and the exhausting of natural resources".

More relevant to the present discussion is Eliot's essay, 'Religion and Literature' in *T. S. Eliot: Selected Prose*, where he champions Christianity in what for him are remarkably combative terms: (Eliot 1935: 41-2) "What I do wish to confirm is that the whole of modern literature is corrupted by what I call secularism, that it is simply unaware of, simply cannot understand the meaning of, the primacy of the supernatural over the natural life". The whole of modern literature corrupted by secularism? Until the publication of *Ash-Wednesday* in 1930, most of Eliot's own poetry is secular in his sense of the word in the quotation above; but although his early poetry does not acknowledge the primacy of the supernatural over the natural, it is nevertheless religious on those occasions when it expresses the sacredness of life, especially life in a seemingly confused, amoral, and soulless age, as in Section IV of *Preludes*: (Eliot 1958: 23)

The notion of some infinitely gentle
Infinitely suffering thing.

And his early work – not only 'Gerontion', *The Waste Land*, and *The Hollow Men* but also 'Rhapsody on a Windy Night', 'La Figlia Che Piange', 'Sweeney Erect', and 'Sweeney Among the Nightingales' – is religious, too, in its celebration of the mystery of our existence. Any poet who expresses his sense of the sacred and his need to celebrate mysteries is responding to the religious impulse and cannot be called secular. A few poets today as in 1935 might fail to understand the concept of the primacy of the supernatural over the natural, but it is more likely that most poets understand the concept and reject it for the alternative belief: that the religious impulse is innate and natural, a feature of our human nature.

When Eliot discusses Christianity and the arts in the later essay, 'The Three Senses of "Culture"' in *Notes Towards the Definition of Culture*, he argues that there should be an interrelationship between religion and culture, and states that it is a widely held error (Eliot 1948: 30) "that culture can be preserved, extended, and developed in the absence of religion". He adds: "This error may be held by the Christian and the infidel". Eliot means doctrinal religion, the religion of an established church, but what matters to artists is their innate religious impulse and sense of the sacred. 'The Three Senses of "Culture"', *The Idea of a Christian Society*, and 'Religion and Literature', all of which express his deep commitment and his profound sense of obligation, were written as reasoned arguments and not as sacred works; a sense of the sacred and of the religious and creative impulses working together appear only in Eliot's poems.

When Eliot was writing 'Religion and Literature', one of the most powerful secular forces at work in Britain and Europe was Marxism, a doctrine and mythology that threatened the existence of the classicist, royalist, Anglo-Catholic culture that Eliot supported. The British poet who was most lastingly influenced by Marxism, or rather, by Marxist-Leninism, was Hugh MacDiarmid, the pseudonym of Christopher Murray Grieve. An early stanza in MacDiarmid's long visionary comedy on Scottish and international themes, *A Drunk Man Looks at the Thistle*, opens with the line: (MacDiarmid 1985: 86) "A greater Christ, a greater Burns, may come". For MacDiarmid, the greater Christ is Lenin, and his greater Burns, I suspect, is MacDiarmid himself. 'First Hymn to Lenin' and 'Second Hymn to Lenin' are the title poems of his collections published in 1931 and 1935; the 'Third Hymn to Lenin' appeared in 1957, shortly after MacDiarmid had publicly declared his support for the Soviet Union's invasion of Hungary.

Long after Lenin and Leninism had been replaced by Stalin and Stalinism, MacDiarmid continued to write of Lenin as a redeemer; his poems to Lenin are not portraits or odes but hymns, songs in praise of a god. In the 'First Hymn' in *The Complete Poems of Hugh MacDiarmid*, Lenin is hailed as Christ's successor come to complete Christ's work on earth, but Lenin's methods are those of the Old Testament God who slaughters his enemies and those whom he thinks might be his enemies: (MacDiarmid 1985: 298)

> As necessary, and insignificant, as death
> Wi' a' its agonies in the cosmos still
> The Cheka's horrors are in their degree;
> And'll end suner! What maitters't wha we kill
> To lessen that foulest murder that deprives
>> Maist men o' real lives?

The mass executions of the Cheka – *Chrezvychainaya Komissiya*, the Extraordinary Commission for the Elimination of Counter-Revolution, Sabotage, and Speculation established by Lenin in 1917 – the killings, says MacDiarmid, are necessary and insignificant. What does it matter, he asks rhetorically, whom we kill? And he uses the pronoun, "we", as if he himself were an agent of the Cheka, enforcing his master's will.

The reader might see a contradiction between the support for killing in the name of Lenin, and in MacDiarmid's claim in the title poem of *The Battle Continues* (MacDiarmid 1985: 905) that the poet, Roy Campbell

> kisses the bloody hands of mass-murderers like Hitler, Mussolini and
> Franco.

The basis of MacDiarmid's accusation is that Campbell supported Franco during the Spanish Civil War of 1936-39. In his poems of Spain Campbell fuses politics and religion. We do not know which of Campbell's poems incited MacDiarmid; two possible poems in *Collected Poems of Roy Campbell Volume II* are (Campbell 1957: 25-6) 'To Mary after the Red Terror' and (Campbell 1957: 54-8) 'Dawn on the Sierra of Gredos'. The neutral reader might feel that support for any murderous tyrant is wrong. The extent of the denunciation of Campbell, and MacDiarmid's assertion of his own righteousness – *The Battle Continues* is around nine hundred lines long – strikes the neutral reader as excessive. Even so, the reader must assume that MacDiarmid knew his own mind, and that his adoration of Lenin and vilification of Campbell and others whom he regarded as his enemies are neither the utterances of the doubter who talks louder and longer in order to silence the doubt, nor of the convert who professes his faith more zealously than someone who was born into the faith and grew up in it. Religious hatred is a common occurrence. The religious impulse can be expressed as hatred as well as love, and the hatred can be codified into a doctrine that cannot tolerate the sacred or the mysterious unless they are sanctioned by that doctrine. What is uncommon is that in some of MacDiarmid's poetry the creative impulse, too, is driven by hatred.

For Eliot, religion is Christianity; for MacDiarmid, it is the post-Christian and anti-Christian apotheosis of Lenin. For Robert Graves, religion is the acknowledgement of pre-Christian goddesses and gods. In his study of magic, religion, and poetry, *The White Goddess*, some of the statements of faith are contrived, whimsical, and self-conscious to the extent that the reader occasionally questions Graves' belief in his pagan pantheon; in many of his poems, by contrast, the faith is more fully imagined and influences his modes of poetic thought and feeling. In the Introduction to *The White Goddess* he states: (Graves 1948: 11-12), "The function of poetry is religious invocation of the Muse; its use is the experience of mixed exaltation and horror that her presence excites". Religious invocation, or the summoning up and the expressing of the religious impulse, is a major function of poetry but not the only

one, and the Muse is not the only realization of the impulse. The chief
deity in Graves' religion, in his prose as in his poetry, is his Muse, and
in the first chapter of *The White Goddess* he identifies the Muse as the
White Goddess: (Graves 1948: 20)

> The test of a poet's vision, one might say, is the accuracy of his por-
> trayal of the White Goddess and of the island over which she rules [...] a
> true poem is necessarily an invocation of the White Goddess, or Muse,
> the Mother of All Living, the ancient power of fright and lust – a female
> spider or the queen-bee whose embrace is death.

Graves' test is arbitrary; a poet can have a true vision of life without
ever portraying the mythological White Goddess on her mythological
island; and true poems, including poems that express religious truths,
can be written on a variety of subjects and themes. The statement is, in
fact, Graves' personal interpretation of his response to the religious and
creative impulses; the words express his religious belief and at the same
time they symbolize his creative methods.

At the centre of his religion is a complex association of ancient ma-
triarchal forces: the Muse, the White Goddess, who in some myths also
takes the form of the Earth Goddess or Earth Mother, Graves' 'Mother
of All Living'; she can even appear in theriomorphic forms, part-human
and part-insect, of the female spider and the queen bee, which symbol-
ize the Devouring Mother whose fecundity demands human sacrifice.
Indeed, in 'War in Heaven', the final chapter of *The White Goddess*,
Graves states that the poet must experience a vision of human sacrifice
before he can understand the nature of poetry: (Graves 1948: 393)

> Poetry began in the matriarchal age, and derives its magic from the
> moon, not the sun. No poet can hope to understand the nature of poetry
> unless he has had a vision of the Naked King crucified to the lopped
> oak, and watched the dancers, red-eyed from the acrid smoke of the
> sacrificial fires, stamping out the measure of the dance, their bodies
> bent uncouthly forward, with a monotonous chant of: 'Kill! kill! kill!'
> and 'Blood! blood! blood!'

Although that statement begins with astrology and ends in melodrama, it is worth considering because of what it reveals of Graves' experience of creativity and religion.

The statement can be read as anthropological fiction, that is, a conjectured reconstruction of the past that is imaginatively true. It is also a re-working of myth. *The White Goddess* contains references to James Frazer's *The Golden Bough: a Study of Magic and Religion*, which in its abridged form, published in 1922, led to a new interest in mythology among British writers. Graves' reference to the crucifixion of the Naked King seems like an echo of Christian mythology, but Graves' mythology is the pre-Christian ritual killing of the king. Graves' statement can also be read in terms of the personification and projection of information – sensations, images, ideas – that is released when nonconscious networks are activated and become conscious. The two interpretations are consistent with each other; it is clear that in Graves' mind creativity and religious activity are centred on actual rituals, some of which were ordeals, and that these ordeals reflect the ordeals of his imagination, painful trials of his creative power, of his faith and of his poetic self.

Rituals similar to the one quoted above from *The White Goddess* but in less histrionic language are re-enacted in poems from all stages of Graves' career: from the glimpsed mysteries of 'The Unicorn and the White Doe' to the huntress, "the laughing, naked queen", in 'Dethronement', and in the late poem, 'Druid Love', especially the second stanza, which begins: "But if the woman be herself a Druid?" One of Graves' most representative expressions of the subject is the entranced love-quest in the poem, 'The White Goddess': (Graves 1975: 157)

> Green sap of Spring in the young wood a-stir
> Will celebrate the Mountain Mother,
> And every song-bird shout awhile for her;
> But we are gifted, even in November
> Rawest of seasons, with so huge a sense
> Of her nakedly worn magnificence
> We forget cruelty and past betrayal,
> Heedless of where the next bright bolt may fall.

The poem is an imaginative re-enactment of what was probably an actual ritual performed in early human societies. At the same time it reveals something of the creative process that is distinctively but not exclusively Graves': the poetic imagination's quest for truth; the ordeal poets must sometimes endure when nonconscious networks are activated and release strange, disturbing visions; the personification of some of the elements in these visions; and the fulfilment – emotional, intellectual, and spiritual – poets experience when imagination gives shape and meaning to religious and creative impulses. Although today's reader is unlikely to believe in Graves' goddesses and gods, the reader can see that the poems are energized by religious faith and the religion is realized in the poems in such a way that the religion is the poetry and the poetry the religion. Graves' biographer, Martin Seymour-Smith, writes in Chapter Seven, '1919-25' of *Robert Graves: His Life and Work*: (Seymour-Smith 1982: 102) "To all intents and purposes, poetry is his religion, and magic (the magic, the mysterious qualities of words) is his means".

Spender and Auden discuss the religious nature of poetry in terms that are less ritualistic and less symbolic than Graves' but no less intense. In 'The Making of a Poem' Spender writes: (Spender 1955b: 58) "It is evident that a faith in his vocation, mystical in its intensity, sustains poets". In the next paragraph he writes: "My sense of the sacredness of the task of poetry began then, [at the age of nine] and I have always felt that a poet's was a sacred vocation, like a saint's". The nature and intensity of Spender's belief in the sacredness of poetry and in the act of writing poetry are similar to Shelley's in *A Defence of Poetry*: the creative impulse is a religious impulse. Both men have been ridiculed for their belief. The ridicule could be an effect of the reader's spiritual impoverishment, but one sometimes feels, especially in Spender's case, that the ridicule is not an expression of outright disbelief but rather the false censure of a reader who is disturbed or embarrassed by statements he regards as socially and artistically inadmissible, by a public display of what he feels should be a private confession, by a disclosure of forbidden knowledge. But at its most intense, its most profound, the creative impulse in poetry is more often a sacred than a secular force.

In 'Making, Knowing and Judging' in *The Dyer's Hand* Auden outlines his concepts of the Primary Imagination and the Secondary Imagination, not in Coleridge's terms but in terms of the sacred and the profane, or secular: (Auden 1963: 54-5) "The concern of the Primary

Imagination, its only concern, is with sacred beings and sacred events. The sacred is that to which it is obliged to respond; the profane is that to which it cannot respond and therefore does not know". Only the Primary Imagination, then, is creative, and its expression is an irresistible response to sacred beings and events, which have their origins in the religious impulse. Auden continues: (Auden 1963: 55) "A sacred being cannot be anticipated; it must be encountered. On encounter the imagination has no option but to respond". The religious impulse cannot be summoned consciously but must occur as if spontaneously, and when it does the poet is impelled to direct his imagination on it. A sense of the sacred, Auden states, is innate and universal. Two paragraphs later he adds: "Some sacred beings seem to be sacred to all imaginations at all times. The Moon, for example, Fire, Snakes and those four important beings which can only be defined in terms of non-being: Darkness, Silence, Nothing, Death". The imagination of the poet today is unlikely to be grasped by the moon, fire or snakes, but it is still haunted by Auden's four great absolutes: literal and metaphorical darkness, silence, nothingness, and the finality of death.

## A Biology of Religion

At the beginning of the twentieth century William James delivered the Gifford Lectures in Natural Religion to audiences of Scottish clergymen in Edinburgh. The lectures were published as *The Varieties of Religious Experience* in 1902. By the time he delivered his tenth lecture, 'Conversion', some members of the audience must have been aware of the range of his intellect and his modes of thought. Even so, some of them might have been troubled when he said: (James 1982: 242) "it is logically conceivable that *if there be* higher spiritual agencies that can directly touch us, the psychological condition of their doing so *might be* our possession of a subconscious region which alone should yield access to them". James makes a similar observation in his lecture, 'Saintliness', where he states: (James 1982: 270) "If the grace of God miraculously operates, it probably operates through the subliminal door". As the earlier chapter, 'Jung, Freud and Creativity', has shown, James discussed nerve cells and cerebral patterns of transmission in

*The Principles of Psychology* in 1890; he knew that the subconscious region was the brain, the biological substrate of the mind. James writes conditionally: *"if there be"*, *"might be"* and "probably". I believe that his views are more positive and that his characteristic avoidance of dogmatic assertion leads him to write as he does; he knows that the concept of a supernatural being has its origin in our human nature.

Jung reaches that conclusion in *Psychological Types* where he states: (Jung 1946: 306) "If we regard the 'soul' as a personification of unconscious contents, so God [...] is also an unconscious content – a personification, in so far as he is personally conceived". And Jung reaffirms this view in his late work, *Answer to Job*, first published in1952, although he makes an aberrant denial of a physical dimension. In the penultimate chapter he writes: (Jung 1964: 169) "God is an obvious psychic and non-physical fact, i.e., a fact that can be established psychically but not physically". Jung makes the same point twice more in the same paragraph. If, as Jung claims, God is known to exist in but not outside the mind, then our concepts of God and our sense of the sacred are innate faculties of mind. *Answer to Job* ends with the rich ambiguity of "the One": (Jung 1964: 180) "even the enlightened person remains what he is, and is never more than his own limited ego before the One who dwells in him, whose form has no knowable boundaries, who encompasses him on all sides, fathomless as the abysms of the earth and vast as the sky".

The One could be God, perhaps in the form of the Holy Spirit who is said to be continuously present in our mind; or, more probably, the One could be the near-infinity of the nonconsciousness that underlies the conscious mind and includes the innate forces which, under the shaping power of the imagination, take the form of the religious impulse.

The philosopher and historian, Johan Huizinga, reaches a similar conclusion thorough an unusual route: the concept of play. In the chapter, 'The Elements of Mythopoesis', in *Homo Ludens: A Study of the Play Element in Culture* Huizinga writes: (Huizinga 1970: 163) "It is impossible, in my view, to make any sharp distinction between poetic personification in allegory, and  the conception of celestial – or infernal – beings in theology". He adds: "Holiness and play always tend to overlap. So do poetic imagination and faith". The faith that Huizinga associates with poetic imagination must surely be the religious impulse and not fixed doctrine. Functions of mind that transform an abstract quality into a person are similar to the functions that transform one kind of religious impulse, the prescriptive kind, into a god. The two processes, personification and deification, could be variations on the same theme. And fundamental to the theme is the mind's fluid and prolific play with multiple identities of godhood and human selfhood. One function, or set of functions, of mind personifies and deifies and then, as if separately and independently, another function or set of functions projects the personified and deified abstractions into worlds outside the mind.

The sophistication of non-invasive brain-scanning techniques has eliminated the need for the open-skull experiments conducted in the midtwentieth century by Wilder Penfield. A modern practitioner, the neurosurgeon V. S. Ramachandran, has identified networks in the temporal lobes of the brain which, when activated, give the patient a sense of spirituality. In the chapter, 'God and the Limbic System', in *Phantoms in the Brain* Ramachandran writes: (Ramachandran 1998: 175) "I've always suspected that the temporal lobes, especially the left lobe, are sometimes involved in religious experience". He adds that all medical students are taught that patients with apoplectic seizures in the left lobe may have religious experiences, and that even in seizure-free periods the patients may become preoccupied with religion. If patients experience the preoccupation in seizure-free periods, there need be no cause-and-effect connection between apoplexy and religion. Ramachandran discusses some case studies and then states: (Ramachandran 1998: 188) "The one clear conclusion that emerges from all this is that there are circuits in the human brain that are involved in religious experience". The neurologist, Antonio Damasio, confirms this in *Looking for Spinoza* when he asserts: (Damasio 2003: 284) "Yet spiritual experiences, religious or otherwise, are mental processes. They are biological processes of the highest level of complexity". In the same chapter, 'God and the Limbic System', Ramachandran refers to the work of the neurosurgeon, Michael Persinger, in Canada.

Persinger was interviewed by the science journalist, Alex Tsakiris, for the multi-media digital series, *Skeptiko*, in December 2009. At an early stage in the interview Persinger says: (Persinger 2009: 3 of transcript) "Our research starts on the basic premise that all experience is generated by brain activity". On that premise, he says of a person's experience: "And if they're natural phenomena, and we think that mystical experiences, including the God experience, the God belief, are natural phenomena, we should be able to reproduce them easily if we have the correct parameters in the laboratory". At several stages in the interview Persinger stresses the need to measure brain activity in laboratory experiments. His measuring device is a transcranial magnetic stimulator, a piece of headgear colloquially known as the God helmet, that directs minute electrical currents to specific sites in the brain and allows the neurosurgeon to identify areas associated with certain emotions and thoughts.

The device cannot, of course read the mind; it may identify an emotion but it cannot predict when a person will experience that emotion outside the laboratory or how the emotion will be expressed. It cannot predict when a poet will next experience the emotion, or the patterns of ideation in the poem. The science journalist, Jonah Lehrer, discusses the power of scanning machines in *Imagine: How Creativity Works*. In the Introduction he states: (Lehrer, 2012: xviii) "Furthermore, this new knowledge is useful: because we finally understand what creativity is, we can begin to construct a taxonomy of it, outlining the conditions under which each particular mental strategy is ideal". There can be no final understanding. Creativity is an interpenetration of the conscious and nonconscious mind, and we shall never know their full extent; for these reasons a taxonomy of creativity is impossible.

An argument against the innateness of the religious impulse is presented by the ethologist, Richard Dawkins, in *The God Delusion* in 2006. I readily agree that doctrinal religion can be a destructive force. Stephen Pinker describes just how exultantly destructive in the chapter, 'The Humanitarian Revolution', in *The Better Angels of Our Nature* (Pinker 2011: 31-56).

Dawkins writes: (Dawkins (2006: 174). "A proximate cause of religion might be the hyperactivity in a particular node of the brain. I shall not pursue the neurological idea of a 'god centre' in the brain because I am not concerned here with proximate questions". What Dawkins calls a "proximate cause" could be a direct source, and what he calls "hyperactivity" could be normal mental activity. Dawkins suggests that religion could be "a by-product of something else", and his something else is inculcation: "Obey your parents; obey the tribal elders, especially when they adopt a solemn, minatory tone". And then he adds a Darwinian interpretation: (Dawkins 2006: 176) "Natural selection builds child brains with a tendency to believe whatever their parents and tribal elders tell them". He does not name Ignatius Loyola, founder of the Jesuit Order in 1540-41, but he quotes the words attributed to Loyola: "Give me the child for his first seven years, and I'll give you the man".

I believe that, in human evolution, the religious impulse and a sense the sacred precede all religious doctrines and need not be defined in doctrinal terms. I know that when children begin to have some understanding of language, around the age of two, they sometimes defy their parents; they learn, from parental example, to say no. On questions of belief, adolescents sometimes try to assert their new identity by rejecting their parents' faith.

In his interview on *Skeptiko* Persinger replies to a question on science and religion: (Persinger 2009: 9 of transcript) "The only difference between a scientist and a religious believer or a mystical believer is the fact that we measure. And once we measure it we can reproduce it experimentally. If you can experimentally reproduce it, you can control it. And then you understand how it works".

Perhaps the difference between the scientist and the believer in a religious faith is greater than Persinger allows. The difference between science and poetry can be great. The scientist and the poet have different views on the nature and purpose of human experience. The scientist measures it; the poet expresses it in a work of art. The scientist seeks to control it; the poet seeks to liberate it. The scientist must reproduce the experience in laboratory experiments; the poet must reproduce the experience in such a way that the end result is not, in fact, a reproduction but a transmutation of experience. And the poetic rule of originality requires that a poet must never exactly repeat an experience; each poem must be new, unique.

# 4

# Poetic Vision

## Visionary Poetry

PROPHETIC AND MYSTICAL VISIONS are rare in English-language po-
etry of the last hundred years. Visionary poetry is a difficult and
dangerous genre. A poem is truly mystical or revelatory only if it offers
a transcendent vision of earthly reality. The vision must strike the reader
as a spontaneous account of a profound experience that fills the creative
imagination with the gift of grace; and the vision must be expressed in
a purity, perhaps a simplicity, of language. Today, poets still speak of
origins, sometimes in mythological terms, but they are unlikely to speak
of a divine creation. We are fascinated by time and the imagination's
transcendence of time, but when we speak of timelessness it is a time-
lessness that is a suspension of time within a temporal rather than an
eternal context. On questions of human identity, we speak more readily
about the state of our minds than the state of our souls, and we are likely
to identify the human spirit as a function of the human, not the divine
mind. Today's poets speak of mortality, including their own, but not of
immortality. Even so, poets still believe that the making of a poem is a
spiritual activity and that good poems – not only great poems but poems
that are honest and well made – are sacred texts. And when the content
of a metaphysical poem goes beyond existing limits of reality and cre-
ates a new and convincing order of reality – past or future, terrestrial or
eternal, dystopian or utopian – the result can be a transcendental vision.

John Milton and William Blake are the great visionaries in English
poetry. Among the visionary poems by British writers in the twentieth
century are Edwin Muir's 'Ballad of the Soul' published in 1925, Hugh
MacDiarmid's *A Drunk Man Looks at the Thistle* published in 1926,
some of Yeats' *Supernatural Songs* published in 1935 and some sec-
tions of Eliot's *Four Quartets*. David Gascoyne's *The Nightwatchers*,
*Megalometropolitan Carnival*, and *Encounter with Silence*, originally

written for radio and then published as one volume, *Night Thoughts,* in 1956, have a visionary quality. Robert Nye has written mystical poems at all stages of his poetic career, from his Juvenilia to *An Almost Dancer* published in 2012. George Szirtes' title sequences, *The Photographer in Winter* published in 1986 and *Metro* published in 1988 are visionary quests in which, through the transfiguring power of the imagination, the poet ransoms human goodness from the squalor of Eastern Europe in the 1940s and 1950s. Among American poets, Wallace Stevens, Theodore Roethke, John Berryman and Anne Sexton offer transcendent visions of life; in a younger generation of Americans, Louise Glück transforms precisely observed terrestrial details into the mystical visions of 'All Hallows', 'Messengers', and the sequences, *The Garden* and *Lamentations* in *Descending Figure* (Glück 1986: 379-80, 385-6).

A transcendental vision can take the form of prophecy or mysticism, both of which often have a religious content. Although this chapter is written in the belief that all forms of poetry, including visionary, are products of the human mind rather than divine or supernatural interventions in human affairs, it is clear that theistic religious beliefs are still integral elements of many people's thoughts, and for that reason the non-theistic poet and critic should take account of these beliefs. There is the belief that is present in creation myths: a divine or supernatural force created the universe and could, if it chose, destroy it; it is a force that is present throughout the universe and yet has an existence beyond it. There is the widespread belief in immortality, the eternal life of the soul after the death of the body, or the eternal after-life of body and soul together. It is understandable that some people should have a vision of an after-life in a heavenly state, not only as a compensation for the brevity or suffering of mortal life but also because the dead continue to live in the minds of the living. Perhaps longevity has partly reduced our need for eternity. Even today it can be argued that, since the faces, forms, and voices of the dead appear in the waking and dreaming minds of the living, the dead might have an existence in some other order of reality. And there remains the belief that a human can commune with a divine force and thus gain an understanding of divinity. Such a belief might require no great leap of faith for people who already believe that they are made in the image of God or gods and that their purpose on earth is to do God's will and to persuade other people to do likewise.

The prophet might genuinely believe that his or her vision is a divinely inspired, divinely authorized, insight into the nature of divinity. Insight might then be expressed as foresight, a foretelling of the deity's plans for the future of the universe.

It is pointless for the agnostic poet or critic to claim that there is no evidence to justify these beliefs or the doctrines that proliferate from them, because it is almost impossible to dispossess someone of a deeply held belief by using reasoned argument. Visionaries, convinced of the divine truth of their vision, will say that religious belief by its very nature cannot be disproved, especially by agnostic arguments. The experiencing of visions is a function of mind that has persisted over thousands of years and in so many civilizations that even the agnostic must accept that the mind is designed to accommodate theistic beliefs. That is, although theistic visions are beyond the belief of agnostics, we must recognize that a mental capacity for such visions is part of our human nature. The agnostic finds it easier to agree, or not to disagree, with the prophet who envisages possible futures in order to invite us to think about what might happen between now and then; that kind of vision is an invitation to reconsider our present beliefs, our values, and the ways in which we conduct our life.

Mysticism is sometimes regarded as a condition of mind that is beyond ordinary understanding, but some mild forms of mysticism are almost commonplace. When we successfully complete a physical or mental task, or when we are so close to completion that can visualize the end result – carpentry, for example, or making a garden, building a wall, or writing a poem – we sometimes feel that we have completed ourselves, or one of the selves that make up our composite self, and that the self in its justifiable satisfaction transcends all other senses of self and all forms of striving, because it is completely at one with a complete world. Another common mystical experience is the kind of sensation one sometimes has when walking alone through woods or along a deserted shore, or sitting on a bench in a city-centre garden and hearing, half-hearing, the hum of traffic; it is the sensation of losing, of voluntarily surrendering, one's personal identity and becoming an integral, fully realized, and fully reconciled part of a universal identity. The feeling is not irrational: we have our origins in the natural world and we depend on natural forces for our survival. Some of us are still aware of our pagan origins, and even the most urbanized people in Britain are predisposed to venerate rivers and lakes, mountains and forests. Most of us live in towns and cities, but we know that even there moments of stillness can find us.

The mystical trance that finds expression in poetry is so similar to the inspirational trance that the two must be variations of the same function of mind. Mysticism of that kind is the essence of several of Traherne's *Centuries*, of many of Blake's poems, of Wordsworth's 'Upon Westminster Bridge' and some sequences *The Prelude* and Eliot's *Four Quartets*. Seamus Heaney reports that he, too, experienced urban mysticism, firstly in San Francisco and then in New York. Of the first experience he says in interview with Dennis O'Driscoll in *Stepping Stones*: (Heaney 2008: 32) "Humanist Joy? Awe? A tremendous sense of what human beings had achieved on earth. Something akin to Wordsworth's revelation on Westminster Bridge". That recollection seems to release a memory of the later experience of mysticism, and in the next paragraph he recalls a morning in Manhattan: "Everything was magnificent and still and outlined with a kind of oxyacetylene definition against the dawn light. Something in me swam out to it and at the same time something from it swam into me. It was like being an inhabitant of the empyrean". Even Byron has moments of mysticism. In *Childe Harold's Pilgrimage*, Canto the Third, stanza LXXII he writes: (Byron s.d.: 142)

> I live not in myself, but I become
> Portion of that around me; and to me
> High mountains are a feeling, but the hum
> Of human cities torture: I can see
> Nothing to loathe in nature, save to be
> A link reluctant in a fleshly chain,
> Class'd among creatures, when the soul can flee,
> And with the sky, the peak, the heaving plain
> Of ocean, or the stars, mingle, and not in vain.

Mysticism in poetry is a form of prayer in which the writer's devotion can be to the natural world, the supernatural, or to both; mysticism expresses a religious experience that can be agnostic or theistic. The experience can also be a form of knowledge. William James admits that his nearest encounter with mysticism was a sense of euphoria induced by nitrous oxide, or laughing gas, but he is aware of mysticism as a natural condition. In 'Mysticism' in *The Varieties of Religious Experience* he writes of mystical experiences: (James 1982: 380-81) "They are states of insight into depths of truths unplumbed by the discursive intellect. They are illuminations, revelations, full of significance and importance [...] and as a rule they carry with them a curious sense of authority for after-times".

Yeats' mysticism still seems indiscriminate. In Section XL of Yeats' *Memoirs – Autobiography* edited by Denis Donoghue Yeats writes: (Yeats 1972: 123) "An obsession more constant than anything but my love itself was the need of mystical rites – a ritual system of evocation and meditation – to reunite the perception of the spirit, of the divine, with natural beauty". Such an intense longing for the mystical state of spiritual unity and completeness is itself the beginning of mysticism. In the same section he adds: (Yeats 1972: 124) "I was convinced that all lonely and lovely places were crowded with invisible beings and that it would be possible to communicate with them". Lonely and lovely places are natural habitats for mystical experiences and for the invisible beings, real or imagined, who are the spirits of these places. Worshipping these spirits, Yeats adds, "would unite the radical truths of Christianity to those of a more ancient world". His translation, with Shree Purohit, of *The Ten Principal Upanishads* in 1937 is an attempt to unite these truths but his expression of the union is not wholly convincing, as the later chapter, "The Poet's Role", will show.

On other occasions Yeats' mysticism seems mere superstition. In Section XXI of *Autobiography* he writes: (Yeats 1972: 70)

> I had a crystal and showed many how to see in it, and an even larger number to see visions according to the method of my Order. A very considerable proportion would pass into trance and see what I called up as vividly as ever with the eye of the body.

The Order was a group of mystics, spiritualist, aspirants and fantasists who formed the Order of the Golden Dawn. If the participants in Yeats' séances passed so readily into a trance, then the trance was likely to have been some form of hypnotism, or self-hypnotism, or a desire to see, a form of sincere pretence adopted by the novice in the presence of the master. How many people made up that "larger number" and "very considerable proportion"? Yeats' superstition included a belief in astrology. In his letter of 17 September 1935 to Dorothy Wellesley in *Letters on Poetry from W. B. Yeats to Dorothy Wellesley* he writes: (Yeats 1964: 27) "I lost your birth date and place of birth and so cannot work at your horoscope". Yeats must have received the information, because on 15 November 1935 he writes to Wellesley to say: (Yeats 1964: 37-8) "My wife and I looked at your horoscope the other night [...] It has greatly surprised me, your profile gives a false impression". He was surprised because the character derived from the horoscope was unlike the character of the real person.

Heaney offers a more positive view of Yeats' beliefs. In *Stepping Stones* Heaney states: (Heaney 2008: 319) "it must also be said that Yeats's construction, bare-handed, of a cosmology and a psychology, if not a theophany, was first of all another proof of intellectual power". I question whether such beliefs are proof of intellectual power but I readily agree with Heaney when he adds that Yeats "wanted endorsement and access to the wisdom of the ages".

Jung, as the chapter, 'Innateness: Conscious and Nonconscious', has shown, practised astrology. Hughes was another practitioner. In *Sylvia Plath: Letters Home – Correspondence 1950-1963*, edited by Plath's mother, Aurelia Schober Plath, Plath states in her letters of 11 May 1960 and December 24, 1960 (Plath 1975: 383) that Hughes cast horoscopes. In an earlier letter, 5 July 1958, Plath tells her mother that she and Hughes consulted a Ouija board. (Plath 1975: 346) Perhaps the word, "superstition", is too harsh; some forms of superstition are not far removed from faith, and many atheists regard all forms of religious faith as superstition.

In their most intense forms, the prophetic and mystical visions of the poet, like the visions of the tribal shaman, are not subject to immediate direct conscious control, and their revelations can sometimes be mistaken for hallucinations. Fantasies and daydreams, the mildest forms of hallucination, are usually benign, but hallucinations in their most acute forms are sometimes expressions of a mental disorder. The two conditions, the visionary and the hallucinatory, are usually associated with intense surges of electrochemical energy that increase the conductivity in the brain and bring about the interpenetration of consciousness and the nonconscious through the activation and recombination of nonconscious neural networks and the creation of new conscious or semiconscious networks. To that extent, the mental process of hallucination is similar to artistic creation. But when a vision or a hallucination is prolonged, then a person's consciousness and sense of identity can be disrupted to the extent that he or she might feel that they are controlled, possessed, by some other person or spirit, or by a god. The other person or spirit is, in fact, a new and inchoate self that is the result of the new or newly recombined neural networks that become encoded for self-identity in the course of the vision; but the networks are sometimes coded for self-identity in such an irregular, perhaps frightening, way that the person cannot accept the self as his or her own.

Hallucinations are partly determined by the particular cortex of the brain that is the centre of the neural activity, and so the experience might be auditory or tactile as well as visual. People affected in these ways might believe that what they see is not the object of their own powers of perception but that of the other person or spirit or god inside their mind. When they speak, they might feel that it is not they who utter the words but the other. In their hallucinations, these people might feel themselves being embraced, or shaken, or struck by their possessors.

The two experiences, transcendental poetic vision and hallucination, have so many features in common that they are sometimes said to be one and the same experience. For over two thousand years there has been the recurring question: Do poets create visions of reality and truth, or do they merely hallucinate? Even today the question is asked: Is creativity a benign or pathological process?

The question will be discussed in the later chapters on madness and poetry. In its simple either-or form the question is a false dilemma because the conditions, benign and pathological, are stages in a mental continuum rather than precisely definable alternatives. But it is clear that visionary artists are less likely than people with mental disorders to be deluded about their personal or professional life, and less likely to project or objectify their mental activity to the extent that they confuse the life of the mind, that is, the visionary world of the poem, with the physical and social world. What is beyond argument is that the mind is designed to function in a great variety of states of consciousness, and that transcendental visions and hallucinations, however painful or dangerous they might be, are natural functions of mind and are probably as old as consciousness itself.

## Mystery in Poetry

For the modern poet, the debate about the elimination of mystery begins with these lines in Keats' *Lamia*: (Keats 1879: 460-1)

> Do not all charms fly
> At the mere touch of cold philosophy?
> There was an awful rainbow once in heaven:
> We know her woof, her texture; she is given
> In the dull catalogue of common things.
> Philosophy will clip an Angel's wings,
> Conquer all mysteries by rule and line,
> Empty the haunted air and gnomed mine –
> Unweave a rainbow.

The physics of the rainbow – the refraction, reflection, and dispersion of sunlight through rain or mist, through a waterfall or the bow-wave of a ship or through eye-lashes moistened by tears – began to be understood as early as the fourteenth century through the work of the German scientist-philosopher, Theodoric of Freiburg. But the refraction, reflection, and dispersion of light, no matter how minutely these processes are explained, remain mysterious to the person whose mind is open to mystery, as Keats' mind usually is. Even someone who understands the physics of the phenomena might still feel, like Wordsworth, his heart leap up when he sees a rainbow, because what he sees is not the physics but a radiant configuration of colours and light. A sense of mystery, like a law of physics, is not out there but in the mind of the poet and physicist.

Keats' rainbow symbolizes the end of a particular mystery and the possible end of other natural mysteries; he fears that science "will clip an Angel's wings". Wordsworth's rainbow in 'My Heart Leaps Up' symbolizes the persistence of mystery in the mind of the poet and in the natural world. And a world or a mind without mystery, Wordsworth says, is not worth living in: (Wordsworth 1956: 62)

> So be it when I shall grow old,
>     Or let me die!

Daniel C. Dennett, the American philosopher of mind and interpreter of neuroscientists' contributions to the understanding of mind, presents the reader with a paradox: as the mysteries of the universe and of humanity are gradually explained, so our sense of wonder grows. In the chapter, 'Explaining Consciousness' in *Consciousness Explained*, Dennett writes: (Dennett 1991: 25)

> Looking on the bright side, let us remind ourselves of what has happened in the wake of earlier demystifications. We find no diminution of wonder; on the contrary, we find deeper beauties and more dazzling visions of the complexity of the universe than the protectors of mysteries ever perceived.

The mystery of the unknown is one of awe, and the mystery of the known is one of illumination and delight, but concepts of demystification can be delusions, because mystery, as an earlier paragraph argued, is not only an inexplicable phenomenon or a problem to be solved in the external, physical world; a sense of mystery is also an innate faculty of mind.

In the same paragraph, Dennett continues: "Fiery gods driving golden chariots across the skies are simpleminded comic-book fare compared to the ravishing strangeness of contemporary cosmology". In using the word, "simpleminded", Dennett is making the rash claim that his mind is more complex than the minds of the Homer poets; but his reference to "the ravishing strangeness of contemporary cosmology" is vitally important, because it is a delight and wonder that follows discovery and is based on knowledge and understanding, however limited, of the actual universe. Homer's gods are personifications, or deifications, projected from his imagination into the heavens. The evolution of consciousness allows new knowledge and understanding of the mind and new modes of thought that partly displace older modes. Dennett concludes: "When we understand consciousness – when there is no more mystery – consciousness will be different, but there will still be beauty and more room than ever for awe". Consciousness will, indeed, be different if we ever understand it, but Dennett is surely mistaken when he predicts the end of mystery. His language – "no diminution of wonder", "deeper beauties and more dazzling visions", "ravishing strangeness", "more room than ever for awe" – is itself the language of mystery. And Dennett uses these words, I suggest, because the kind of knowledge he discusses is mysterious.

Dennett's assaults on mystery have continued. In the chapter, 'Universal Acid', in *Darwin's Dangerous Idea: Evolution and the Meanings of Life* he writes: (Dennett 1995: 74) "There is simply no denying the breathtaking brilliance of the designs to be found in nature". Breathtaking, but not mysterious, says Dennett. In 'A Self of One's Own' in the Chapter, 'Are You Out of the Loop?' in his later work, *Freedom Evolves*, Dennett states: (Dennett 2004: 254)

> Mental contents become conscious not by entering some special chamber in the brain, not by being transduced into some privileged and mysterious medium, but by winning the competition against other mental contents for domination in the control of behavior.

There are no special chambers in the brain but there are specialized areas and functions that are open and interconnected: the language areas of the brain transduce, or convert, one kind of energy, electrochemical, into a different medium and different energy, language. And language is what Dennett says it is not: a "privileged and mysterious medium". It is privileged in the sense that it is only through language that we can discuss all other features of the brain and the external physical world; it is mysterious in the sense that we cannot know the origin and evolution of language because we cannot know the origin of consciousness, which is the prerequisite for language; and we may never understand all the functions of the brain. In the chapter, 'Explaining the "Magic" of Consciousness', in *Sweet Dreams: Philosophical Obstacles to a Science of Consciousness* Dennett states (Dennett 2005: 57) that consciousness is "exquisitely ingenious in its operation, but not miraculous or even, in the end, mysterious".

Richard Dawkins, by contrast, is a celebrant of mystery. Wonder is the subtitle of *Unweaving the Rainbow: Science, Delusion and the Appetite for Wonder*, and a sense of wonder runs throughout the book. In the chapter, 'Barcodes in the Stars', for example, he writes: (Dawkins 1999: 40) "Mysteries do not lose their poetry when solved. Quite the contrary; the solution often turns out more beautiful than the puzzle and, in any case, when you have solved one mystery you uncover others, perhaps to inspire greater poetry". And in 'What's Wrong with Religion?' in *The God Delusion* he writes: (Dawkins 2006: 283) "The truths of evolution, along with many other scientific truths, are so engrossingly fascinating and beautiful; how truly tragic to die having missed out on all that!"

Mystery in a poem can be discussed but never finally explained. We read a poem several times, perhaps over intervals of years. We enjoy the poem at several levels and to that extent we understand it, but on each reading we find that our enjoyment has changed, and on each reading we feel that we cannot fully possess the poem. We feel no gap in our delight or understanding, and yet we feel that something eludes us. Obvious examples of poetic mystery are Coleridge's 'The Rime of the Ancient Mariner' and 'Christabel'. Many of Shakespeare's sonnets, even after centuries of critics' annotations, have this elusive element. Examples from the last century include Wallace Stevens' 'Sunday Morning', 'The Idea of Order at Key West' and 'Final Soliloquy of the Interior Paramour'. Theodore Roethke creates a different quality of mystery in the title poem of *The Lost Son* published in 1948, and 'In a Dark Time' and 'Infirmity' in *The Far Field* published in 1964. Reading these poems again, I feel haunted and happily perplexed. Seamus Heaney suggests that a sense of mystery is almost a duty for the maker of poems when he says in interview in *Stepping Stones*: (Heaney 2008: 203) "You have been mysteriously recompensed by the words and you owe some fidelity to the mystery".

## Myth in Poetry

The true source of poets' mythologizing powers is the creative imagination. The works of James Frazer, Freud and Jung led to a renewed interest in myth among creative writers in the twentieth century, but what matters for poets is the act of mythopoesis in which the making of a poem can be the making or re-making of a myth. A poem can take its starting point and even its subject matter from a knowledge of myth, but poets can discover the poetic truth of myth only through imaginative participation, that is, by enacting or re-enacting the myth in their imagination. The interaction of the poetic imagination with the religious and creative impulses can lead to acts of mythopoeia through which poets envisage and create the worlds about which they write. The myth expressed in the poem might then have the originality and independence of the poem as a work of art.

In their long, mythological narrative poems, Alfred Tennyson, Matthew Arnold, William Morris and Algernon Charles Swinburne are more intent on writing entertainment, which is a valid poetic purpose, than on mythopoesis. Tennyson's *Idylls of the King*, which was written as separate poems between 1842 and 1885 and was later grouped as a continuous sequence; Arnold's *Tristram and Iseult* published in 1852 and his long poem on Norse myth, *Balder Dead* published in 1855; Morris' Nordic-Teutonic *Story of Sigmund the Volsung And The Fall of the Niblungs* published in 1876; and Swinburne's *Tristram of Lyonesse* published in 1883 – these re-workings of myths all have similarities in subject matter, characterization, and narrative structures. Even the prosodies are similar: *Idylls of the King* and *Balder Dead* are in blank verse; the others are in rhyming couplets.

These poems are not mythopoeic; they are historical fictions, like *The Faerie Queene* or the narrative poems of Scott, some of which – *The Lay of the Last Minstrel* published in 1805, *Marmion* published in 1808, and *The Lady of the Lake* published in 1810, all in rhyming couplets – were critical and commercial successes. Scott's novels were even more successful, and it was partly through their success that historical fiction began to be seen as the domain of the novelist rather than the poet. More importantly, in terms of the comparative development of the English novel and English poetry, the novel also became the medium for the portrayal of contemporary urban life. Charles Dickens' *Oliver Twist* was published serially in 1837 and 1838; Elizabeth Gaskell's *Mary Barton: a Tale of Manchester Life*, appeared in 1848; George Eliot's *Adam Bede* in 1859. Compared with these novels, which give fairly realistic accounts of some aspects of urban life, the historical fictions of Tennyson, Arnold, Morris, and Swinburne are a superior kind of escapist fantasy. Poets in the twentieth century adopt a more rigorous approach to myth.

Robert Graves was so convinced of the truth of Celtic and Mediterranean myths that he felt impelled to declare their influence on the creative imagination in that remarkable poetic credo, *The White Goddess*. Many of Graves' poems on mythical subjects and themes generate an added creative tension through the contrast between the violence of their contents and the accomplished craft of their forms. The poems also give the impression that the myths have been assimilated by his imagination to the extent that myth is his natural, his necessary, mode of thought and expression. Eliot's use of tribal myth in *The Waste Land*, by contrast, is obviously second-hand, borrowed for the occasion rather than assimilated and imagined. The poem is an important work of mythopoesis, but Eliot's Notes on *The Waste Land* show that his use of myth is a contrivance that partly blurs the distinction between artifice and artificiality. Edith Sitwell's *Gold Coast Customs* and its explanatory Notes (Sitwell 1982: 237-53) give a similar impression. Sitwell is more convincing in *Three Poems of the Atomic Bomb*: 'Dirge for the New Sunrise', 'The Shadow of Cain', and 'The Canticle of the Rose', (Sitwell 1982: 368-378) where she re-creates Christian, Old Testament, and tribal myths in a unified vision of the present, a vision intensified by the threat of the ultimate holocaust of nuclear war.

Eliot's *Ash-Wednesday*, the sections of which were written as separate poems, is an effective juxtaposition of Christian, Old Testament, and Dantean myths; the poem achieves its unity through Eliot's creation of a complex ideational figure that is itself mythical in its movement from themes of the Old Testament to the New, from agony to stillness, and from Purgatory to Paradise. The result is a great mythical poem that almost meets the requirement for religious literature that Eliot states in his essay, 'Religion and Literature': (Eliot 1955: 35-6) "What I want is a literature which should be *un*consciously rather than deliberately and defiantly, Christian". *Ash-Wednesday* does not meet the requirement fully because there is an element of calculation, of deliberation, in the interweaving of the myths.

Eliot is a greater, more daring and innovative poet than his immediate contemporary, Edwin Muir, but Muir's assimilation of myths – classical, Biblical, tribal, Jungian, and uniquely personal – is as fully imagined as Eliot's, and more wide-ranging. As I try to show in *The Golden Harvester: the Vision of Edwin Muir* (Aitchison a 1988), much of Muir's best poetry is mythopoeic. He writes of Eden and the Fall, of the mysteries of time, of the various myths of the human journey: the lost way, exile, ordeal, pilgrimage, and homecoming; he writes of Christian and non-Christian redemption, of Christian incarnation, and of Jungian incarnation through continual individuation and realization of the self. With the additional evidence of Muir's *An Autobiography*, an earlier version of which was entitled *The Story and the Fable* in order to stress the fabulous dimension of our existence, we can see that Muir thought of the life of the imagination, and to an extent his personal, historical life, in mythical terms.

Towards the end of his parallel career as poet and literary journalist, Muir reviewed Ted Hughes' first collection of poems, *The Hawk in the Rain* in 1957, and noted that Hughes creates a world that is both real and mythical. Perhaps Muir recognized in the younger poet's work some of his own mythical preoccupations, including the human and the animal orders of creation and the differentiation of human and animal, themes that Muir explores in 'The Animals', 'The Days', 'The Horses', and 'The Late Swallow' in his great collection, *One Foot In Eden,* published in 1956 (Muir 1991: 193-233). Like Muir, Hughes is able to see the real world as mythical because of the mythologizing power of the creative and religious impulses and the poetic imagination.

Hughes' most sustained exploration of myth is *Shakespeare and the Goddess of Supreme Being* published in 1993, where he claims to discover mythologies in fifteen of Shakespeare's plays. Each play is approached in the same way, and what could have been an open investigation becomes a fixed mode of interpretation, a methodology, and his interpretations become formulaic. This extract from the chapter, 'The Tragic Equation Matures and Mutates', is typical of the work: (Hughes 1993: 254)

> Macbeth, who suffered a so to speak preliminary phase of his Tarquinian fate when he moved towards murdering Duncan/Banquo, now steps into the major phase, where his Boar self, combined with (possessing) the Adonis self of Duncan/ Banquo (the monarchy in which his own Adonis self was invested) becomes the mad Tarquin – the tyrant who

will now rape and destroy Scotland (repeatedly described as his victim,
a woman near death, no longer 'our mother, but our grave', etc.)

Hughes' greatest exploration of myth is in his poetry. Some of the power in his poems comes from his recognition of the divergence of humans and animals from what he sees as their common origin, from his recognition of the persistence of primitive forces in the modern mind and, sometimes implicitly rather than explicitly, from his recognition that these primitive forces are unresolved and that we delude ourselves in thinking that we have outgrown them. Poems and animals coincide in Hughes' mind because it was a natural habitat for all manner of creatures. The necessity of the coincidence and the inevitability of human conflict with animals occurred to Hughes in a dream of a creature, part-fox and part-human, he had while he was an undergraduate at Cambridge University. The dream-creature, a fox, is unlike 'The Thought-Fox' in *The Hawk in the Rain*. His brief account of the dream appears in 'The Burnt Fox' in *Winter Pollen* where he writes: (Hughes 1994: 9)

> across the room towards me came a figure that was at the same time a
> skinny man and a fox walking erect on its hind legs. [...] I saw that
> its body and limbs had just now stepped out of a furnace. Every inch
> was roasted, smouldering, black-charred, split and bleeding. It came up
> until it stood beside me. [...] At the same time it said: 'Stop this – you
> are destroying us.'

The dream that emerged from his nonconscious mind into consciousness was a revelatory myth whose power sustained him in his mythopoeic celebration of primordial mysteries for the rest of his life.

## Beauty, Horror and Truth in Poetry

For a few poets and many readers there is only one kind of poetic truth. When Keats imagines the Grecian urn saying "'Beauty is truth, truth beauty'", he understands that beauty is not only the ideal world of the people and the landscape depicted on the urn but also the urn as a work of art and thus the objectification of the artist's ideal of beauty. The beauty of the urn will persist, Keats writes, 'When old age shall this generation waste'; and the poet in his mortality is tormented by the everlasting beauty of the urn: (Keats 1879: 241)

> Thou, silent form! dost tease us out of thought
> As doth eternity.

In his imagination the beauty of the urn and of the world it depicts are as if eternal; the urn is both a physical object and an abstract ideal, a concept of beauty so absolute that it must, in Keats' view, be a kind of truth.

A year or so before he wrote the ode, 'On a Grecian Urn', Keats wrote that astonishing letter of November 1817 to Benjamin Bailey. In the letter, one of several insights into the nature of poetry and the poetic imagination is this: (Keats 1952: 67) "What the imagination seizes as Beauty must be truth". The letter continues:

> I am certain of nothing but of the holiness of the Heart's affection and
> the truth of Imagination – What the imagination seizes as Beauty must
> be truth – whether it existed before or not – for I have the same Idea
> of all our Passions as of Love they are all in their sublime, creative of
> essential Beauty.

Keats' surging imagination outpaces his syntax as if he were making spontaneous, instantaneous discoveries in the act of writing the letter. Thoughts and emotions merge in a complex ideational flow that is not entirely coherent but is clearly the expression of a great discovery, a discovery that has perhaps been half-formed, semi-conscious, until the moment of realization. And in that moment the urgency, the importance of the discovery makes it a belief, an item of faith, a truth. For Keats in the course of writing the letter, truth is the play of imagination on beautiful things and on ideas of beauty; the truth of beauty, or truth in beauty, is an ideal, an absolute, and thus a projection of inner reality onto the external world as well as an inner recognition of external beauty.

In December 1817, just a few weeks after writing to Bailey, Keats wrote to his brothers, George and Thomas: (Keats 1952: 70) "the excellence of every Art is its intensity, capable of making all disagreeables evaporate, from their being in close relationship with Beauty and

Truth". The "close relationship" is, of course, in the mind of the poet. And on this occasion Keats' sense of truth in beauty differs fundamentally from that in the letter to Bailey or in 'On a Grecian Urn'. He is writing with enthusiasm about a painting by Benjamin West, *Death on a Pale Horse*, which he describes as "a wonderful picture".

West's was one of several pictures with the same title in the exhibition of art works by William Blake and his contemporaries in the Tate Gallery in London in the spring of 2006. The picture, in landscape format and approximately four feet by two feet, portrays the Four Horsemen of the Apocalypse not as messengers of death but as dashing Hussars. *Death on a Pale Horse* is dynamic and rhythmic, and West's media, ink and wash, give the picture a lightness of execution.

In the same paragraph Keats adds: "but in this picture we have unpleasantness without any momentous depth of speculation excited, in which to bury its repulsiveness". He then gives the example of *King Lear* to illustrate the idea that all disagreeables evaporate when they are related to beauty and truth. It is as if in the act of writing the letter to his brothers – Keats was then twenty-two years old – he discovers the paradoxical aesthetic of the mature artist who finds satisfaction in giving imaginative expression to the harsher truths of the human condition, and who finds beauty in the well-made play, or painting, or poem in which the harsh truths are expressed. These things are clear to the reader, and yet one feels that there is an even greater complexity in Keats' understanding of beauty and truth.

Edgar Allan Poe, by contrast, divorces beauty from truth. In 'The Poetic Principle' in *The Poetical Works of Edgar Allan Poe* he states (Poe 1850: 225) that beauty is transcendental; a sense of the beautiful is "An immortal instinct", and the search for beauty is "Inspired by an ecstatic prescience of the glories beyond the grave" and is "a struggle to apprehend the supernal Loveliness". Truth and beauty, Poe argues, are incompatible: (Poe 1858: 227-8)

> In the contemplation of Beauty we alone find it possible to attain that pleasurable elevation, or excitement, *of the soul*, which we recognize as the Poetic Sentiment, and which is so easily distinguished from Truth, which is the satisfaction of the Reason.

It is through reason that Poe reaches that conclusion, and through reason that he reaches the contradictory conclusion, that the beautiful is true, in *Eureka: A Prose Poem*. *Eureka* is a prose dissertation on astronomy and religion, and on the cosmos and the terrestrial world. On nebular theory, that is, the theory that the cosmos was formed from gases and then from clusters of stars, Poe states: (Poe 1895: 73-4) "From whatever point we regard it, we shall find it *beautifully true*. It is by far too beautiful, indeed, *not* to possess Truth as its essentiality".

Coleridge discusses beauty in his letter of August 1829 to Joseph Henry Green. The letter is a delighted but not entirely coherent response to what he calls Green's "theory of the Beautiful", a theory that leads Coleridge, in the act of writing the letter, to formulate a concept of beauty that extends beyond aesthetics. He writes: (Coleridge 1988: 267)

> Not only in the whole circle of the Fine Arts but in practical Morals, it
> will have a most salutary influence to have an admitted principle – that
> the Beautiful is the centripetal Power, which dare never be *out of Act*
> even under the boldest and apparently wildest centrifugation.

The central and centralizing force that beauty exerts cannot, must not be displaced even by the strongest of opposing forces. Coleridge adds: (Coleridge 1988: 267)

> Another useful corollary is, that the Beautiful is an *Idea* – the *spirit* of this
> or that object – but not the object in toto – as Beauty adequately realized.
> As you truly observed, it is the subjective in the form of the objective – a
> fortiori, not the objective in contradistinction from the Subjective.

Beauty lies not in the object itself or the object as a whole; the beauty that is thought to be a characteristic feature of the object is a concept that is realized, made real, in the mind of the viewer. And so the concept that leads Coleridge to state that beauty "is the subjective in the form of the objective" is more subtle and complex than the statement that beauty is in the eye of the beholder. Coleridge concludes: "We behold our own light reflected from the object as a light bestowed *by* it. The Beauty of the object consists in its fitness to reflect it". The light, or the sense of beauty, that we project onto the object seems like a light, a beauty, that emanates from the object. An object can be called beautiful only when it is fit – one assumes that fitness includes the object's size, shape, colour and texture – to reflect or represent the sense of beauty projected by the observer.

For poet and reader alike, the recognition of beauty – in a poem or other artifact, a landscape, a thought, a human face or body – and the pleasure that comes from the recognition, are natural functions of mind. Most readers and observers do not need to search for the truth as widely or as deeply as the poet; for readers, the act of recognizing beauty and the truth of beauty is an end in itself; and for some readers beauty is not only a sufficient truth but the only truth of art. In the Western world, the concept of beauty and the physical configurations that are regarded as beautiful are not absolutes, but the concept and some of the preferred images have remained remarkably constant over time. The animals painted some ten thousand to twenty thousand years ago in the caves at Altamira and Lascaux – the horses, bison, aurochs and deer must have seemed to tremble as if alive when they were seen by the wavering light of flaming torches, the mysterious gift of light – are regarded as beautiful today. And the human figures sculpted in Greece more than two thousand years ago, like the figures on Keats' urn, are still seen as celebrations of the beauty of the human form. For the public at large, then, an aesthetic of beauty is the only truth of art; art that acknowledges horror is regarded as perverse, and not true art. Artists can feel impelled to celebrate the beautiful, and through the act of celebration – the making of the poem, the painting, the piece of music – they re-create the beauty; but they also feel impelled to recognize horror. Poets who willfully ignore horror give a restricted, and to that extent a false, vision of the world.

Is it paradox or plain contradiction to say that pain, disease, and death are beautified by the artistry of the poem in which they appear? Poets know that they must confront horror, because it is part of the truth of the human condition. This problem, like so many other problems in poetry, is confronted and partly answered by Eliot. In 'Matthew Arnold' in *The Use of Poetry and the Use of Criticism* Eliot writes: (Eliot 1933: 106)

> It is of advantage to mankind in general to live in a beautiful world; that
> no one can doubt. But for the poet is it so important? We mean all sorts

of things, I know, by Beauty. But the essential advantage for a poet is
not, to have a beautiful world with which to deal: it is to be able to see
beneath both beauty and ugliness; to see the boredom, and the horror,
and the glory.

And by confronting the horror, by admitting it to the creative imagina-
tion and making from it a work of art, poets make the horror imaginable,
containable by the imagination, and also meaningful. The immediate
reality of horror will always have the power to horrify; if we ever lost
that sense or horror we would lose part of our humanity. But we cannot
live our lives in a continuing state of shock; that, too, would be a threat
to our humanity. We cannot by an act of will banish the memory of the
horror, and so we must find a way of living with it. Art shows us one
of the ways. A work of art can incorporate and imaginatively assimilate
the horror so that it becomes the meaning or part of the meaning of the
completed work. The finished work is not then an escape from painful
reality; it commemorates that reality in a way that makes the memory
bearable, understandable, and sometimes beautiful.

Physical horror is also mental horror in that horror is a state of mind.
How, then, might the poet confront and transform a horror that is en-
tirely or mainly in the mind? In trying to understand these things, and
searching still for the truths of poetry, our understanding is blocked not
so much by the paradox of the power of art to transfigure horror as by a
failure to understand or even to identify some crucial function or func-
tions of mind. For the poet, that part of the mind remains a mystery. At
some points in *Winter Pollen* Hughes seems to penetrate that mystery.
In 'The Hanged Man and the Dragonfly' he writes: (Hughes 1994: 91)
"New art awakens our resistance in so far as it proposes changes and
inversions, some new order, liberates what has been repressed, lets in
too early whiffs of an unwelcome future". We sometimes resist new art
because it makes a new kind of demand of our imagination and requires
us to re-assess our existing values and perhaps to re-order our mind. But
such re-ordering is likely to be preceded by an experience of disorder,
perhaps chaos, and it is understandable that we should regard some new
art as disturbing and as "an unwelcome future". In the same paragraph
Hughes adds: (Hughes 1994: 91)

But when the incidental novelty has been overtaken or canonized, some other unease remains. At least, where the art is serious and real (one supposes, major) it remains. An immanence of something dreadful, almost (if one dare say it) something unhuman. The balm of great art is desirable and might even be necessary, but it seems to be drawn from the depths of an elemental grisliness, a ground of echoless cosmic horror.

Even when a new work of art is assimilated by the reader or observer, even when it is understood or partly understood, it can continue to disturb. Perhaps Hughes' observation, that a major new work of art retains a dreadful, almost unhuman immanence, is prompted by his awareness that the work originates in and is partly shaped by mental forces that are nonconscious, unpredictable, sometimes uncontrollable, and are thus not readily recognized as human. The grisliness – literally, horror or terror – would then be the fear that one's mind might be possessed by unhuman or supernatural forces. Hughes' metaphor of echolessness suggests that there is nothing that reflects sound, that is, no boundaries to contain the power of the new work; and the cosmic horror is the projection of these fears into the external world; or, more probably, the cosmos is the mind, its neurons as innumerable as stars. Perhaps Hughes is also referring to a particular condition or function of imagination, the kind of openness or suggestibility that prevents us from becoming inured to horror but leaves us forever vulnerable.

Hughes develops the theme of horror as truth in his intricate analysis of Coleridge's poetry, 'The Snake in the Oak'. He writes of Coleridge's creation, Geraldine, the woman-serpent, the snake in the oak, in 'Christabel': (Hughes 1994: 441)

Though his vision of her is one of terror, he will speak of her only as "surpassing fair". Though he sees her as the Goddess of Death and the rotting sea, as well as the Goddess of Life and of the effulgent sea of birth, he will worship her as the wholly beautiful.

The transposition of the image of corruption, "the rotting sea", from 'The Ancient Mariner' is appropriate. Hughes writes of Coleridge and Geraldine as Graves writes of his White Goddess, as forces of good and evil, bringers of life and death; but Hughes knows, perhaps more consciously than Coleridge or Graves, that Geraldine and the White God-

dess are creatures of these poets' minds. When a poet creates such a god-
dess, he must worship her in order to praise the life-force and propitiate
or appease the death-force. Hughes continues: (Hughes 1994: 441-2)

> This is not a poetic or religious perversity. It is a commonplace of the
> mystical life. Perhaps of the life of the dedicated scientist also. It is a
> simple recognition of the natural and presumably biological law that
> whatever is perceived as reality emits a compelling fascination indistin-
> guishable from beauty. And his female presented herself to Coleridge's
> unusual awareness as the ultimate reality, therefore the ultimate truth,
> therefore the ultimate beauty.

Reality can, indeed, exert "a compelling fascination", but Hughes is
mistaken in stating that this is indistinguishable from the fascination ex-
erted by beauty. We respond to beauty with fascination and delight; we
respond to horror with fascination and revulsion. Can we make sense
of Hughes' three-in-one resolution: 'the ultimate reality, therefore the
ultimate truth, therefore the ultimate beauty'?

Geraldine, writes Coleridge, is "Beautiful exceedingly!" Our rec-
ognition and enjoyment of beauty are innate; the delight that we find
in some symmetries and configurations can be so great that we feel
the beauty and delight to be kinds of goodness: how could someone so
beautiful be other than good? But Geraldine is also the woman-serpent,
the theriomorphic devouring female who seduces, and thus spiritually
devours, both Christabel and her father, Sir Leonine. The evil in Geral-
dine's mind is contained within the beauty of her face and body in such
a way that the irresistible allure of her beauty makes the horror, too,
irresistible. Coleridge finds these elements in Geraldine because he put
them there; she is the personification of these things in his mind; she
is the realization, the making real, of horror, truth, and beauty; and in
these ways, perhaps, she is Hughes' three-in-one. But can there be, as
Hughes claims, ultimate forms of these things? Can there be an ultimate
form of truth?

Poets yearn for ultimate understanding, ultimate truth. When they
pursue an idea to the limits of their understanding, the limits of imagi-
nation, they sometimes have the feeling that the idea continues beyond
these limits. Eliot expresses this experience when he writes in 'The Mu-

sic of Poetry': (Eliot 1958: 57) "If, as we are aware, only a part of the meaning can be conveyed by paraphrase, that is because the poet is occupied with frontiers of consciousness beyond which words fail, though meanings still exist". Poets long to follow the meaning, the truth, into that beyond, and sometimes they succeed. They must search for and create the truth of the experience in the poem in progress; they must realize, and they must exhaust, the creative impulse that is the motive power of the poem; and they must meet the artistic need for originality. In order to achieve these aims, poets are sometimes driven beyond the limits of the imagination; and in order for that to happen, they must extend or re-combine their existing neural networks or create new networks, the effect of which is to extend the limits of the imagination. When that occurs, poets knows that they have entered the longed-for beyond and have created an ultimate truth of the imagination; ultimate, that is, until they are impelled to repeat the search in their next poem.

# 5

# Madness

## Madness and Poetry

WHEN PLATO DESCRIBES POETS AS MAD his purpose is usually political, but his observations in *The Republic* and in *Ion* give the impression that he genuinely believes poets to be mad and that he assumes that some at least of his readers agree with him. In *Ion*, for example, he writes: (Plato 2001: 11) "For the poet is a light and winged and holy thing, and he has no ability to create until he has been inspired and is out of his senses, and reason is no longer in him". In Plato's view, inspiration is a divine force that breathes and speaks through the mouth of the poet. Plato makes the claim in order to argue that the poet is not personally responsible for the creation of the poem; by implication, if the poet's inspiration is divine, then his madness, too, is divine. Today, most poets accept that they are responsible for the poems they write and for the mental processes that produce the poems.

Aristotle, Plato's pupil, is more concerned with the artistry, the craft, and the practical criticism of poetry, but he, too, raises the question of the poet's sanity. In the *Poetics,* which was written around 330 BC, he states: (Aristotle 1955: 33-4)

> Hence it is that poetry demands either great natural quickness of parts, or an enthusiasm allied to madness. By the first of these we mould ourselves with facility to the imitation of every form; by the other, transported out of ourselves, we become what we imagine.

Aristotle is referring to two levels of creative consciousness and the corresponding creative processes: inventiveness and imagination. He describes the poet not as being mad but as having an enthusiasm that is related to madness. For Aristotle, enthusiasm – originally, the condition of being inspired or possessed by a god – could be synonymous with

Platonic inspiration, but Aristotle refers to enthusiasm as a mental condition and process in which "we become what we imagine", not what the gods require us to imagine. And the experience of being "transported out of ourselves" is the experience in which poets in the grasp of creative imagination suspend their sense of self in order to realize the identity of the subject of the poem.

The experience is the same as the one Keats notes in his letter of 22 November 1817 to Benjamin Bailey: (Keats 1952: 68) "or if a Sparrow come before my Window I take part in its existence and pick about the Gravel". That is, poets in the act of writing must ignore their everyday identity in order to identify with the subject, which cannot be realized creatively, poetically, in any other way. The experience is necessary not only for the poet; it is the entirely natural experience of anyone whose attention is caught and held by anything in the external world or in the world of the mind.

Some three centuries after Aristotle, Horace concludes *The Art of Poetry*, written around the year 20 BC, with his description of the mad poet of the Roman era: (Horace 1955: 76)

> Beyond doubt, he is mad and, like a bear that has succeeded in breaking through the barriers of his cage, your poet, with his wearisome readings, puts all to flight, unlearned and learned alike; but if he catches any one, he clings to him, and bores him to death by his recitals and adheres to his skin till gorged with blood, a veritable leech.

The behaviour of Horace's poet, unlike Plato's or Aristotle's, could be described as psychotic, and Horace shows the psychosis to be active between poems and not only during the creating of them. But the portrait he paints is obviously a comic stereotype, a grotesque caricature whose wild antics do not represent the real behaviour of real poets but are an unruly kind of play through which Horace satirizes the conventional view of the mad poet.

At the beginning of the twentieth century the workings of the mind of the creative writer began to be discussed in psychological, and especially Freudian, terms, and the generic term, "madness", began to be replaced by clinical terms that identify mental disorders more precisely. As the earlier chapter on Freud and Jung has shown, Freud expresses his contempt for creative writers and creative writing. One of the great ironies of literary life in the twentieth century is that so many writers accepted the reductive, determinist doctrine of a man who despised them and their work. By contrast, Freud's younger contemporary, Jung, made several rigorous, original and sympathetic studies of the mental processes involved in artistic creation.

Jung's fundamental approach to literature is clearly stated in 'On the Relation of Analytical Psychology to Poetry', in which he also dissociates himself from the views of Freud. He writes: (Jung 1971a: 813) "In order to do justice to a work of art, analytical psychology must rid itself entirely of medical prejudice; for a work of art is not a disease, and consequently requires a different approach from the medical one". And this statement in 'Psychology and Literature' in *Psychological Types* indicates Jung's attitude to visionary art: (Jung 1946: 186-7) "The vision is not something derived or secondary, and it is not a symptom of something else. It is true symbolic expression – that is, the expression of something existent in its own right, but imperfectly known".

Freud imposes the same procrustean dogma on all writers, whereas Jung is willing to listen to writers and, as far as is consistent with any psychological approach, to judge writers in their own terms. Despite his positive and sympathetic approach, Jung admits to uncertainty about meaning in visionary art; the vision is true symbolic expression, he says, but of something that is imperfectly known. The vision is imperfectly known because it cannot be fully transduced from its nonconscious state into consciousness but must be expressed as symbolism, which is the natural mode of expressing a vision. Symbols are essentially non-linguistic modes of thought that cannot be fully represented in words. If symbols were reduced to specific referents, then the poet's vision would be reduced to a declarative statement that would falsify the mysterious nature of the vision.

On the related question of the possible pathological content of visionary poetry, and thus the madness or sanity of the poet, Jung is equally positive in his approach and equally uncertain in his conclusions. Although he states in 'On the Relation of Analytical Psychology to Poetry' that the work of art is not a disease, in 'The Problem of Types in Poetry' in *Psychological Types* he states: (Jung 1946: 238)

> When apprehension of the collective unconscious reaches a depth where conscious expression can no longer grasp its content, it cannot be decided at once whether it is a morbid product we have to deal with or whether something quite incomprehensible because of its extraordinary depth.

Jung acknowledges that there are instances when he cannot tell if a work of literature is pathological because – the admission is in stark contrast to Freud's assertions on literature – the work's complexity makes its meaning incomprehensible. Jung clearly implies that the responsibility for the incomprehension is his own, not the writer's, but if the complexity takes the form of incoherence or wilful obscurity, then the responsibility is the writer's. That is, the writer must create a coherent and unified work of art while still respecting the complex mystery of the vision.

In 'On the Relation of Analytical Psychology to Poetry' Jung restates his view that the creative impulse is an autonomous complex, and he defines a complex as: (Jung 1971a: 816) "a psychic formation that remains subliminal until its energy-charge is sufficient to carry it over the threshold of consciousness". A neuroscientific description is consistent with Jung's: the "psychic formation" is a set of neural networks that can be activated and made conscious by the firing of neurons and the discharge of neurotransmitters. Jung adds that an autonomous complex is not subject to conscious control and can neither be inhibited nor voluntarily reproduced. Here we may disagree with the claim that there is a complete division between the creative impulse and consciousness. The poet is sometimes conscious of a neural agitation that is the stirring of the creative impulse; and the poet knows that the creative impulse must be subjected to conscious control, especially at the final editing stage of the poem, because without some control the impulse could not be realized as a coherent linguistic structure.

Although poets cannot command the creative impulse to appear, they can sometimes activate it by a conscious process of propitiation. Poems often have a starting-point in the form of a semi-conscious agitation or yearning that might develop into a phrase, an image, or an idea; poets then search for other phrases, images, and ideas that might be related to the starting-point, and they make notes of what they find. They combine and recombine the phrases in the hope that some combination will serve as a linguistic votive offering that fires the creative imagination and quickens the electrochemical conductivity of the brain so that imagination can activate the creative impulse and then engage in continuous interaction with it. This deliberate method is used, sometimes successfully, by poets who are unable to compose by inspiration and are unwilling to wait for the wholly spontaneous activation of the creative impulse.

Of the spontaneous activation of the creative impulse, or creative complex, Jung writes in 'On the Relation of Analytical Psychology to Poetry': (Jung 1971a: 816) "In this respect it offers an analogy with pathological processes, since these too are characterized by the presence of autonomous complexes, particularly in the case of mental disturbance". But how analogous are the spontaneous working of the creative impulse and the working of those autonomous complexes that are associated with mental disturbance? Jung forecloses the argument in his next sentence: "The divine frenzy of the artist comes perilously close to a pathological state, though the two things are not identical". The concept of the act of composition being undertaken in a divine frenzy is similar to Plato's concept in *Ion* (Plato 2001: 12). But if poets compose not in a divine frenzy but in a more controlled state of imaginative excitation, as many poets do, and if they believe that their mental condition is human and natural rather than divine or supernatural, then the creative mind is not close to, and certainly not perilously close to, a pathological state. The fact that Jung does not consider this more controlled and painstaking method of composition, and does not allow that the creative impulse can be subjected to some degree of conscious control, leads him to relate the mental processes of creativity more closely than necessary to pathological mental processes. On the question of the poet's madness, then, Jung's overall attitude is one that could be described as affirmative doubt: it is likely, but not certain, that the poet is sane. Despite the uncertainty, Jung's analyses of the creative processes are largely compatible with neuroscientific analyses, and they are still of value to the poet and critic today.

Recent commentators adopt a fundamentally different approach to the question of the poet's sanity or madness, but their conclusions are no more clear-cut than Jung's; indeed, the subject is so complex that there may never be clear-cut conclusions. Jung's methods are interpretative and subjective; Kay Redfield Jamison's methods in *Touched with Fire: Manic-Depressive Illness and the Artistic Temperament* are based on diagnostic surveys and are investigative and statistical. Jamison, a psychiatrist, also takes account of the findings of neuroscience, and in Chapter 1, 'That Fine Madness', she writes: (Jamison 1993: 3)

> Due to the extraordinary advances in genetics, neuroscience, and psychopharmacology, much of modern psychiatric thought and clinical practice has moved away from the earlier influences of psychoanalysis and toward a more biological perspective.

Psychopharmacology, the study of the therapeutic effects of chemicals on the functioning of the minds of patients, can be as intimately personal a practice as, and more demonstrably effective than, the application of Freudian doctrine or Jungian myth. Psychopharmacology cannot cure psychopaths but it can pacify them.

Jamison's main investigations are these: a biographical survey of thirty-six major British and Irish poets born between 1705 and 1805 (Jamison 1993: 63-71); a diagnostic survey, conducted in 1989, of forty-seven eminent British writers and artists (Jamison 1993: 75-84); and a review of the academic literature on the mental health of writers and artists. From her historical study, Jamison concludes that, compared with the general population, the thirty-six poets had a higher than normal incidence of manic-depressive illness, of cyclothymic disorders, that is, of intense mood swings from elation to despair, of committal to asylums and madhouses, and of suicide. The results of her diagnostic survey in 1989 show that over sixty per cent of the playwrights had been treated, mainly by psychotherapy, for depression; that fifty per cent of the poets had been treated by drugs, psychotherapy, and hospitalization for extreme mood disorders; and that there was a much higher incidence of affective illness, and a higher than normal use of alcohol and non-prescribed drugs among the writers than the painters and sculptors. Over eighty per cent of the people interviewed said that their most intensively creative periods of work coincided with manic episodes that lasted from a week to a month. That is, almost all the writers and artists were at their most productive during the manic, or elated, cycle of manic-depression and lesser cyclothymic disorders. Jamison admits that the sample groups in these two surveys are small, but she states that her findings are consistent with her wide-ranging review of the literature on the subject.

Jamison also says that it is not clear whether there is a causal relationship between mood swings and creativity. Most poets would probably be comforted by these observations; if poets were manic-depressive, and if there were a direct cause-and-effect relationship between manic episodes and creativity, then it could be said that poetry is a product of manic states of mind. But these observations are counterbalanced and to an extent contradicted by some of her conclusions. For example, in Chapter 4, 'Their Life a Storm Whereon They Ride', she states: (Jamison 1993: 105)

> Two aspects of thinking in particular are pronounced in both creative and hypomanic thought: fluency, rapidity, and flexibility of thought on the one hand, and the ability to combine ideas or categories of thought in order to form new and original connections on the other.

It seems likely that the fluency, rapidity, and flexibility found in the two forms of thought, the creative and the hypomanic, are accompanied by similar levels of electrochemical conductivity in the brain and with similar but different sets of neural networks that are activated by similar but different neurotransmitters. The increased conductivity activates a larger than normal number of neural networks at what is sometimes a faster than normal speed; the recombinations of ideas and categories of thought noted by Jamison reflect the recombinations of neural networks.

These patterns of thought and the mental conditions that accompany the patterns are probably more complex than those outlined by Jamison. Fluent, rapid, flexible, and recombinative creative thinking is the kind of thinking the poet recognizes as inspiration, that is, the mental condition and the mental processes in which the creative imagination interacts with the creative impulse in such a way that nonconscious information is transduced spontaneously and instantaneously into consciousness and language. But creative thinking is not, of course, always fluent, rapid, and flexible. Non-inspirational modes of creative thinking are usually much slower, more deliberate, more evaluative, and thus more likely to be fully conscious than inspirational modes. The method of composition does not, of course, determine the quality of the finished work; a poem that reaches its final form after twenty drafts can be as fresh and immediate a work of art as a poem written in a one-hour sitting.

Anthony Storr also finds similarities between the psychotic person and the creative artist. In 'Escape From Reality?' in *Music and the Mind* he writes: (Storr 1992: 104) "it appears likely that the mentally ill and the creative may share a difficulty in dealing with sensory input from the external world, whether this takes the form of speech, non-verbal sounds, or emotional pressure". If the difficulty is shared, then it is likely that the neural networks associated with the difficulty are also shared; that is, the problem lies not in external reality but in the inner reality of mind. In the same paragraph Storr makes this distinction: "The mentally ill are overwhelmed by the threat of confusion and disorder. The creative meet the challenge by creating a new order in their works and thus master the threat". For the creative artist, this prospect of mastery seems comforting, until one notes that the artist is impelled, or propelled by the momentum of the creative impulse, to face the challenge of disorder constantly in the making of new and original poems. There is no final mastery of the disorder.

Storr then discusses depression. He names several composers who suffered from the illness: Robert Schumann, Hugo Wolf, Berlioz, Rachmaninov and Tchaikovsky, and he adds: (Storr 1992: 104) "This condition can be so extreme that it prevents production altogether, but *liability* to depression and the threat of its recurrence can act as a spur to creativity". Here again Storr's conclusion seems comforting. Today, creative artists continue to create even when their liability to depression is controlled by the continuous use of prescribed anti-depressant drugs; that is, the liability to depression can be reduced without depressing the creative impulse.

Day Lewis in Chapter X of *A Hope for Poetry* refers to the mental illness of four eighteenth-century poets: William Collins, Christopher Smart, William Cowper, and William Blake, and then he suggests: (Day Lewis 1944: 67) "This madness, the poet's sense of responsibility to nothing but his own inner voice, is perhaps his only way of preserving poetic integrity against the influences of a perverse generation". Madness, far from "preserving poetic integrity", destroys it by destroying the integrity of the mind. If the poet listens only to his inner voice and rejects external and social realities, then he might go mad; but the best works of the four poets named by Day Lewis are clearly the expressions of sane minds. Christopher Smart, for example, writes lucidly of his madness, but not in a state of madness, in his poem, 'Hymn to the Supreme Being on Recovery from a Dangerous Fit of Illness': (Smart 1984: 429)

> But, O immortals! What had I to plead
>     When death stood o'er me with his threat'ning lance,
> When reason left me in the time of need,
>     And sense was lost in terror or in trance?
> My sick'ning soul was with my blood inflamed,
> And the celestial image sunk, defaced and maimed.

Day Lewis' concept of "a perverse generation" is probably a fallacy; there are poets in every age who claim that their particular generation is particularly perverse. In the same paragraph, Day Lewis contrasts these eighteenth-century poets with the poet of the 1930s: (Day Lewis 1944: 67) "Madness is a luxury that he cannot afford; and a condition the more difficult for him to attain in proportion as he is conscious of its defence-mechanism nature". He implies that madness is an option and that the twentieth-century poet's awareness of the functions of mind makes madness a less likely condition than it was in earlier centuries. It is as if the poet, being aware of the defence mechanism, does not need that mechanism for his defence. Day Lewis was writing at a time when what passed for knowledge of the mind was mainly psychoanalytical doctrine; but knowledge of that doctrine, or of neuroscience, does not make one immune from madness. Madness and sanity are determined by mental conditions that are different from factual knowledge or theories of mental conditions.

A simple assertion of the writer's sanity is not enough. Charles Lamb debates the subject of madness and the poet in his essay, 'Sanity of True Genius', first published in *The New Monthly Magazine* in May 1826 and reprinted in *The Works of Charles Lamb*. Lamb considers the claim, "That Great Wit is Allied to Madness", which is prompted by the line, "Great Wits are sure to Madness near alli'd", in Part 1, line 163 of Dryden's long satirical poem, 'Absalom and Achitophel' written in 1681. For Lamb and Dryden the term, "wit", is the creative imagination.

We can accept Lamb's opening statement: (Lamb 1904: 511) "So far from the position holding true, that great wit (or genius, in our modern way of speaking) has a necessary alliance with insanity, the greatest wits, on the contrary, will ever be found to be the sanest writers". There is, as Lamb says, no "necessary alliance". He continues: (Lamb 1904: 53) "The greatness of wit, by which the poetic talent is here chiefly to be understood, manifests itself in the admirable balance of all the faculties. Madness is the disproportionate straining or excess of any one of them". A balance of all the faculties might be admirable if it were attainable, but it is not a necessary element in the creative process. If "straining or excess" of a mental faculty is grossly disproportionate, the creative process might be disrupted; but when the creative imagination is at work it is often a disproportionate force in the poet's mind. If all faculties were in equal proportion, the creative imagination could not prevail.

The line that immediately follows "Great Wits are sure to Madness near alli'd" in 'Absalom and Achitophel' is "And thin Partitions do their Bounds divide". There are no partitions, not even thin ones, in the mind; if there were, Lamb might not have experienced madness in his personal life. For six weeks in the winter of 1795-96 he was detained in Hoxton lunatic asylum in London. In September 1796 his sister, Mary Ann, stabbed their mother to death with a table-knife. Mary Ann, too, was detained in Hoxton but was later released in a remarkable act of charity by doctors and magistrates when Charles formally agreed to act as his sister's constant guardian.

Philip Larkin, too, asserts the poet's sanity. In 'Big Victims', a review of the complete poems of Emily Dickinson and Walter de la Mare, in *Required Writing: Miscellaneous Pieces 1955-1982*, Larkin states: (Larkin 1983: 191-97) "Poetry is an affair of sanity, of seeing things as they are. The less a writer's work approximates to this maxim, the less claim he has on the attention of his contemporaries and of posterity". But different poets see things differently and express what they see in uniquely distinctive ways. And if Larkin's robustly common-sense view – seeing things as they are – were to prevail, there might be no visionary poetry. Larkin is more convincing when at an earlier point in 'Big Victims' he offers the ironic observation: "Writers are usually on surprisingly affable terms with their neuroses". Such affability clearly implies that a poet's neuroses do not prevail over his creativity; instead, a creative part of the poet's mind understands the neurotic part well enough, or each part understands the other well enough, to engage in dialogue or politely ignore each other.

Poets whose minds are gripped by emotion cannot write lucid poems about the emotion because the actuality of an emotion is a disabling experience, a state of mind that impedes creative thought and the creative use of language, as the later chapter on emotion will show. The neural networks for the creative imagination cannot function while the networks for the emotion are active. The real proof of what Day Lewis calls "poetic integrity" is that poets who suffer from mental illness can, in their lucid states of mind, write well-made poems, including poems on the subject of illness itself.

## Madness, Sanity and Confessional Poetry

Some American poets of the twentieth century assimilate their experience of mental illness in ways that allow them to make good, and in some cases great, poems on the subject. Allen Ginsberg's *Howl* (Ginsberg 1985: 126-133) explores states of being so extreme that they express the near-annihilation of mind and spirit. *Howl* has been discussed for more than half a century, but some things have to be re-discovered by successive generations; and a new approach to poetry may make new discoveries.

Ginsberg names the nineteenth-century French poet, Arthur Rimbaud, in several of his later poems: 'Ignu', 'Kansas City to Saint Louis', 'Pertussin', 'Car Crash III', 'Memory Gardens' and 'Manifesto'. Rimbaud does not appear in *Howl* and yet the first section of the poem acts out Rimbaud's revolutionary ultra-Romantic theory. In his celebrated letter of May 15, 1871 to his friend, Paul Demeny, published in *A Season in Hell* and *The Illuminations*, Rimbaud states: (Rimbaud 1973: 7) "The Poet makes himself a visionary through a long, immense and reasoned deranging of the senses." Rimbaud's "reasoned deranging" is the condition in which Section I of *Howl* is expressed. Ginsberg's derangement is reasoned because he is reflecting, not hallucinating; the poem is written as one long sentence but within that sentence the syntax is orderly and grammatical, clearly the work of a reasoning mind.

Rimbaud commends "All the forms of love, of suffering, of madness"; and of the poet he states: "he tries to find himself, he exhausts in himself all the poisons, to keep only their quintessences." Love, suffering, madness and a fluctuating sense of self are primary subjects in *Howl*; Rimbaud's poisons are Ginsberg's drugs and his bleakly ironic "turpentine in Paradise Alley". Rimbaud states that the poet "becomes among all men the great invalid, the great criminal, the great accursed one"; (Rimbaud 1973: 7) Ginsberg writes of friends and acquaintances "who crashed through their minds in jail". And Rimbaud's "supreme Visionary" could be Ginsberg's "archangel of the soul". Rimbaud's best-known literary expression of his reasoned derangement is his prose-poem, 'Une Saison en Enfer', 'A Season in Hell'; if that work influenced *Howl*, then the influence is tenuous: *Howl* is an independent expression of a unique creative imagination.

Anne Sexton's letters about the life of the mind during the making of poems show her acute awareness of the different states of sanity and madness. The letters are collected in *Anne Sexton: A self-portrait in Letters* edited by Linda Gray Sexton and Lois Ames. Writing on circa October 6, 1958 to her fellow-poet, W. D. Snodgrass, she states: (Sexton 1977: 40) "I have really been alive for only a year"; that is, she feels she did not begin to live until her creative imagination impelled her to write. She felt that if she had not begun to write she would have ended her life sooner than she did. In her letter to Snodgrass of February 1, 1959 she says: (Sexton 1977: 51) "The thing that seems to be saving me is the poetry". She makes similar statements in successive letters to Snodgrass: "All is an emotional chaos. Poetry and poetry alone has saved my life", on June 9, 1959 (Sexton 1977: 81); "The life of poetry is saving me (I hope) as some things are as bad as I've ever known", (Sexton 1977: 107) on May 10 or 11, 1960; "Only poetry saves me (and by poetry I don't mean getting famous but the writing of it)", (Sexton 1977: 111) in her letter written between August 6 and 8, 1960.

Five years later, on August 12, 1965, Sexton makes an emphatic statement on madness, sanity and poetry in her letter to an admirer who sent her some of his poems: (Sexton 1977: 267)

> As for madness ... hell! Most poets are mad. It doesn't qualify us for anything. Madness is a waste of time. It creates nothing. Even though I'm often crazy, and I am and I know it, still I fight it because I know how sterile, how futile, how bleak ... nothing grows from it'.

In her excited, sometimes exultant, correspondence with Snodgrass she discovers that her poetic self is whole, in contrast to the fragmented personal self that had tormented her for years and would continue to torment her until her death. In her letter to Snodgrass on February 1, 1959 she writes of the prospect of being published and observes: (Sexton 1977: 52) "But, I remind my self's self, I've got to stay sane to do it". In a letter to Louis Simpson on March 7, 1960 she discusses poetic voice and the poetic self: (Sexton 1977: 100) "I do what I do because I don't know how to be someone else. Therefore I dedicate myself to write my best self". Her best self, her sane self, is the creator of her best work, notably the religious sequences, *Angels of the Love Affair* and *The Jesus Papers* in *The Book of Folly* in 1972, and the sequence, *O Ye Tongues* in *The Death Notebooks* in 1974.

Ginsberg and Sexton are not alone in assimilating their experience of mental illness in ways that allowed them to make good, and sometimes great, poems on the subject. Robert Lowell's final sentence in 'Afterthought', the prose epilogue to *Notebook* is: (Lowell 1970: 263) "In truth I seem to have felt mostly the joys of living; in remembering, in recording, thanks to the gift of the Muse, it is the pain". Through the association of the gift and the pain, Lowell transmutes suffering into art. *Notebook* includes one of Lowell's most elegantly measured expressions of suffering, the sequence of three unrhymed sonnets of 'Alcohol'. (Lowell 1970: 82) The sequence leads the reader from the anguish of "burning in the sun of the universal bottle" in the first sonnet, to the demonic "I am a worshipper of myth and monster" in the second, to the sad, self-deprecatory state of acceptance in the final line of the sequence: "you are no larger than the shoe you fit". In 'For John Berryman', also in *Notebook*, Lowell salutes and commiserates with a fellow-sufferer.

Many of the poems in Berryman's *Dream Songs* speak lucidly of extreme states of mind: (Berryman 1972: 71) "the brainfever bird" in "a crazy land" in Song 5, which ends with the exquisite, elegiac tenderness:

> an image of the dead on the fingernail
> of a newborn child.

Song 29 speaks of a seeming infinity of grief and anxiety: (Berryman 1972: 78)

> if he had a hundred years
> & more, & weeping, sleepless, in all them time

lines that are partly echoed in the couplet in Song 305: (Berryman 1972: 144)

> I sing with infinite slowness finite pain
> I have reached into the corner of my brain.

And in the opening line of Song 172: (127) "Your face broods from my table, Suicide", Berryman is thinking not only of the death of Sylvia Plath but of his own death.

In their poems on alcoholism, madness and suicide, Berryman, Lowell and Sexton answer one of the fundamental, recurring questions of poetry and poetics: Are there subjects that are unsuitable for poetry? The answer, of course, is no; any subject can be shaped into a poem by the creative imagination. The intimate, autobiographical nature of some of Berryman's, Lowell's and Sexton's work was once termed confessional in the pejorative sense that the poems speak of experience that should not be mentioned outside the confession box of the Roman Catholic Church, or outside the psychiatrist's consulting room. Things that are said in the consulting room, for example, Anne Sexton's dialogues with her analysts – a transcript of one dialogue appears as 'Appendix: Therapy Tape' (Middlebrook1991: 401-3) in Diane Wood

Middlebrook's *Anne Sexton: a Biography* – do not explain the poems. A patient's state of mind during a consultation is different from the state in which poems are made. The poems, as Sexton says repeatedly in her letters, are expressions of sanity.

When a poem disturbs a reader, poet and reader are jointly responsible for the disturbance, but the poet is never responsible for a reader's moral indignation, especially when the reader's response includes self-righteousness. Could contemporary readers have been shocked by the confessions of Berryman, Lowell and Sexton if those readers knew Walt Whitman's *Children of Adam*? In 'From Pent-up Aching Rivers' Whitman states that he is (Whitman 1987: 125-7)

> singing the phallus,
> Singing the song of procreation.

In 'I Sing the Body Electric' he writes of (Whitman 1987: 127-36)

> love-flesh swelling and deliciously aching,
> Limitless limpid jets of love hot and enormous.

When in 'A Woman Waits for Me' he states: (Whitman 1987: 136-7) "Sex contains all, bodies, souls", he means heterosexual lovemaking. 'Spontaneous Me' is even more sexually explicit: (Whitman 1987: 138-40)

> Love-thoughts, love-juice, love-odor, love-yielding, love-climbers,
>   and the climbing sap,
> Arms and hands of love, lips of love, phallic thumb of love, breast of
>   love, bellies press'd and glued together with love.

Whitman's celebration of sexuality is more explicit than the confessions of a later generation of American poets. Allen Ginsberg pays homage to Whitman in the early work, 'Love Poem on Theme by Whitman', where Ginsberg writes of breasts, cock, hot hips and buttocks, hands between thighs, and the white come flow.

Bodily functions such as excretion, ejaculation and menstruation are entirely natural and are not in themselves disgusting. The distinction is obvious: even when the subject of a poem is, or seems to be, disgusting, the disgust can be contained and made imaginable in the finished poem. If the poem contains the disgust in this way, then the poem as a work of art is not disgusting.

Theodore Roethke achieves a healing vision that transcends illness. Among previously uncollected work in Roethke's *Collected Poems* is 'Meditation in Hydrotherapy', a poem of six octosyllabic couplets that are as tightly structured as some of the poems in his first collection, *Open House* in 1941, but with an almost colloquial simplicity – (Roethke 1968: 248) "My past is sliding down the drain" – that allows the poet to see a pattern in his fragmented life. The ambiguous final line: "I soon will be myself again", could be ironic, implying that the self will be same old sick self; it could be an expression of hope for the future; or, when his past has slid down the drain, an acknowledgement of his mortality.

In two other late poems, 'In a Dark Time' and 'Infirmity' in *Sequence, Sometimes Metaphysical*, Roethke draws on his experience of illness to create a vision of wholeness. Imagery of darkness alternates with imagery of light in 'In a Dark Time'. In the line: (Roethke 1968: 231) "My shadow pinned against a sweating wall", the shadow is at once a metaphysical self, the unacknowledged self that is the shadow that Jung discusses in *Memories, Dreams, Reflections* (Jung 1971b: 273-4) and elsewhere in his work, and the shadows on the wall of Plato's cave in *The Republic*. (Plato 1956: 278-286) The light, too, is metaphysical: "All natural shapes blazing unnatural light". By the final stanza the dark and the light are as one: "Dark, dark my light"; and the poem ends with a transcendental religious vision of a sublime unity:

> The mind enters itself, and God the mind,
> And one is One, free in the tearing wind.

The language in 'Infirmity' (Roethke 1968: 236) is more openly religious than the language of 'In a Dark Time'. Through its juxtaposition of images, and the concepts that underlie the images – the sacred and the secular, the spiritual and the physical, the eternal and the temporal – 'Infirmity' evolves into a poem of redemption and then, as if inevitably, into a poem of death and resurrection. The seemingly paradoxical invocation, "Sweet Christ, rejoice in my infirmity", is a plea for divine recognition of the poet's human frailty, a frailty illustrated by the playful banality of fluid on the knee and "a shoulder full of cortisone". And this is followed by a paradoxical statement of faith:

> Thus I conform to my divinity
> By dying inward, like an aged tree.

The poet imagines "a pure extreme of light" that "Breaks on me as my meager flesh breaks down". And as the flesh grows corrupt, so "The soul delights in that extremity": the nearer he comes to death, the nearer he comes to the release and realization of his eternal soul.

Roethke offers another paradox in what seems like a reversal of the expected transformation from the finite to infinity: "The eternal seeks, and finds, the temporal". But in finding the temporal, the eternal changes the darkness into light, and on his death the poet will be freed from the torment of earthly elements: "I move beyond the reach of wind and fire". In the penultimate stanza the poet suggests that through the intensity of his delight in the natural world, "the green of summer", and his life in that world, he discovers a spiritual completeness: "My soul is still my soul". And the successive figures of transmutation lead the poet to the conclusion:

> How body from spirit slowly does unwind
> Until we are pure spirit at the end.

'Infirmity' – the reader's mind provides the counter-matching word, "infinity" – is a triumph of sanity over madness.

# 6

# Poetic Voice

VOICE IN POETRY IS ACHIEVED when the poet uses written language in ways that represent premeditated speech. When the poetic voice is persuasive and readers are receptive, readers feel that they are being addressed directly by the poet and can hear the poet's voice spontaneously reciting the poem inside their heads. Philip Larkin makes that point in his interview with Robert Phillips of *Paris Review* in 1982; the interview is published in Larkin's *Required Writing: Miscellaneous Prose* 1955-1982, where Larkin states: (Larkin 1983: 57-76) "When you write a poem, you put everything into it that's needed: the reader should 'hear' it just as clearly as if you were in the room saying it to him". Margaret Atwood in '*Duplicity*: The Jekyll Hand, the Hyde Hand, And the Slippery Slope' in *Negotiating with the Dead* claims that what the reader hears is illusory. On the question of a writer finding his voice, she writes: (Atwood 2002: 42) "Of course he has done no such thing. Instead, he has found a way of writing words down in a manner that creates the *illusion* of a voice". The experience is not illusory; it is a natural function of the auditory imagination, which is, in turn, a function of the auditory cortex. In silent reading we should be aware of, or susceptible to, the sounds of words and intonation contours because these are essential elements in poetry. It is these elements, the phonology of a poem, that are lost in translation from one language to another.

I. A. Richards, who is often concerned about ways in which functions of mind and properties of language combine in a poem, discusses the linguistic nature of this effect in 'The Analysis of a Poem' in *Principles of Literary Criticism*: (Richards 1925: 118)

> Visual sensations of words do not commonly occur by themselves. They have certain regular companions so closely tied to them as to be only with difficulty disconnected. The chief of these are the auditory

image – the sounds of the words in the mind's ear – and the image of
articulation – the feel in the lips, mouth, and throat, of what the words
would be like to speak.

Richards repeats these ideas in *Science and Poetry*, first published in
1925, and 'Introductory' in *Practical Criticism*. The sensations he de-
scribes in *Science and Poetry* are the common and yet extraordinarily
complex experiences of readers of poetry; the complexity lies in the
fact that the experience involves not only two but all four systems of
language use: reading, writing, hearing and, because silent readers hear
the speech sounds in their auditory imagination, speaking.

This multiplicity of functions, which is a natural feature of the
language-processing areas of the brain, is reinforced by the phonetic
nature of English spelling. Although the twenty-six characters of the
English alphabet cannot consistently represent all the sounds of all
the words in the English language, anyone who is literate in English
can see and hear the connections between the written and the spoken
word. Edward Carney offers a persuasive defence of English spelling
in 'English Spelling Is Kattastroffik' in *Language Myths* (Carney 1998:
32-40). Most readers are so familiar with the parallelism of the writing
system and the sound system of English that, either involuntarily or at
will, they can read a text in such a way that the written word is simul-
taneously decoded and re-encoded in speech sounds. In jargon terms,
English orthography and phonology are isomorphic. The isomorphism
operates mainly from writing to speech rather than from speech to writ-
ing; that is, when we read a text we can hear the words in our auditory
imagination, but when we hear speech we seldom visualize the written
forms of the words.

In poetry, the parallels between writing and speech are reinforced
further through the general acceptance, by poets and readers alike, that
the spoken form is the primary form of the poem and the written text a
secondary form. Lyrical poems are still regarded as forms of song, bal-
lads as sung stories, narrative and epic poems as forms of story-telling,
odes and elegies as forms of oratory. The agreement that speech is the
primary form of a poem is no mere convention or received opinion but
is central to the craft and art of poetry. Poets choose words and phrases
not only for their meanings but also for the sounds, the pitch and stress
of syllables and words, and the fluctuating pitch of intonation contours

in lines and sequences of lines. Poets listen to the sound of the poem as it takes shape, and they sometimes utter syllables, words, phrases, and lines aloud to hear if they sound right in the poem and to hear the extent to which they reflect the natural rhythms and intonations of spoken English. Some poets also try to hear whether the sounds of the poem in progress are consistent with the sound of their poetic voice.

In 'Words and the Word' in *Secondary Worlds*, Auden extends the idea of the poet addressing the reader by suggesting that there is an audible dialogue between poet and reader: (Auden 1968: 130) "One can never grasp a poem one is reading unless one hears the actual sound of the words, and its meaning is the outcome of a dialogue between the words of the poem and the response of whoever is listening to them". Eliot, too, refers to a dialogue between the poet and the reader when he states in 'The Music of Poetry' (Eliot 1955: 58) that poetry is "one person talking to another". But in a later essay, 'Poetry and Drama', first published in 1950, Eliot discusses voice in terms of a monologue rather than a dialogue. He contrasts the different voices in a verse drama with the single poetic voice: (Eliot 1955: 75) "In writing other verse, I think that one is writing, so to speak, in terms of one's own voice: the way it sounds when you read it to yourself is the test. For it is yourself speaking". There is, of course, no contradiction between poets talking to themselves and talking to readers; poets do both. But there could be disagreement about the voices poets actually hear when they read their poems silently.

Richards stresses the importance of the auditory imagination. A slow and silent reading of a poem, he says, (Richards 1925: 119) "will sound mutely in the imagination somewhat as it would if read aloud". Richards was writing in 1925 and might not have taken full account of the fact that speakers in the act of speaking cannot hear the actual sounds of their voices. His references to the auditory imagination suggest that he knew that a conceptual auditory image, that is, an image generated within the mind, activates the same areas of the brain as an external image perceived by the senses.

Brain-scanning machines have shown that the auditory areas of the brain or, for poets and readers, the auditory imagination, function in similar ways when we read silently, when we read aloud, and when we listen to someone else reading aloud. Oliver Sacks, the physician and author of several works on the brain, discusses some brain-scanning studies in *Musicophilia: Tales of Music and the Brain*. He states (Sacks 2011: 34) that the studies "have shown that imagining music can indeed activate the auditory cortex almost as strongly as listening to it".

In the same paragraph as the one referred to above, Richards adds:

> But the degree of correspondence between the image-sounds and the actual sounds that the reader would produce, varies enormously. Many people are able to imagine word-sounds with greater delicacy and discrimination than they can utter them.

That is, most people can hear and understand a greater range of accents or dialects than they themselves can speak. Most of us who speak a regional or social dialect of English are able to imagine speech sounds in other dialects, including received pronunciation, but we are seldom able to reproduce the sounds of dialects other than our own. When we attempt that kind of reproduction we may feel that it is clumsy mimicry; on these occasions it is as if there is no neural pathway from the auditory cortex to the vocal tract.

A poet's auditory imagination involves the same functions of brain and mind as actual physical hearing but without an external stimulus. For the poet, auditory imagination is a function of the auditory cortex and poetic imagination. And since the auditory imagination is involved in language processing, it must be related to the language areas of the brain. In the act of composition, what the poet hears are imagined, idealized speech sounds. Shakespeare did not compose his poems and plays in a Warwickshire accent; his contemporary, Walter Ralegh, did not compose his sonnets in the Devonshire accent that he spoke all his life. Derek Walcott's speaking voice locates him in the West Indies, and Edwin Muir retained his Orkney accent until his death in 1959, but there are no traces of insular accents in their poems. Heaney reads his poems in an Irish accent, but the voice of his auditory imagination, his poetic voice, the voice that emerges from the printed page, is not Irish, not even when Heaney's subject is Ireland. In these and in most other cases, with the obvious exception of dialect poetry, the evidence of the poems is clear.

There is other, more commonplace, evidence of the occasional accentlessness of the auditory cortex and the language areas of the brain.

All speakers of British English have a regional, social, or regional-and-social accent, but when we listen to a speaker for a few minutes, or when we engage in dialogue lasting a few minutes, we cease to be aware of the speaker's accent. What we then hear are accentless speech sounds; or rather, what we hear are not so much the external sounds of the speaker as the meanings into which the sounds are transduced in our minds. This topic, the relationship or lack of relationship between one's auditory imagination and the actual sound of one's speech, is the main subject in Tony Harrison's poems in *The School of Eloquence* in his *Selected Poems*; it is also the subject of many of Tom Leonard's poems in *Intimate Voices*; and in that frequently quoted poem by e. e. cummings, 'ygUDuh', (cummings 1960: 52), the slurred diction and lurching, irregular rhythms are designed to echo the speech of a drunken, uneducated racist. Harrison and Leonard contrast the speech of their original language community, Harrison's Leeds and Leonard's west-central Scotland, with the sounds of received pronunciation, and so they ask, and partly answer, questions of social class and of social and personal identity.

Received pronunciation – "received" meaning handed down, as in received wisdom or received opinion – emerged as the social and professional dialect of educated middle-class speakers in south-east England. Today it is still regarded as the dialect of an educated middle class, but it is also regarded apolitically as a linguistic standard and is the pronunciation that is indicated in British English-language dictionaries. Only a minority of British speakers uses the exact phonetic range of received pronunciation, but regional versions of it, sometimes known as paralects, are widely used throughout Britain. Although the great majority of British speakers do not use received pronunciation, they are familiar with its sound, mainly because it has been used on network, or nation-wide, broadcasts by announcers since the earliest days of the British Broadcasting Corporation; indeed, the term, "BBC English", was used as an alternative for "received pronunciation" in the middle years of the twentieth century. When John, later Lord, Reith became director-general of the BBC in 1927, he appointed announcers – Godfrey Adams, Freddie Grisewood, Alvar Liddell, John Snagge, and others – whose speech, Reith thought, contained no trace of an accent. Reith himself had a noticeable Scottish accent. The announcers' accent was, in fact, that of the prestige middle-class dialect, and Reith's reason for appointing them was that their speech was intelligible to listeners throughout Britain. Voices speaking received pronunciation were heard by everyone who owned what was then called a wireless set, and they are still heard, in slightly different and slowly changing forms, on network radio and television broadcasts.

This stanza from Tony Harrison's 'Long Distance', for example, is clearly meant to be read in an urban Yorkshire accent that diverges from the received pronunciation standard: (Harrison 1984: 133)

> Ah've allus liked things sweet! But now ah push
> food down mi throat. Ah'd sooner do wi'out.
> And t'only reason now for beer's to flush
> (so t'dietician said) mi kidneys out.

And the lines below, from Tom Leonard's 'Parokial', are meant to be heard as the urban demotic English speech of west-central Scotland. The semi-phonetic spellings make the words visually as well as phonetically alien, even to speakers of the dialect because, unlike literary Scots, the dialect has no agreed written form; Leonard creates a new orthography for his speech community when he writes: (Leonard 1984: 40)

> goahty learna new langwij
> sumhm ihnturnashnl
> noah Glasgow hangup
> bunnit husslin.

Apart from such exceptions, the poet in the act of composing, and the silent reader, hear an idealized voice, and in Britain that voice speaks received pronunciation. When a spoken language has a standardized prestige dialect, then the voice the poet hears is likely to speak a version of that dialect.

Denise Levertov, who was born in England and lived in America from 1948, discusses this question in her essay, 'Linebreaks, Stanza-Spaces and the Inner Voice' in *New & Selected Essays*. Of the inner voice she writes: (Levertov 1992: 92)

> What it means to me is that a poet, a verbal kind of person, is constant-
> ly talking to himself, inside of himself, constantly approximating and
> evaluating and trying to grasp his experience in words. And the 'sound'
> inside his head, of that voice is not necessarily identical with his literal
> speaking voice, nor is his inner vocabulary identical with that which
> he uses in conversation. At their best, sound and words are song, not
> speech. The written poem is then a record of that inner song.

The different voice the poet hears inside her head, and her different use
of language, reflect the difference between poetry and ordinary speech.
Levertov's second last sentence is ambiguous. Lyrical poems can be
read and heard by the reader as songs, but by asserting the primacy of
song over speech she could also be asserting the primacy of music over
poetry; but poetry is more directly related to speech than to music. Per-
haps Levertov's song is a rhythmic, melodic, slightly incantatory form
of speech.

Seamus Heaney is mistaken, then, in 'Feeling Into Words' in *Find-
ers Keepers* when he says of the poet's voice: (Heaney 2002: 16) "a
poetic voice is probably very intimately connected with the poet's natu-
ral voice, the voice that he hears as the ideal speaker of the lines he is
making up". The ideal speaker is the poetic self, but the poetic self can
be as far removed from the everyday self as the ideal voice is from the
natural voice. And because speakers cannot hear their own voice in the
same way as their listeners, they cannot be certain of the sound of their
natural voice unless they listen to recordings of themselves from time
to time. Heaney is more convincing in 'Learning from Eliot' when he
quotes the first ten lines of section II of Eliot's *The Hollow Men*, the
sequence that begins: "Eyes I dare not meet in dreams". Heaney states:
(Heaney 2002: 28)

> I love the lines quoted above because of the pitch of their music, their
> nerve-end tremulousness, their treble in the helix of the ear. Even so, I
> cannot with my voice make the physical sound that would be the equiv-
> alent of what I hear on my inner ear.

Heaney returns to the question of the relationship between the spoken
word and poetry in *Stepping Stones* where he says to his interviewer:
(Heaney 2008: 129)

I've always confined myself to words I myself could have heard spo-
ken, words I'd be able to use with familiarity in certain companies.

We can read a work of prose attentively without fully activating our
auditory cortex, but we cannot read a poem attentively without activat-
ing both the cortex and the auditory imagination. The cortex allows us
to hear the words; the imagination allows us to hear the words creating
a work of art.

A poet's inner vocabulary, Levertov rightly states, is not the same
as the vocabulary she uses in ordinary conversation. In any discussion
of a person's individual use of language, the jargon term, "idiolect", is
useful. The word was coined in the mid-twentieth century by analogy
with the word, "dialect", to denote a person's uniquely distinctive use
of language, mainly in speech but also in writing. Everyone's personal
use of language is unique because everyone's experience of language
– speaking, listening, writing, reading, thinking – is unique; and be-
cause everyone's neuronal networks are unique, so everyone's memory
and imagination are also unique. Uniqueness of idiolect does not mean
that every person's every utterance is original; all of us, including poets,
make use of ready-made expressions, but poets should use second-hand
language only for a particular purpose and to create an original effect.
In writing, then, the uniqueness of a person's idiolect is determined by
the mind and the ways in which the mind uses language; in speech,
the uniqueness is partly determined by the physical quality, or timbre
– soft, squeaky, gravelly – of the speaker's voice. These factors alone
will make a poet's use of language, and thus his poetic voice, unique,
but they do not in themselves make the poet's voice interesting; textual
analysis of a poet's work could establish a statistical uniqueness that
might be of no literary significance. Don Foster discusses this kind of
linguistic analysis in *Author Unknown,* published in 2000.

Poets' voices become recognizably their own, and a positive feature in
their poetry, only when they clearly understand some of the properties
of language and when their language is a product of the creative imagi-
nation. Then, poets use language so precisely that some words, phrases,
and syntactic structures will be used only in their poetry; indeed, some

words and phrases, and many longer linguistic units, will appear only in one poem, and not in their other writings.

The poet's voice is related to the poetic self and the poetic persona; if the voice is too obviously imposed on the poem then, like a false persona, the voice will sound false. But poets at the beginning of their career may have no sense of their voice or poetic self, and in their uncertainty they sometimes assume a voice – street-wise, or manly, or satirical – without hearing that it is false. Through practice, through the search for the truth of experience, and through a knowledge of and respect for language, poets will find their real poetic voice; or rather, they will create that voice.

In the course of a single poem a poet's tone of voice can fluctuate, especially at the transition point where the subject of the poem becomes the theme. In the course of a career spanning, say, forty to fifty years, the poet's voice should change as he or she explores new experiences in new ways; such change is likely to be expressed in a different use of language, a different vision of life, and perhaps in different forms. Eliot's voice in the early poem, 'The Love Song of J. Alfred Prufrock', is different from his voice in *Four Quartets*, and the development of his poetic voice is accompanied by a development of imagination and vision. Such change can be difficult for poets because it requires them to change their poetic imagination. Eliot himself is aware of the difficulty. Change can also be difficult for those readers who, having gained an understanding of a poet's work and become familiar with his voice, are disconcerted to find the understanding contradicted in a new collection of poems written in a new, perhaps unrecognizable, voice. Eliot himself, Siegfried Sassoon, Auden, Williams and MacDiarmid, confused some of their readers in that way.

Heaney makes similar observations in 'Yeats as an Example' in *Finders Keepers:* (Heaney 2002: 107)

> He [Yeats] bothers you with the suggestion that if you have managed to do one kind of poem in your own way, you should cast off that way and face into another area of your experience until you have learned a new voice to say that area properly.

And then Heaney suggests that change and renewal can be achieved through "revision and slogwork" and by practicing the craft of poetry:

(Heaney 2002: 107) "He [Yeats] encourages you to experience a trans-
fusion of energies from poetic forms themselves, reveals how the chal-
lenge of a metre can extend the resources of the voice". C. Day Lewis
in *The Poet's Way of Knowledge* discusses this need for change: (Day
Lewis 1957: 21)

> If I have perfected a language of my own, I may have to discard it be-
> cause its very perfection induces facility – the poet's greatest danger:
> a much-used idiom, like a well-worn path, will lead the poet's steps
> insensibly away from the theme he should be searching for, to some
> familiar and exhausted one.

In changing their voice, poets face the wider challenge of developing
the creative imagination, exploring new experience or finding new ways
to express existing experience, and expressing their changing vision of
life. In making some or all of these changes, poets will also change their
poetic self. The struggle can be painful: one's everyday self changes au-
tomatically over time, from a momentary mood to a religious belief that
changes over decades; by contrast, poetic self and poetic voice change
only when poets create change consciously in the poetic imagination, in
their use of language and form, artistry and craft.

# 7

# Emotion in Poetry

POETRY CANNOT REPRESENT THE FULL mental or physical experience of emotion. In theatre, cinema, and television an actor can simulate hysterical laughter, drunken rage, or terror; poetry cannot offer that kind of verisimilitude. If poets in the course of writing a poem were to re-create the actual emotion, they would experience an agitation of mind that would defeat the creative process by reducing their control of thought and language and by making it impossible to exercise the craft and artistry needed to shape the emotion as an element of the experience in the poem or as a figure in the poem's overall structure. The disturbance aroused by the actual emotion would also shout down the affective, partly spontaneous commentary that poets maintain as they write, the emotional thinking or thoughtful emoting that is not part of the experience in the poem but is an essential part of the experience of making the poem.

In the normal course of composition, the poet experiences the mental process described by Northrop Frye in the Second Essay in *The Anatomy of Criticism*: (Frye 1973: 83)

> a process stumbling through emotional entanglements, sudden irrational convictions, involuntary gleams of insight, rationalized prejudices, and blocks of panic and inertia, finally to reach a completely incommunicable intuition.

Frye's description partly echoes William James' concept of the stream of thought and consciousness in 'The Stream of Thought' in *The Principles of Psychology*; the act of thinking is not an exclusively intellectual process; it also includes emotional, non-rational mental activity. The fact that Frye expresses the mental processes so precisely shows that neither they nor the final intuition are incommunicable.

A more recent commentator, Anthony Storr, reaches a similar conclusion. In 'The Significance of Music' in *Music and the Mind* Storr writes: (Storr 1992: 74)

> We like to describe the processes of thought as continuous, as a 'train
> of thought' inexorably proceeding by logical steps to a new conclu-
> sion. Yet it is more like floundering about in a slough of perplexity, a
> jumble of incoherence, relieved by occasional flashes of illumination
> when a new pattern suddenly emerges. Ordered, coherent progression
> of thought is a retrospective falsification of what actually happens.

Storr's description of the process, like Frye's and James', confirms that we can pursue trains of logical thought to their conclusions, although the trains may travel through various mental states.

Of Eliot's various observations on emotion, some of which are contradictory, one of the best known and yet ambiguous appears in the early essay, 'Hamlet and His Problems': (Eliot 1950: 100)

> The only way of expressing emotion in the form of art is by finding an
> 'objective correlative'; in other words, a set of objects, a situation, a
> chain of events which shall be the formula of that particular emotion;
> such that when the external facts, which must terminate in sensory ex-
> perience, are given, the emotion is immediately evoked.

The term, "objective correlative", has proved to be a minor distraction in literary criticism and poetics. Robert Browning expresses similar functions of mind and forms of artistry in the closing lines of 'The Book and the Ring', which is the final section of *The Ring and the Book*, first published in 1869: (Browning 1903: 291)

> But Art, – wherein man nowise speaks to men,
> Only to mankind, – Art may tell a truth
> Obliquely, do the thing shall breed the thought,
> Nor wrong the thought, missing the mediate word.

And Browning speaks of the grandeur of such art:

So write a book shall mean beyond the facts,
Suffice the eye and save the soul beside.

Eliot's objective correlative is similar to a leitmotiv in music, that is, a recurring musical phrase or theme that identifies a person or a circumstance. In the popular arts, an obvious example of the objective correlative is cinema music: John Williams' low-pitched chords of double basses tell us that the great white shark is close; Bernard Herrmann's high-pitched staccato music shrieks at us and tells us that the psychotic murderer is about to strike again.

In poetry the objective correlative is language itself; within a poem the correlative can take a variety of forms: a single image, a metaphor, a symbol, irregular or fluid rhythm; even the sound of a word, euphonious or cacophonous, can create an emotional stir. Through these and other devices the poem becomes expressive of an emotion rather than a direct expression of it; that is, the poem represents an emotion without re-creating it. Words that denote emotion, for example, "horror", "rapture", "grief", will not be emotive if they simply state the emotion without expressing it. And attempts to intensify emotion in a poem can lead to melodrama: "ravenous jealousy", "crucified by guilt", "an incandescent rage", "ambushed by love", "fear like a cancer gnawing at his bowels". The effect of such phrases is to inflate the currency of the language of poetry and bring about linguistic and emotional bankruptcy. Even dressed as they are in metaphor, such phrases are too hackneyed and too explicit to make an appeal to the imagination; the language is emphatic, but it is the emphasis of bombast.

The various states of mind discussed in the last few paragraphs lead to the conclusion that the affective element in poetry is often feeling rather than emotion. Feeling, too, is difficult to define, but if emotion and feeling are regarded as stages in a gradience, then the feeling of sadness can be seen as relating to the emotion of grief, just as the feelings of happiness, anxiety, and contempt are related to the emotions of joy, fear, and hatred. Emotion is a mainly unthinking, or unreasoning, condition that is designed to lead to action, whereas feeling is a less intense condition that is often accompanied by reflective forms of thought. The poet usually expresses feeling and reflection rather than emotion and an urge to action. This is widely understood, and no real confusion is caused when the words, "emotion" and "feeling", are used in discussing poetry. The neurologist, Antonio Damasio, recognizes this when he writes in *Looking for Spinoza*: (Damasio 2003: 28) "Emotions and feelings are so intimately related along a continuous process that we tend to think of them, understandably, as one single thing". But the difference in meaning between the two leads to a paradox.

In order to write effectively about emotion the poet will use his memory and understanding of emotion rather than try to re-create an actual emotion; but the acts of remembering and editing memories for the purpose of a poem are intellectual rather than emotional processes; and the kind of cognition that we call understanding is partly intuitive but mainly intellectual. Poetic craft, artistry and linguistic problem-solving are also partly intuitive but mainly intellectual. Put simply, the paradox is this: the expression of emotion in poetry owes as much to the poet's intellect as to his or her capacity for emotion. How, then, should we respond to the frequently quoted definition that poetry is "emotion recollected in tranquillity"?

The first response is to quote the words in their context in the Preface to the second and later editions of *Lyrical Ballads*: (Wordsworth 1956: 740)

> I have said that poetry is the spontaneous overflow of powerful feelings: it takes its origin from emotion recollected in tranquillity: the emotion is contemplated till, by a species of reaction, the tranquillity gradually disappears, and an emotion, kindred to that which was before the subject of contemplation, is gradually produced, and does itself actually exist in the mind.

An emotion recollected in tranquillity and subjected to contemplation is clearly not the raw original but a related feeling; and when the tranquillity disappears, what Wordsworth experiences is still not the original emotion but a variety that is similar to the one that was the subject of contemplation. The emotion that "does itself actually exist in the mind" is not, as Wordsworth's next sentence makes clear, the emotion that will appear in the finished poem but is the pleasure he feels in the act of composing:

> In this mood successful composition generally begins, and in a mood similar to this it is carried on; but the emotion of whatever kind, and in

whatever degree, from various causes, is qualified by various pleasures, so that in describing any passions whatsoever, which are voluntarily described, the mind will, upon the whole, be in a state of enjoyment.

Whatever the subject or emotion of a poem might be, Wordsworth, unlike his friend Coleridge, enjoys the act of writing.

Eliot in 'Tradition and the Individual Talent', first published in 1919, dismisses Wordsworth's view of emotion: (Eliot 1955: 29)

> The business of the poet is not to find new emotions, but to use the ordinary ones and, in working them up into poetry, to express feelings which are not in actual emotions at all. And emotions which he has never experienced will serve his turn as well as those familiar to him.

Wordsworth, too, uses ordinary emotions, or "the general passions and thoughts and feelings of men". The feelings expressed in a finished poem can, as Eliot says, differ in kind and degree from the initial emotion. As the poem develops, so the emotion in the poem and the poem's overall emotional effect also develop, even to the extent that the emotional content of the finished poem might not be a representation of an actual emotional experience but something that is created in the course of writing the poem. Poets need not have personal experience of emotions they express in a poem; they can use vicarious experience and can develop a latent or potential emotion into a representation of the emotion in question; that is, the poet can imagine emotion.

In his next sentence, Eliot states: "Consequently we must believe that 'emotion recollected in tranquillity' is an inexact formula. For it is neither emotion, nor recollection, nor, without distortion of meaning, tranquillity". Wordsworth does not, of course, offer a formula. Eliot's denial of emotion contradicts his claim earlier in the same paragraph that the poet uses ordinary emotions, including some that he has not experienced, and edits them – "working them up" – for the poem. The denial also contradicts the final paragraph of 'Tradition and the Individual Talent', where he states: (Eliot 1955: 30) "There are many people who appreciate the expression of sincere emotion in verse [...] But very few know when there is expression of significant emotion which has its life in the poem and not in the history of the poet". Eliot also denies that recollection takes place, but the recollection of emotion or of memories that are charged with emotion is usually part of the creative process, even if the original recollection is not included in the final version of the poem. The poet cannot express emotion or feeling in a poem without recognizing, that is, remembering, the nature of the emotion or the feeling, or without recognizing the kind of experience with which the emotion or feeling is associated, even if the experience never occurred in fact but is created in the course of creating the poem. Eliot rejects the word, "tranquillity", but it is likely that the "serene and blessed mood" in 'Lines Composed a Few Miles above Tintern Abbey' (Wordsworth 1956: 163-5) was Wordsworth's actual state of mind, a creative trance, in the process of composing. Readers can agree with Eliot when, towards the end of 'Tradition and the Individual Talent', he states: (Eliot 1955: 30) "Poetry is not a turning loose of emotion", but we cannot agree – and on the evidence of Eliot's own words quoted above, he himself does not agree – that poetry is "an escape from emotion". There can be no escape from the emotion that is often part of the experience in the poem and is almost always part of the meaning of a memory; no escape from the connotations, often emotional, of words and phrases; and no escape from the attendant emotion – in Wordsworth's case, pleasure, in Coleridge's, anguish – that accompanies the act of creating.

# 8

# Thought in Poetry

Attempts to define thought and thinking are likely to be as controversial and inconclusive as attempts to define emotion and feeling, partly because thought takes as many forms as emotion and feeling, and partly because there is no firm agreement on the nature of these forms. William James in his "stream of thought, of consciousness" discussion in 'The Automaton-Theory' (James 1983: 132-47) in *The Principles of Psychology* compares the processes of thought to a river and then, in the chapter, 'The Stream of Thought', (James 1983: 236) to a bird's "alternation of flights and perchings." The images of the river and the bird are readily understood; the neurological reality is more complex. James writes: (James 1983: 236-7)

> Let anyone try to cut a thought across the middle and get a look at its
> section, and he will see how difficult the introspective observation of
> the transitive tract is. The rush of the thought is so headlong that it al-
> most always brings us up at the conclusion before we can arrest it.

The attempt to get a look at a section of thought is like trying to grasp the flowing river or the flying bird. James continues: "Or if our purpose is nimble enough and we do arrest it, it ceases forthwith to be itself". And James concludes that the attempt is like "a snowflake caught in the warm hand", or "like seizing a spinning top to catch its motion". (James 1983: 237) James' poetic metaphors are as precise as the clinical, analytic language in which he discusses the findings of experimental psychology.

Thought can be said to include ideas, concepts, and theories; opinions, beliefs, and values; purpose and intention; analysis, assessment, problem-solving, and decision-making; intuition, insight, and revelation; recollection, reminiscence, reflection, and meditation; conception, creation, and invention; reasoning; debate; plotting in the form of con-

spiring or deceiving and plotting in the form of planning and sched-
uling. If in addition to these forms of thought we include the mental
processes involved in creating or enjoying a painting, a sculpture or of
piece of music, or the mental processes involved in sports and games,
then it is clear that many forms of thought are independent of language.
Thought without language? The possibility is still denied by some who
write about the mind.

Peter Carruthers in Chapter 2 of *Language, thought and conscious-
ness: An essay in philosophical psychology* states: (Carruthers 1998:
40) "human conscious thinking involves sentences of natural language"
and "It is images of *natural language sentences* which are the primary
vehicles of our conscious thoughts". In the same chapter he adds: (Car-
ruthers 1998: 51) "my conscious thinkings take place in English and
not 'in a supposedly innate, universal, symbolic system'". In his final
chapter Carruthers subverts his thesis when he states: (Carruthers 1998:
262) "Mathematicians, scientists, and composers certainly engage in a
kind of thinking, and thinking which is genuinely propositional; but this
thinking need not be mediated by natural language".

The thinking of mathematicians, scientists and composers emerges
from mental faculties that Carruthers denies: innate, universal, sym-
bolic systems. Many mental activities are possible only through innate
potentialities; some mental faculties are universal in the most funda-
mental sense: the structure of the human brain, and to some extent its
infrastructure, is the same in all human groups; most forms of human
communication, including non-verbal communication, are symbolic
systems: they refer to, or symbolize, things other than themselves.

Among twentieth-century philosophers, Ludwig Wittgenstein is the
most emphatic in asserting the divisibility of thought and language.
In paragraph 5.6 of *Tractatus Logico-Philosophicus,* first published
in 1921, he makes that much quoted statement: (Wittgenstein 1974:
56) "*The limits of my language* mean the limits of my world". But we
experience the world – not only arts, crafts, mathematics, sports and
games but also loving, voyaging, gardening, driving a car and operat-
ing machines – without the use of language. Wittgenstein repeats his
assertion in a different form in paragraph 6.62: (Wittgenstein 1974: 57)
"The world is *my* world: this is manifest in the fact that the limits of
*language* (of that language which I alone understand) mean the limits

of *my* world". As an aside we could say that if Wittgenstein alone understands a language then it cannot be a form of communication; the self-contained system is solipsistic.

Wittgenstein returns to the related subjects of thought, language and experience in paragraph 96 of *Philosophical Investigations* where he states: (Wittgenstein 1972: 44) "Thought, language, now appear to us as the unique correlate, picture, of the world. These concepts: proposition, language, thought, world, stand in line one behind the other, each equivalent to each". Thought and language, says Wittgenstein, give us a picture, that is, a nonlinguistic representation of the world. And he repeats the equation of the linguistic and the visual in Section II xi of *Philosophical Investigations*: (Wittgenstein 1972: 215) "But if a sentence can strike me like a painting in words, and the very individual word in the sentence is like a picture". These observations partly contradict his assertions in the earlier work, the *Tractatus*, but the contradiction, or concession, also appears in paragraph 6.522 of the *Tractatus*: (Wittgenstein 1974: 73) "There are, indeed, things that cannot be put into words. *They make themselves manifest.* They are what is mystical". Some forms of self-contradiction are inevitable in the evolving life of an individual mind. What strikes the reader and delights the poet in the quotation above is Wittgenstein's belief that some things are both manifest and mystical.

In effect, thinking includes most forms of abstract, symbolic, conscious mental activity. Not all these forms of thought appear as the subjects or themes of poems, but some of the forms are used by poets in arriving at the finished poem. No poem need express significant thought, but every poem is a product of thinking; and the thinking that goes into the making of a poem – one might call it poetic intelligence – is as important as the thought that appears in the poem.

Thought and emotion are usually interactive in poetry, and the identifying of sensory stimuli and the assessing of emotional experiences are forms of thought. When we identify an external stimulus as red or rough or round, we make an abstract symbolic representation of the stimulus. The process is almost automatic; it is also commonplace, but in a work like this the process must be discussed. In *Looking for Spinoza* the neurologist, Antonio Damasio, summarizes the pattern of sense perception: (Damasio 2003: 200) "And yet, the images we experience are brain constructions *prompted* by an object, rather than mirror reflections of the object".

When the poet and reader transduce perception into language, the simple abstraction, the roughness of the bark of an oak tree, leads to the general abstraction of roughness, and the physical quality is abstracted to a concept. Brain and mind are designed to interact in ways that represent physical reality as thought; they interact in similar ways to represent emotion as thought. When we see two pairs of lips touch in a certain way, the occurrence is identified and abstracted in the word, "kiss", and then, perhaps, further abstracted in the word, "love", so that love is both the thought and the emotion. The expression on a man's face is identified and abstracted as the word, "scowl", and then, more abstractedly, as the word and the concept, "contempt", so that contempt, too, represents both the thought and the emotion.

In a poem, the images and ideas triggered by the words, "kiss" and "scowl", are likely to be imaginative re-enactments of the occurrences, momentary dramas that have an immediacy and physicality. Words at the second level of abstraction, "love" and "contempt", are clearly not re-enactments but interpretations. The different effects of the two levels of abstraction can be likened to the difference between a first-hand account of an eyewitness and a second-hand, paraphrased account. And because immediacy and physicality are more readily imaginable, most poets today prefer to use words at the first level of abstraction. Poets sometimes change to the second level, that is, from language that represents physical reality and emotion to language that represents thought and emotion, when they develop the subject of a poem into a theme and set the particular act, the kiss or the scowl, in the wider human context of love or contempt. That kind of transition is more likely to be effective if the poet first persuades the reader to make the imaginative re-enactment; that is why many poets try to avoid the language of thought in favour of a language of physicality and physical immediacy.

Some of Eliot's views on thought in poetry appear in 'Poetry and Philosophy', abstracted from his essay of 1927, 'Shakespeare and the Stoicism of Seneca'. Eliot refers to poets who are said to be thinkers: Shakespeare, Dante, and Lucretius, and poets who are not: Swinburne and Tennyson, and then he states: (Eliot 1955: 53) "But what we really mean is not a difference in quality of thought, but a difference in quality of emotion. The poet who thinks is merely the poet who can express the emotional equivalent of thought". But, as an earlier paragraph suggested, there is a faculty, or sub-faculty, that can be called poetic intelligence, which is not quite the same as poetic imagination but is a knowledge and understanding of how to choose the subject of a poem, how to relate the subject to the theme, how to create an appropriate semantic field, how to structure internal figures within the overall structure of the poem, and how and when to bring a poem to its conclusion. The effectiveness of the expression of emotion, and to that extent the effectiveness of the poem, will be influenced by the quality of the poet's thinking during the act of composition.

Eliot himself acknowledges the importance of thought in the making of a poem when he writes in the same paragraph: "To express precise emotion requires as great intellectual power as to express precise thought". This acknowledgement of intellectual power is contradicted by his later statement in the same essay on the function of poetry: "But if this function is not intellectual but emotional, it cannot be defined adequately in intellectual terms". If, on the other hand, the content and function of poetry are both intellectual and emotional, it can be defined, or rather, discussed, only by using both sets of terms. Eliot's denial is puzzling; *The Waste Land, Ash-Wednesday, Four Quartets*, and other poems contain complex and sophisticated thought and are clearly the work of a powerful intellect; and his criticism is, of course, an intellectual activity. If poetry contains no real thought and has no intellectual function, to what, apart from emotion, does the critic apply his intellect?

Perhaps Eliot means a certain kind of thought. In 'Shakespeare and the Stoicism of Seneca', referring again to Shakespeare's thought, he states: (Eliot 1955: 55) "If Shakespeare had written according to a better philosophy, he would have written worse poetry". This idea of an opposition between poetry and philosophy partly echoes the view that Eliot expresses in his letter of 6 January 1915 to Norbert Wiener, the mathematician and a founder of cybernetics, in *The Letters of T. S. Eliot: 1898-1922*, edited by Valerie Eliot. Eliot writes: (Eliot 988: 80) "In a sense, of course, all philosophizing is a perversion of reality. [...] It is an attempt to organize the confused and contradictory world of common sense, and an attempt which invariably meets with partial failure – and with partial success". His view of philosophy in the letter and the essay on Seneca is partly influenced by his experience as a student of philosophy at Harvard and Cambridge universities. His dissertation for Harvard was a study of the writings of the British philosopher, Francis Herbert Bradley.

Coleridge, by contrast, in Chapter XV of *Biographia Literaria*, states: (Coleridge 1956: 179) "No man was ever yet a great poet, without being at the same time a profound philosopher. For poetry is the blossom and fragrancy of all human knowledge, human thoughts, human passions, emotion, language". And in his Notebook for March 1806, he ends a sustained discussion of Shakespeare with the words: (Coleridge 2002: 102)

> Lastly, he – previously to his Drama – gave proof of a most profound, energetic & philosophical mind, without which he might have been a very delightful Poet, but not the great dramatic Poet/ but this he possessed in so eminent a degree that it is to be feared.

For Coleridge, philosophy is thought, and especially original thought. But the meaning of the word, "philosophy", changed in the century between Coleridge and Eliot; one assumes that philosophy for Eliot means logical, rational, systematic thought, the kind of thinking and writing that excludes emotion, symbols, metaphors and other figurative language, connotations and even personal experience.

It is the kind of philosophy that Wittgenstein refers to in Part I, paragraph 109 of his daring exploration of language and mind, *Philosophical Investigations*, where he writes: (Wittgenstein 1972: 47) "Philosophy is a battle against the bewitchment of our intelligence by means of language". The poetic imagination is one way in which our intelligence is bewitched by language. In paragraph 194 Wittgenstein observes: (Wittgenstein 1972: 79) "When we do philosophy we are like savages, primitive people, who hear the expressions of civilized men, put a false interpretation on them, and then draw the queerest conclusions from it". And in paragraph 261 he suggests that in the pursuit of a thought, language – and thought itself – can be lost. Some poets will recognize the state of mind: (Wittgenstein 1972: 93) "So that in the end when one is doing philosophy one gets to the point where one would like just to emit an inarticulate sound". These observations echo a statement in his earlier work, *Tractatus Logico-Philosophics*. In paragraph 4.003 Wittgenstein writes: (Wittgenstein 1974: 19) "Most of the propositions and questions to be found in philosophical works are not false but non-sensical". Wittgenstein usually works from first principles; his starting points are often his rigorous assessments of his own experience, with few references to the work of other philosophers. His observations are paradoxical: intimate and yet impersonal.

Poetry cannot be written in the logical language of reductive reasoning, but reason can be creative and revelatory. Reason is one of the main functions of mind and one of the great features of our humanity; to reject reason is to reject a vital part of our inheritance. Day Lewis offers that view of reason in 'Broken Images' in *The Poetic Image*: (Day Lewis 1947: 133) "A poetry which excludes the searchings of reason and the prompting of the moral sense is by so much the less impassioned, the less various and human, the less a product of the whole man at his full imaginative height". Antonio Damasio writes of the neurological interdependence of emotion and reason in *The Feeling of What Happens*: (Damasio 1999: 42) "Well-targeted and well-deployed emotion seems to be a support system without which the edifice of reason cannot operate properly". Reason is not a threat to other forms of thought or to emotion and feeling; it combines with them as an equal element in the poetic imagination. An imagination that includes reason is more likely than an unreasoning imagination to discover truths of the human condition. Reason can also be a force for artistry and craft in poetry, as Day Lewis argues in *The Poet's Way of Knowledge*. He compares the poet and the scientist, and he concludes: (Day Lewis 1957: 23-4)

> The poet, on the other hand, must not only imagine but reason – that is to say, he must exercise a great deal of consciously directed thought in the selection and rejection of his data: there is a technical logic, a poetic reasoning in his choice of words, rhythms and images by which a poem's coherence is achieved.

This argument, conducted against the received opinion of the time, is daring and original: craft and artistry in poetry, and the meaning that is revealed through craft and artistry, are products of reason as well as emotion.

One of the main celebrants of ideas in poetry is Matthew Arnold. In 'The Function of Criticism at the Present Time' in *Essays in Criticism*, first published in 1865, Arnold writes: (Arnold 1865: 4-5) "Now in literature, – I will limit myself to literature, for it is about literature that the question arises, – the elements with which the creative power works are ideas, the best ideas, on every matter which literature touches, current at the time". It seems certain that Arnold has in mind the older meaning of "idea", a standard of thought to be aimed at, as well as its neutral meaning, a concept.

In his essay, 'Matthew Arnold', in *The Use of Poetry and the Use of Criticism*, (Eliot 1933: 113) Eliot claims that Arnold's literary values are disturbed by confusing poetry and morals in the attempt to find a substitute for religious faith. But if poetry is regarded as a spiritual force, then it is not a substitute for faith but a faith in its own right, as earlier chapters on poetry and religion have shown. What strikes the reader of Arnold's 'The Function of Criticism at the Present Time' and 'The Study of Poetry' is that he achieves a union of the intellectual and the spiritual through literature, largely because he believes that spirituality can be expressed as effectively through literature as through religious faith. In 'The Function of Criticism at the Present Time', referring to creative literary genius, Arnold states: (Arnold 1865: 5)

> its gift lies in the faculty of being happily inspired by a certain intellectual and spiritual atmosphere, by a certain order of ideas, when it finds itself in them: of dealing divinely with those ideas, presenting them in the most effective and attractive combinations, making beautiful works with them, in short.

In 'The Study of Poetry' in *Essays in Criticism, Second Series*, first published in 1888, Arnold repeats his conviction that ideas are the essence of poetry: (Arnold 1888: 9-10) "But for poetry the idea is everything; the rest is a world of illusion, of divine illusion. Poetry attaches its emotion to the idea; the idea is the fact". If, as seems likely, Arnold is now using the word, "idea", as a synonym for thought, then we agree that the emotion in a poem is supported by the thought, but we cannot agree that "the idea is the fact"; that is, that the reality of poetry lies entirely or mainly in the thought in the poem. Arnold overstates the importance of ideas in poetry just as, in the next paragraph of 'The Study of Poetry' he overstates the importance of poetry generally: "Without poetry, our science will appear incomplete; and most of what passes with us for religion and philosophy will be replaced by poetry".

A belief in the importance of ideas in literature and the belief that literature can satisfy intellectual as well as emotional needs are features of Lionel Trilling's work. In 'The Meaning of a Literary Idea' in *The Liberal Imagination*. He argues: (Trilling 1970: 288)

> we as readers know that we demand of our literature some of the virtues which define a successful work of systematic thought. We want it to have – at least when it is appropriate for it to have, which is by no means infrequently – the authority, the cogency, the completeness, the brilliance, the hardness of systematic thought.

Without some of these qualities a body of poetry can seem like an accumulation of separate fragments that become less and less important as one follows another. The fact that Eliot's poetry has some of the qualities of systematic thought makes his views on the subject seem like wilful aberrations.

Auden, by contrast, notes the importance of ideas and logic in poetry. In 'Writing' in *The Dyer's Hand*, he observes: (Auden 1963: 26)

> Verse is also certainly the equal of prose as a medium for the lucid exposition of ideas; in skilful hands, the form of the verse can parallel and reinforce the steps of the logic.

Among poets who have presented ideas through their poetry are Milton in *Paradise Lost*, Pope in his *Essay on Criticism* and *Essay on Man*, Jonathan Swift in *On Poetry* with its ironic subtitle, *A Rhapsody,* Wordsworth in *The Prelude*, Gerard Manley Hopkins in many of his poems and Edwin Morgan in *Sonnets from Scotland*. Richard Wilbur expresses the interdependence of ideas and feelings in his autobiographical essay, 'On My Own Work' in *Poets on Poetry*, where he writes: (Wilbur 1966: 171)

What poetry does with ideas is to redeem them from abstraction and submerge them in sensibility; it embodies them in persons and things and surrounds them with a weather of feeling; it thereby tests the ability of any ideas to consort with human nature in its contemporary condition.

# 9

# Meaning

## Meaning in Poetry

A CONTINUING ORTHODOXY IN SOME branches of literary theory is the denial of meaning in works of literature, an attitude as absurd as that of those twentieth-century philosophers and psychologists who denied the existence of mind. If an agreed system of symbols can consistently represent features of physical reality and the life of the mind, then that system expresses meaning. Writing and speech, in poetry or any other linguistic forms, are two such systems. Literary theorists' fear of meaning, and the language in which they express that fear, show that much of modern literary theory is irrelevant to literature, possibly because the theorist is ignorant or fearful of, or hostile to, the workings of the creative impulse and the poetic imagination.

Poets and readers know that one of the fundamental needs of mind is the need to find meaning in human experience, and that the need can be met through the writing and reading of poetry. Meaning in poetry can be lexical, connotative, variously figurative, phonological, rhythmic, and visual. In addition, meaning in poetry is usually experiential and artistic. Experiential meaning is the significance or the value of the human experience in a poem; readers are more likely to find meaning in poems where the experience is recognizable and significant to them. Artistic meaning is the nature of the poem as a work of art: its degree of originality of language, voice, and vision; the presence or absence of rhythmic patterns, rhyme, and other musical effects; the poem's overall structure, and within that structure the formality or informality of stanza patterns and internal figures.

Literary theorists are afraid of meaning for several reasons: some academic orthodoxies, as the opening paragraph suggests, deny the existence of meaning because the task of identifying the various kinds of meaning in a poem is a complex one that makes demands of the readers' imagination as well as their intelligence. Interpreting a poem is essentially a subjective, introspective activity. Literary theorists claim that there is objectivity and science – the science of linguistics and the pseudo-science of semiology or semiotics, which cannot have the status of physical science – in their methods, and so the theorists claim to reject subjectivity and introspection. But no topic, either scientific or artistic, can be pursued without inner thought and reference to the editor or assessor who is present in the mind of the physical scientist and social scientist as well as the artist. Any sustained process of reasoning involves not only subjectivity and introspection but also some of the feelings and emotions that inevitably accompany that process.

Literary theory takes no account of the creative process or the working of the creative imagination; indeed, some theorists, notably Michel Foucault in 'What Is an Author?' and Roland Barthes in 'The Death of the Author' in *Modern Criticism and Theory* edited by David Lodge are hostile to the creative writer in ways that sometimes remind one of Plato's and Freud's hostility. Foucault, for example, writes of the author: (Foucault 1988: 209) "The author is therefore the ideological figure by which one marks the manner in which we fear the proliferation of meaning". And Barthes, towards the end of 'The Death of the Author', states: (Barthes 1988: 70)

> We know now that a text is not a line of words releasing a single 'theological' meaning (the 'message' of the Author-God) but a multi-dimensional space in which a variety of writings, none of them original, blend and clash. The text is a tissue of quotations drawn from innumerable centres of culture.

The clumsy sarcasm suggests an unreasoning enmity, and Barthes relates sarcasm to truth in the Preface to the 1957 edition and later editions of *Mythologies*: (Barthes 1984: 12) "What I claim is to live to the full the contradiction of my time, which may well make sarcasm the condition of truth". In literature, satire is one condition of truth; sarcasm is the product of a lesser imagination. The experience in a poem, and the language in which that experience is expressed – connotative, figurative, rhythmic, melodic – seldom has a single meaning. Some poems are prompted by a religious impulse and express a sense of the sacred, but in modern poetry the religious element is seldom theistic and, contrary to what Barthes claims, the poet as author never assumes the authority of God or a god. Fearing the proliferation of meaning, and denying that the creative writer is capable of originality, the literary theorist cannot admit the possibility that a mature poet may have a uniquely distinctive poetic voice and might also have a unique vision of life. The effect of these failures is to make modern literary theorists incapable of responding to poetry as poetry.

Their professional stance on the question of meaning is clearly false, because it is almost impossible to read a poem even casually without responding to some of the features in the poem: the lexical and connotative meanings of words, the nature of visual and other sensory images, the sounds of words and the presence of rhyme and other musical effects, the rhythms, and the visual patterns formed by the lengths of lines and stanzas. It would take a sustained effort of will and considerable practice before a reader could fail to respond to all these features in a poem. If one reads a poem with an open or half-open mind, then one's mind will respond to some at least of these features, because the responses are produced by the automatic, natural, and largely nonconscious language-processing functions of the brain. The language areas in the brain of the reader automatically decode the marks on paper, the graphemes, into images, ideas, emotions, sounds, and thus into meanings; the brain also notices, perhaps only vaguely, the visual patterns on the page.

Similarly, the spoken word cannot normally be heard only as an acoustic pattern, a range of phonemes shaped by movements of the tongue and lips as they articulate the streams of sound produced by the vocal tract. What the speaker utters and the listener hears can be described as an acoustic sequence of hums and hisses and buzzes and clicks, but these sounds are heard automatically and instantaneously as speech sounds: phonemes, syllables, words, and thus meanings. The nature of language and mind are such that the reader of a poem, or the listener to a poem, responds spontaneously to meanings in the words and other features of the poem.

These responses are, in fact, the beginning of interpretation; inferring the meanings in a poem is a natural and to some extent an automatic process. Conscious sensory perception – and sometimes nonconscious perception – is inescapably linked with cognition; information is automatically relayed from our senses to our existing bodies of knowledge, our schemata or schemas. If, as literary theorists claim, there is no meaning in a work of literature or, as some of them claim, no meaning that can be identified as literary meaning, then there can be no meaning, and certainly no literary meaning, in the writings of literary theorists. Why do they continue to read and write about literature if it has no meaning? Do they assume that their own writings, unlike the literature they write about, have meaning? If theorists deny the existence of meaning in literature, then they must have some purpose other than the discussion of literature.

An obvious underlying danger is that a theory, by its very nature, is a concept that cannot fully encapsulate the actuality it claims to represent. Another danger is that theorists coin special jargon to express their concepts. Tzvetan Todorov noted this danger his *Introduction to Poetics*. In his opening chapter, 'Definition of Poetics', Todorov warns of (Todorov 1981: 12)

> a danger of over-theorization: in a movement that is itself in accord with the principles of poetics but skips all intermediary stages, increasingly formalized versions of poetics are being proposed, in a discourse that no longer has anything but itself for its object.

The present situation is worse than Todorov feared. Critical schools consisting of bands of literary theorists have emerged not as mediators but as obfuscators, not only between the creative writer and the ordinary reader but also between themselves as theorists and creative writers as artists. As a result the theorists speak only to each other. Some of them mistakenly identify themselves as scientists but a poem, unlike a scientific experiment, cannot be replicated; each poem should be original, unique, and should not be reducible to measurable physical properties or predictable linguistic structures. The current crisis about meaning in literature is a crisis for the theorist and not the poet, whose main allegiance is to the creative impulse and the creative imagination.

❦

The frequently quoted lines: (MacLeish 1935: 122-3)

> A poem should not mean
> But be

by Archibald MacLeish have been used as an excuse for bad poetry and bad criticism. The lines are the conclusion to the poem, 'Ars Poetica', in *Poems*, first published in 1935, in which MacLeish writes that a poem should also be "mute", "Dumb", "Silent", and "wordless". MacLeish would be mistaken if he were saying that a poem should be silent; the sounds of its words are so central to a poem's meaning, and its being, that even when we read silently we hear the sounds of the words in our auditory imagination. But MacLeish knows, of course, the fundamental importance of sound in poetry. 'Immortal Autumn', the poem that immediately follows 'Ars Poetica' in the collection, has the opening line: (MacLeish 1935: 124) "I speak this poem now with grave and level voice". What MacLeish might be saying in 'Ars Poetica' is that, ideally, a poem should be transmitted as if effortlessly and wordlessly from the imagination of the poet to the imagination of the reader. In such a spontaneous transmission the reader realizes words' referents and connotations – feelings, thoughts and physical realities – rather than the words themselves.

Perhaps it is this process of transmission that Laura Riding and Robert Graves have in mind when they write in the chapter, 'Modernist Poetry and the Plain Reader's Rights' in *A Survey of Modernist Poetry*, first published in 1927: (Graves and Riding 2002: 10)

> The poem is not the paper, not the type, not the spoken syllables. It is as invisible and as inaudible as thought; and the only method that the real poet is interested in using is the one that will present the poem without making it either visible or audible, without turning it into a substitute for a picture or for music.

If 'Ars Poetica' is read as a play with paradox – a mute, dumb, silent, and wordless poem – it is not so much an attack on meaning as an attack on those who demand that a poem should have a literal, unambiguous meaning that can be paraphrased in prose.

In 'The Virgin and the Dynamo' in *The Dyer's Hand* Auden comments on MacLeish's words: (Auden 1963: 68)

> It has been said that a poem should not mean but be. This is not quite accurate. In a poem, as distinct from many other kinds of verbal societies, meaning and being are identical. A poem might be called a pseudo-person. Like a person, it is unique and addresses the reader personally.

A poem has meaning and being as a work of art and also in the aspect of human existence expressed in the experience in the poem. Auden takes a different view of meaning in poetry in the essay, 'Writing', in *The Dyer's Hand*: (Auden 1963: 23) "however esoteric a poem may be, the fact that all its words have meanings which can be looked up in a dictionary makes it testify to the existence of other people". The other people are the readers and, although it is unfashionable to admit it, one agrees that a poet's use of language can be influenced by a legitimate concern for the reader. But by stressing the dictionary, or lexical, meanings of words, Auden partly ignores other kinds of meaning; and when we look up a word in a dictionary, we often find that it has two or more meanings, a condition sometimes known as polysemy by linguists and as ambiguity by poets and critics.

In terms of semantics alone, meaning can be lexical, referential, contextual, connotative, metaphorical, symbolic, and grammatical. Connotations, metaphors, and symbols do not have fixed semantic values; their meanings are influenced by the semantic and sometimes moral and emotional values invested in them by the poet and then by the reader. Referential meaning, that is, the entity or referent to which a word or phrase refers, partly depends on the reader's knowledge of the referent. For example, the meaning of "and a cockerel comes striding with its Quetzalcoatl plumes" in 'Salsa' in *The Arkansas Testament* (Walcott 1987: 72) by Derek Walcott depends for part of its meaning on the fact that Quetzalcoatl was, and to an extent still is, the nature god of peoples in Mexico and Central America, that the god's symbol and the peoples' totem is the bird, quetzal, and that the male bird has iridescent green plumage with a scarlet and gold under-body. The fabulous reference brings fabulous connotations.

The particular sense of a word is usually clarified by the context, but the nature of the English language – its vast and constantly changing vocabulary, the multiple meanings of many words, the infinite number of possible sentences and syntactic structures within sentences – is such that ambiguity cannot always be avoided. And the nature of poetry, concerned as it is with human experience, will often be ambiguous because it is seldom possible to attach specific, circumscribed meanings to experience, or moods, or feelings, or the fusion of feeling and thought in poetry. Indeed, William Empson in later editions of *Seven Types of Ambiguity*, first published in 1930, states that all good poetry is ambiguous. The mind is designed to tolerate ambiguities; if it were not, life would be a state of constant perplexity.

Empson's definition of an ambiguous poem remains valid today: (Empson 1984: x)

> We call it ambiguous, I think, when we recognize that there could be a puzzle as to what the author meant, in that alternative views might be taken without sheer misreading. If a pun is quite obvious it would not ordinarily be called ambiguous, because there is no room for puzzling. But if an irony is calculated to deceive a section of its readers I think it would ordinarily be called ambiguous, even by a critic who has never doubted its meaning.

Ambiguity is not the same as obscurity. The possible meaning or meanings of an ambiguity are usually apparent, and so questions about ambiguity are always questions about meaning and not, as the literary theorist might claim, about the absence of meaning. A reader could perhaps, by exhaustive analysis, identify almost everything a poem expresses, as Empson does in some sections of *Seven Types of Ambiguity*, but it is more likely that every reader will make a different response, because every reader's knowledge and understanding of language, poetry, and experience is different.

Spender offers a positive view of the division between being and meaning. In 'A Ritualist Sensibility' in *Eliot* he writes: (Spender 1975: 17)

> For the relationship between the work of art as art, and its being 'about' something, is a dialectical one of fruitful conflict. The energy of the struggle between 'saying' and 'being' within the work may indeed be the most significant energy communicated.

This kind of dialectical relationship is essentially a metaphysical debate that cannot finally be resolved, but it can, as Spender says, be "one of fruitful conflict". The energy generated by this conflict can be a powerful element in a poem and one that can reveal the tensions released in the process of creation. Total explanation is unnecessary and undesirable, but some degree of paraphrase, of telling in different words, is necessary in teaching, reviewing and criticizing, or simply discussing poetry. One of Empson's main methods of explanation in *Seven Types of Ambiguity* is paraphrase, but for Empson paraphrase is used as a supplement to and not a substitute for the poem.

Poets are celebrants of mysteries but they are also a participants in and observers of human experience, and it is their duty as poets to try to understand the significance of experience and to offer that understanding to the reader. Until these two conditions of mind, mystery and understanding, have been transduced and in that sense paraphrased into language, the sense of mystery and the understanding of experience cannot be realized by the poet, and so are not available to the reader. But even then the natures of language and mind are such that, whatever the poet may wish, the varieties of meaning in poetry produce inevitable paradoxes: the poet will almost certainly write unintended as well as creative ambiguities, and the reader will almost certainly find meanings or shades of meaning of which the poet is unaware.

## Recognising Meaning

We live most of our lives without asking what life and living mean; but we are inescapably anthropocentric as a species and egocentric as individuals, and so there are occasions when our innate curiosity leads us to ask questions about the significance of our existence and of the experiences that fill that existence. Poems sometimes answer these questions of meaning; indeed, one of the main functions of poetry is to discover the significance, the relevance, the value of human experience. When the poet is honest and the poem well made, poet and reader gain some understanding of the experience, including experience of the life of the mind, that forms the subject or the theme of the poem; and to understand the experience in a poem is to understand that part of the poem and the meaning of that part of our existence.

One of the delights in reading poetry is that, in recognizing the meaning of the experience in the poem, we recognize the meaning of our own experience. It is as if a personal experience were in a state of semantic suspension until, by apprehending the significance of the poet's experience, we apprehend the significance of our own. The human experience in a poem retains its uniqueness but at the same time it is recognizable as a shared human experience. Perhaps this is what Keats means in his letter to John Taylor in February 1818: (Keats 952: 07) "I think Poetry should surprise by a fine excess and not by Singularity – it should strike the Reader as a wording of his own highest thoughts, and appear almost a Remembrance".

What makes this sharing of experience possible is the fact that readers, through their intelligence and imagination, can recognize the experience in the poem, and through the act of recognition readers can recombine and extend their own experience of life, including the life of the mind. We know much more than we experience directly and personally. Most of our knowledge and some of our understanding of life is acquired through our mediated, or secondary, experience as students, readers, listeners, and viewers. We can have some understanding of jealousy without ever having felt jealous, some understanding of exile without having been exiled, and some understanding of another person's pain without having suffered exactly the same kind of pain. That much is clear enough, but mysteries remain. We are sometimes unaware of our mediated experience and forgetful of our direct experience until, in reading a poem, we have the shock of recognition and realize that we know things about ourselves that we did not know we knew. The poet's imagination quickens the reader's, increasing the conductivity in the reader's brain and activating neural networks encoded for secondary experience in ways that give the experience a greater relevance, making it seem primary rather than secondary.

What is certain is that, if a poem contains a representation of experience that the reader recognizes, then that poem has meaning for that reader. Most forms of human experience are non-linguistic, and language cannot fully represent all forms of experience; but language can represent most kinds of experience in ways that are recognizable to the reader. For poet and reader alike, then, a poem expresses the meaning of an experience and the meaning of that part of our existence that is realized by the experience. For the poet, the need for meaning is unlikely to be satisfied until the demands of the creative impulse are satisfied; indeed, the meaning is partly determined by the way the poet satisfies the creative impulse on each particular occasion. And because the creative impulse can be satisfied only through the creative imagination, the meaning in the experience in the poem is not discovered but created by the poet. A poet may feel that the real meaning of a poem lies in the act of writing it; when the poem is complete, its meaning is different.

This mental faculty or set of faculties that makes possible the meeting of minds is discussed by the neuroscientist, Antonio Damasio, in *The Feeling of What Happens*. Damasio argues that emotion, and to an extent reasoning, involve several areas of the brain, (Damasio 1999: 51) "beginning at the level of the brain stem and moving up to the higher brain". In the chapter, 'Core Consciousness', he says we can understand each other because: (Damasio 1999: 85) "we, as human beings, in spite of remarkable individual traits that make each of us unique, share similar biological characteristics in terms of the structure, organization, and function of our organisms".

Within a poem's unique linguistic structure there are patterns of experience that we as readers can recognize as our own, and in that act of recognition readers affirm the truth of the experience and the truth of the poem. A poet can achieve a state of being that has something in common not only with the fundamental identities of most other poets but also with most other members of the culture. This wider act of recognition is an essential feature of our humanity.

## Subject, Theme and Experience in Poetry

The subject matter of a poem is usually introduced in the first few lines and might continue to be developed until the end of the poem. Many poems also have an underlying theme, a level of significance that is usually expressed less explicitly than the subject and becomes apparent only towards the end of the poem, and perhaps only after two or more readings of the poem. The reader is sometimes led to the theme by a feeling that the full significance of the poem is greater than the sum of the significance of its parts.

Although the subject matter and the theme of a poem can each contain the various kinds of meaning outlined above, it might be useful to regard the subject as the semantic starting-point and the theme as the semantic destination of the poem. Poets might develop the subject of a poem by means of intelligent craft, but they can discover the theme of the poem only by means of the creative imagination and in a process that extends craft into artistry. Metaphors of discovery are sometimes used to describe the emergence of the theme, but the theme is not some pre-existing thing waiting to be found; it must be created by the poet. The theme can be the realization of a deeper or wider significance in the subject matter; or it can be developed so as to contrast with the subject in ways that are usually converse or obverse rather than contradictory. Theme can be formed as a semantic strand running parallel to but separate from the subject until the two coincide; or, as in Thomas Hardy's 'Convergence of the Twain' (Hardy 1991: 306-7), the subject, vainglorious life represented by *The Titanic* and its passengers, and the theme, mortality as "A shape of ice", collide. In some poems, the parallel strand seems to unravel subliminally, as if the poets themselves were only semi-conscious of the deeper significance until it becomes explicit, or less implicit, towards the end of the poem.

Dramatic monologues – Browning's, and Wordsworth's three great portrait monologues: (Wordsworth 1956: 90) 'The Last of the Flock', (Wordsworth 1956: 18-29) 'The Female Vagrant' ("My Father was a good and pious man"), which was later edited into the sequence, 'Guilt and Sorrow', (Wordsworth 1956: 115) 'Her Eyes Are Wild', originally titled 'The Mad Mother' – monologues can create a subliminal or delayed meaning if the real nature of the speaker's identity and state of mind become apparent only towards the end of the monologue. Two of the earliest monologues in English poetry, 'The Wanderer' and 'The Seafarer', are monologues within monologues. In the inner monologues, the speakers tell of physical journeys that are the subjects of the poems; as the poems develop, the subjects become themes of exile and pilgrimage, and the speakers' states of mind can be seen as states of the human spirit.

The movement from subject to theme, from one level of significance to another, deeper, level, is what Eliot is referring to in the Conclusion to *The Use of Poetry and the Use of Criticism* when he writes: (Eliot 1933: 151)

> The chief use of the 'meaning' of a poem, in the ordinary sense, may be
> to satisfy one habit of the reader, to keep his mind diverted and quiet,
> while the poem does its work upon him: much as the imaginary burglar
> is always provided with a bit of nice meat for the house-dog.

That is, while the reader's attention is focused on the subject matter, the poet is developing the theme of the poem. In the sonnet, the reader is often aware of the exact point at which the poet introduces the theme; it is usually in the last six lines, the sestet, that follow the first eight lines, the octave.

In portrait poems, too, the reader can sometimes detect the point where the poet modulates from subject to theme and opts for one theme rather than another. To be effective, a portrait poem must have a detailed particularity that brings the subject to life: Sidney Keyes' 'William Wordsworth' (Keyes 1945: 35-6); R. S. Thomas' 'Cynddylan on a Tractor' (Thomas, R.S. 1955: 54); Seamus Heaney's early poem, 'Docker' (Heaney 1966: 41); Adrienne Rich's two grandmothers, 'Mary Gravely Jones' and 'Hattie Rice Rich' (Rich 196: 292-3) But the theme of a portrait poem could be that a person's real identity is unknowable; or the theme could be the idea that, despite the uniqueness of the person who is the subject of the poem, there is a common humanity that links that person with the poet and the reader. Such paradoxes of nearness and estrangement appear in several of Sylvia Plath's poems, not only the much anthologized 'Daddy', (Plath 1965: 54-6) but also 'The Beekeeper's Daughter' (Plath 1972: 75) 'Child' (Plath 1971a: 120 and 'Widow' (Plath 1971b: 38-9).

In the course of the twentieth century that pattern – the movement from subject to theme and from one level of meaning to another – became the dominant pattern. Cleanth Brooks in 'Irony as a Principle of Structure', first published in 1949, writes as if that kind of poetic figure were compulsory: (Brooks 1971: 1041)

> The poet does not select an abstract theme and then embellish it with
> concrete details. On the contrary, he must establish the details, must
> abide by the details, and through his realization of the details attain to
> whatever general meaning he can attain. The meaning must issue from
> the particulars.

Although the pattern of meaning described by Eliot and Brooks is the main pattern in twentieth and twenty-first century poetry, it is not a twentieth-century development. The first three lines of Burns' 'Tam O' Shanter' (Burns 1950: 1) depict the end of a busy market day:

> When chapman billies leave the street,
> And drouthy neibors neibors meet,
> As market-days are wearing late.

Keats' 'The Eve of St Agnes' opens with those sharply defined, intensely sensuous images of cold: (Keats 1879: 312)

> St Agnes' Eve – ah, bitter chill it was!
> The owl, for all his feathers, was a-cold;
> The hare limped trembling through the frozen grass.

The first stanza of Tennyson's poem on the same theme, 'St Agnes' Eve', is both physical and transcendental: (Tennyson 1881: 123)

> Deep on the convent-roof the snows
> Are sparkling to the moon:
> My breath to heaven like vapour goes
> May my soul follow soon.

Matthew Arnold's verse drama, *Empedocles on Etna* opens with the finely imagined detail in the lines spoken by Callicles, the young musician: (Arnold 1903: 436)

> The mules, I think, will not be here this hour;
> They feel the cool wet turf beneath their feet
> By the stream-side, after the dusty lanes
> In which they have toil'd all night.

In previous centuries the poet could introduce the theme in the first lines of a poem, and could do so in a language of abstract generalization that is not usually acceptable today. For example, the first stanza of Andrew Marvell's 'The Definition of Love' is: (Marvell 1901: 73-4)

> My love is of a birth as rare
> As 'tis for object, strange and high;
> It was begotten by Despair
> Upon Impossibility.

Wordsworth opens 'Influence of Natural Objects' (Wordsworth 1956: 71-2) in a language that is deliberately universal and transcendental, and in words that he also uses in Book I of *The Prelude*: (Wordsworth 1956: 499)

> Wisdom and Spirit of the universe!
> Thou soul, that art the Eternity of thought.

Tennyson states the themes of *In Memoriam* in the prefatory stanzas that are designed to establish a timeless, divinely decreed order of reality and to affirm the poet's faith in that order: (Tennyson 1881: 286)

> Strong Son of God, immortal Love
> Whom we, that have not seen thy face,
> By faith, and faith alone, embrace,
> Believing where we cannot prove.

*In Memoriam* moves from a divine to a human order of reality, from the eternal to the temporal and mortal.

# 10

# The Poet's Role

## Poet or Citizen?

CONCEPTS OF THE POET'S ROLE CHANGE over time. Plato feared that the independent and divergent mind of the poet would threaten the ordered society of the ideal state. In Book Ten of *The Republic* he writes: (Plato 1956: 384)

> But you will know that the only poetry that should be allowed in a state is hymns to the gods and paeans in praise of good men; once you go beyond that and admit the sweet lyric or epic muse, pleasure and pain become your rules instead of law and the principles commonly accepted as best.

The role that Plato prescribes for the poet is political, not artistic: poets would be required to meet the demands of the autocratic rulers of the autocratic state and to share, or pretend to share, the rulers' values and beliefs. Poets would be prevented from expressing pleasure, pain and all thoughts and emotions that could distract listeners and readers from the common cause of the republic, or from the particular cause of Plato. Wordsworth, by contrast, states in the Preface to *Lyrical Ballads* that the production of pain and pleasure is part of the poet's role: (Wordsworth 1956: 738) "What does the poet? He considers man and the objects that surround him as acting and re-acting upon each other, so as to produce an infinite complexity of pain and pleasure". Philip Sidney and Shelley attribute even greater powers to the poet. Sidney in *An Apology for Poetry*, first published in 1595, and Shelley in *A Defence of Poetry* repeat the Platonic idea that a principal role of the poet is to promote moral virtue and spiritual well-being. As poets they do not, of course, share Plato's ideas of social control. Instead, they idealize the poet and exaggerate his powers to the extent that parts of Sidney's argument in

*Apology for Poetry* strike the modern reader as sophistry, and Shelley's as fantasy. Sidney states that the poet's role is (Sidney1947: 25) "winning the mind from wickedness to virtue", and he describes poetry in these terms: (Sidney1947: 61) "the ever-praise-worthy Poesie is full of virtue-breeding delightfulness, and void of no gift that ought to be in the noble name of learning".

Ben Jonson offers a similar panegyric. In *Timber or Discoveries*, published in 1641, four years after his death, Jonson states of poetry: (Jonson 1951: 263) "it nourisheth and instructeth our Youth; delights our Age; adorns our prosperity; comforts our Adversity; [...] the wisest and the best learned have thought her the absolute Mistress of manners; and nearest of kin to Virtue".

Shelley's concept of the poet is this: (Shelley 1956: 135) "A poet, as he is the author to others of the highest wisdom, pleasure, virtue and glory, so he ought personally to be the happiest, the best, the wisest, and the most illustrious of men". And then, without apparent irony, he asserts, "the greatest poets have been men of the most spotless virtue". Sidney and Shelley write as if the persuasive powers of the poet could bring about the kind of order that Plato says the poet would destroy; indeed, Sidney, Jonson and Shelley believe that poetry is the constant spiritual companion of poets, and a force that can purify the mind of the reader. Poets and readers today can find spiritual companionship, but we doubt the purifying powers of poetry.

Wordsworth, too, seems to think that his poems will improve the moral condition of his readers. In his long and fulsome letter of May 1807 to Lady Beaumont, the wife his benefactor, Sir George Beaumont, Wordsworth states: (Wordsworth 1984: 99) "I doubt not that you will share with me an invincible confidence that my writings [...] will co-operate with the benign tendencies in human nature and society, wherever found; and that they will, in their degree, be efficacious in making men wiser, better, and happier". In the same letter Wordsworth recognizes the limits of a poet's role when he writes:

> It is an awful truth, that there neither is, nor can be, any genuine enjoyment of Poetry among nineteen out of twenty of those persons who live, or wish to live, in the broad light of the world among those who either are, or are striving to make themselves people of consideration in society.

Without readers, the poet has no role; and without poetry, Wordsworth implies, a person has no soul.

Wordsworth does not claim that the poet is a superior person; he knows that in his own life there is a difference between private morality and his public reputation. In a letter to James Gray in 1816 – the letter appears as 'Letter to a Friend of Burns' in *Wordsworth's Literary Criticism* – he states: (Wordsworth 1925: 212) "It is, I own, comparatively of little importance, while we are engaged in reading the *Iliad*, the *Eneid*, the tragedies of *Othello* and *King Lear*, whether the authors of these poems were good or bad men; whether they lived happily or miserably". He is saying not only that the great poet is not necessarily a good man; he is also saying, in a boldly independent statement for the time, that the question is irrelevant to the enjoyment of poetry.

By the second decade of the twentieth century few poets believed that their work could have the power to perfect the reader. Robert Graves is an exception. In his third lecture as Oxford Professor of Poetry in 1965, he states: (Graves 1965: 156) "My own ineradicable view of poets, as opposed to dramatic or literary show artists, is that one cannot separate them from their work: a flaw in character will always reveal itself as a flaw in poetic craft".

Eliot in 'Tradition and the Individual Talent' makes a clear distinction between the man as poet and as citizen: (Eliot 1955: 28) "Impressions and experiences which are important for the man may take no place in the poetry, and those which become important in the poetry may play quite a negligible part in the man, the personality". Yeats states the case succinctly. In *Journal* part 8 in *Memoirs – Autobiography* he writes: (Yeats 1972: 140-1) "The poet's enemies are those industries that make a good citizen. A good poet is a good citizen turned inside out". The personality of the citizen is not the same as the self of the poet; creativity requires a divergent mind, whereas good citizenship requires a great deal of conformity.

When Eliot discusses the subject in *Notes towards the Definition of Culture*, the reader feels that Eliot's view has been confirmed by actual personal encounters: (Eliot 1948: 23)

> An artist of any kind, even a very great artist, is not for this reason alone
> a man of culture: artists are not only often insensitive to other arts than

those which they practise, but sometimes have very bad manners or
meagre intellectual gifts.

Even the accomplished and educated artist is a philistine when he
assumes the persona of an oaf. The poet and critic Donald Davie in
'Postscript 1966' in *Purity of Diction in English Verse* admits that he,
Kingsley Amis and other members of the 1950s' group known as The
Movement, had (Davie 1967: 198) "a streak of aggressive philistinism
that ran through all our thinking".

Auden, too, stresses the difference between the man and the poet, and
perhaps, like Eliot, he writes from direct experience when he states in
'Words and the Word' in *Secondary Worlds*: (Auden 1968: 135) "There
may be certain falsities of heart that so corrupt the imagination as to
render it impotent to create, but there is no comprehensible relation
between the moral quality of a maker's life and the aesthetic value of
the works he makes". And Auden is so opposed to the idealized role
that Shelley claims in the final sentence of *A Defence of Poetry*, "Poets
are the unacknowledged legislators of the world," that he responds in
'Writing' in *The Dyer's Hand* with the dismissive statement: (Auden
1963: 27) "'The unacknowledged legislators of the world' describes the
secret police, not the poets".

In contrast to Eliot and Auden, Williams makes claims as grand and
absolute as Shelley's. In 'Caviar and Bread Again: a Warning to the
New Writer', he states: (Williams 1969: 102) "It is he, the poet, whose
function it is, when the race has gone astray, to lead it – to destruction
perhaps, but in any case, to lead it". And in the same essay Williams as-
serts that the poet has "the most vital function of society: to recreate it in
every part, and so set the world working or dancing or murdering each
other again, as it may be". In a later essay, 'The Basis of Faith in Art',
Williams contradicts himself. Like Shelley, he now sees the writer's
role as a force for good; (Williams 1969: 194) the writer's role is "to
crystallize his findings in a durable form for social confirmation, that
society may be built more praiseworthy". A similar concept of the en-
hancement of the human condition appears in Williams' essay, 'Against
the Weather: a Study of the Artist' (Williams 1969: 97-8):

If I succeed in keeping myself objective enough, sensual enough, I can
produce the factors, the concretions of materials by which others shall

understand and so be led to use – that they may the better see, touch, taste, enjoy – their own world *differing as it may* from mine.

Williams, like Shelley, over-reaches himself. Their claims reflect the importance they, and not society at large, attach to poetry. Their aspiration to grandeur results in grandiosity.

## The Poet and Society

Do poets now have any social role? In 'Imperfect Critics' in *The Sacred Wood* Eliot writes of the isolation of the artist: (Eliot 1950: 32) "The arts insist that a man shall dispose of all that he has, even of his family tree, and follow art alone. For they require that a man be not a member of a family or of a caste or of a party or of a coterie, but simply and solely himself". If poets are possessed by their art, then they might be drawn to make an apostolic renunciation of the world, but not usually as absolutely or dramatically as Eliot describes in the quotation above. By contrast, in the Preface to *The Sacred Wood* he makes that equivocal statement: (Eliot 1950: viii) "Poetry is a superior amusement: I do not mean an amusement for superior people. I call it an amusement, an amusement *pour distraire les honnêtes gens*, not because that is a true definition, but because if you call it anything else you are likely to call it something more false". The statement, "Poetry is a superior amusement", is similar to Wordsworth's in his Essay Supplementary to the Preface to *Lyrical Ballads*, where he states (Wordsworth 1956: 743) that poetry is "a species of luxurious amusement".

Five years later, Eliot, in the Introduction to *The Use of Poetry and the Use of Criticism*, and in a deliberately absurd echo of Walter Pater's claim in 'The School of Giorgione' in *The Renaissance: Studies in Art and Poetry* that – the italics are Pater's – *"All art constantly aspires towards the condition of music"*, Eliot states: (Eliot 1933: 32) "From one point of view, the poet aspires to the condition of the music-hall comedian". The condition to which the comedian aspires, Eliot adds, is popularity; he does not say that the music-hall comedian gained popularity from the pleasure, the gift of laughter, he gave to audiences.

Robert Graves, too, recommends that the poet renounce society. In 'Fabulous Beasts' in *The White Goddess* he states: (Graves 1948: 358)

"He must achieve social and spiritual independence at whatever cost". Graves organized his own life in such a way that he achieved not only a large degree of social and spiritual independence but also a degree of financial independence. He earned large sums from his lecturing in the United States and even greater sums from his novels of imperial Rome, *I Claudius* and *Claudius the God*, both published in 1934. When the novels were dramatized for BBC Television in 1976 they became best-sellers. But Graves made so many lavish gifts of money and property to his family and friends that he never felt financially secure.

Wallace Stevens, who worked as a company lawyer until shortly before his death in 1955, reaches a similar conclusion about the writer and society when he states in 'The Noble Rider and the Sound of Words', first published in 1942: (Stevens 1971: 977) "Then I am interested in the role of the poet and this is paramount. In this area of my subject I might be expected to speak of the social, that is to say, the sociological or political, obligation of the poet. He has none". Stevens is saying that the poet has no civic role, no social obligation whatsoever. This chapter will show that elsewhere in the same essay Stevens assumes the most intimate of poetic roles.

Spender gives opposite advice in 'Greatness of Aim' in *The Making of a Poem*: (Spender 1955b: 44) "The most important task is for the poet to grasp at as much of modern life as he is capable of imaginatively digesting, and turn it into his rich and strange poetry, through channels of form which he can only discover for himself". The poet is not required to adopt Eliot's or Graves' or Spender's attitudes to society, but Spender's recommendation of involvement in contemporary life, an involvement that is imaginative as well as social and physical, seems the healthier idea in that it recognizes the existence of the social world and the world of external realities. Spender's advice partly echoes Emerson's in 'Poetry and Imagination' in *Letters and Social Aims*. Emerson urges poets: (Emerson s.d.: 581) "to convert the vivid energies acting at this hour, in New York, and Chicago and San Francisco, into universal symbols [...] American life storms about us daily, and is slow to find a tongue". When *Letters and Social Aims* appeared American life had already found a tongue: the first edition of Whitman's *Leaves of Grass* was published in 1855.

Poets are free to isolate themselves physically from society and to isolate their art from that of their contemporaries, but when poets ask that their work be published they are asking for that most intimate of social roles: an imaginative presence in the mind of the reader. And if their work is published, read, and enjoyed, then poets play an important social role in that their poems are the vicarious realization of readers' undeveloped creativity and at the same time a vicarious satisfaction of readers' creative needs.

Wordsworth in the Preface to *Lyrical Ballads* makes it clear that he understands the extent to which the poet is a spokesman for the reader and thus for certain sections of society, and he makes it clear that the understanding is possible because of his knowledge of some of the ways in which the mind of the poet and of the reader actually work: (Wordsworth 1956: 738) the poet's "passions and thoughts and feelings are the general passions and thoughts and feelings of men". He knows, with an exceptional prescience for his time, that a poet's imaginings arise: "from the structure of his own mind [...] without immediate external excitement". Wordsworth is familiar, too, with the paradox that the poet can represent the reader only because the poet's mind diverges from the reader's in particular ways: (Wordsworth 1956: 737)

> He is a man speaking to men: a man, it is true, endowed with more lively sensibility, more enthusiasm and tenderness, who has a greater knowledge of human nature, and a more comprehensive soul, than are supposed to be common among mankind.

Does Wordsworth exaggerate? Perhaps the qualities he claims exclusively for the poet are more widespread in society than he allows. Even so, the poet's mind, partly through the particular qualities of innate faculties and partly by developing these qualities through the writing of poetry, is more attentive than other minds to some kinds of experience and some features of our humanity. And because the poet can see and hear things that other people cannot, there are some truths that only the poet can tell.

F. R. Leavis recognizes the importance of this role. In 'Poetry and the Modern World' in *New Bearings in English Poetry*, first published in 1932, Leavis writes: (Leavis 1963: 19)

> Poetry matters because of the kind of poet who is more alive than other people, more alive in his own age. He is, as it were, at the most con-

scious point of the race in his time. [...] The potentialities of human
experience in any age are realized only by a tiny minority, and the im-
portant poet is important because he belongs to this [minority].

It is not that poets, as members of a society, have more, or more impor-
tant, experiences than non-poets, but that they understand the signifi-
cance of experience more clearly than most other people in society.

Ted Hughes in 'Concealed Energies' in *Winter Pollen* makes an
unconvincing claim when he writes: (Hughes 1994: 27) "In any social
group, the imaginative writers are the most visible indicators of the
level and energy and type of the imagination and other vital mental
activities in the whole group". Hughes is saying that the creative writer
indicates what is occurring in the imagination and mental life of the
non-writing majority, as if the majority were of one mind and as if the
poet could read that mind. In his next sentence Hughes describes the re-
lationship between the poet and society in terms that read like psycho-
analytic or shamanic myth: "What happens in the imagination of those
individuals chosen by the unconscious part of society to be its writers,
is closely indicative of what is happening to the hidden energies of so-
ciety as a whole". The claim is unconvincing. If what Hughes calls "the
unconscious part of society" is truly unconscious, then it cannot make
choices in the usual meaning of the word, because choice implies a con-
scious selection. A creative writer is not chosen by society, conscious or
nonconscious; the person chooses to be a writer. The imagination of the
creative writer is not "closely indicative" of what is happening to the
"hidden energies" of the rest of society; if, as Hughes says, the energies
are hidden and society is unconscious, then no one can be aware of the
energies. Writers express the truths of shared human experience, but
they are able to tell these truths only because they have developed their
imagination in ways that diverge from the imagination of most other
language users.

Hughes' mythological view partly echoes an even more ritualistic
concept of the poet's social role. In 'Postscript 1936' in *A Hope for Po-
etry*, Day Lewis refers to the pre-history of art, and then he states: (Day
Lewis 1944: 89) "from these earliest days, the history of the poet has
been the history of the misfit trying to justify himself to society. Just as
the poem is, in a sense, the scapegoat of the poet's sense of guilt; so the
poet is in turn the scapegoat of society". Such mythologizing is unchar-

acteristic of Day Lewis' critical approach; he has been seduced by an idea that, on closer inspection, is implausible. A poem is as likely to be the result of the poet's sense of joy as a sense of guilt; and English-language poets have never been scapegoats in the usual sense of the word; that is, they have never been wrongly and arbitrarily accused of being responsible for the ills of society.

When Eliot discusses the poet's role in 'A Talk on Dante' in 1950, he writes of the poet's responsibility to, and thus his relationship with, the language in which he writes. The poet's relationship with the readers can only be through the medium of language, and the poet's greater understanding of language, along with his understanding of the expression of emotion in language, says Eliot, enhance the lives of the readers: (Eliot 1955: 101)

> The task of the poet, in making people comprehend the incomprehensible, demands immense resources of language; and in developing the language, enriching the meaning of words and showing how much words can do, he is making possible a much greater range of emotion and perception for other men, because he gives them the speech in which more can be expressed.

In going beyond the previous limits of his imagination, the great poet can, as Eliot claims, make the incomprehensible imaginable and thus comprehensible. Modern linguists might question whether any one person can influence the meanings of words in a way that enriches rather than simply extends the meanings; and neuroscientists might argue that most people whose brains are intact are biologically programmed to have a full range of emotions and perceptions. And yet Eliot is surely right in claiming that poets, through their understanding of language and experience, can make the reader aware of a fuller dimension of the reader's humanity.

Wallace Stevens, despite his claim that the poet has no social obligations, accepts what an earlier paragraph in this chapter described as the intimate social role of the poet's imaginative presence in the mind of the reader. In 'The Noble Rider and the Sound of Words' Stevens says of the poet's role: (Stevens 1971: 977) "I think that his function is to make his imagination theirs [the readers'] and that he fulfils himself only as he sees his imagination become the light in the minds of others. His role, in short, is to help people to live their lives". Stevens' concept of the relationship between poet and reader is similar to Eliot's concept of the poet offering the reader a greater range of emotion and perception. But Stevens, unlike Eliot, implies that there is a degree of reciprocity in the relationship. If, as Stevens says, the poet is fulfilled only when he knows that his imagination has activated the reader's imagination then, through his knowledge of that fulfilment, the poet knows that his relationship with the reader is not simply one-way: he knows that the reader, by confirming the value of his, the poet's, imaginative life, is completing the cycle of creation.

Roy Fuller, like Stevens, earned his living as a company lawyer. In his lecture, 'Both Pie and Custard', delivered when he was the Oxford Professor of Poetry and published in *Owls and Artificers*, Fuller notes the nature of Stevens' achievement as a poet: (Fuller 1971: 72) "I know of no other poet who in his work was so constantly alive to what I would characterize as poetry's supreme task – to delineate the life of man in relation to nature unconsoled by any supernatural idea". The earlier chapter on religion and poetry discussed Stevens' belief in the divinity of the imagination. Fuller's concept of the role of the poet and the functions of poetry are far removed from Sidney's and Shelley's; indeed, through Fuller's admission of agnosticism, his concept is removed from Eliot's and Graves'. In the same paragraph Fuller, aware that Stevens is sometimes accused of writing only about poetry and not about human society, adds: "So that if 'poetry' can be said to be the subject matter of all Stevens' poems, that subject matter is in fact all that makes a mysterious nature meaningful – or unmeaningful – to humankind". That is, in serving poetry, the poet is also serving society by showing that there is meaning in the mystery of life. By that measure, all poets who are concerned with the truth of the experience in their poems and who are true to their craft and art have a potential social function.

In 'A Talk on Dante', as an earlier paragraph has shown, Eliot discusses the poet's duty to language and the reader; in 'The Unity of European Culture', the Appendix to *Notes towards the Definition of Culture*, he implies that the poet has a duty to poetry and to other poets: (Eliot 1948: 114) "When a great poet has lived, certain things have been done once and for all, and cannot be achieved again; but, on the other hand, every great poet adds something to the complex material out of which future poetry will be written". The poet's interrelationship with his successors and his predecessors produces a particular kind of continuity, the mythological poetic succession. And since poetry is a medium for expressing truth, the poet plays the role of servant to truth as well as to poetry.

Spender expresses these roles perfectly towards the end of 'The Making of a Poem' when he writes: (Spender 1955b: 62)

> Then, perhaps, literature becomes a humble exercise of faith in being all that one can be in one's art, of being more than oneself, expecting little, but with a faith in the mystery of poetry which gradually expands into a faith in the mysterious service of truth.

These grand, abstract roles seem incompatible with the role outlined by Heaney in 'The Place of Writing' in *Finders Keepers*: (Heaney 2002: 234) "One of the first functions of a poem, after all, is to satisfy a need in the poet. The achievement of a sufficient form and a fulfilling music has a justifying effect within his life". The poet's first reason for writing is to satisfy the creative urge through the working of the poetic imagination. Publication and readership are secondary reasons; there is, after all, enough poetry in the world to satisfy an infinite number of readers for an infinite period of time. But the poet must continue to write in order to keep alive those spiritual faculties of mind – the creative imagination and a sense of the sacred – that are essential elements of our humanity. Even if poets write only for themselves, they must continue in their role as witnesses and celebrants of their age; they must, as Spender says, "keep a faith in the mysterious service of truth". Without such faith, poems would be lesser achievements: less original, less accomplished and less truthful in representing and interpreting human experience.

## Poetic Persona

The poetic self cannot be the same as the poet's personality; in the act of writing, the poet's personality is suspended. Geoffrey Hill in an interview with John Haffenden in *Viewpoints* refers briefly to a possible connection between the two kinds of identity: (Hill 1981: 86) "But if, by personality, we mean the true selfhood of a person, then it would be foolishness to deny the connection between poetry and a man or woman's self". The phrase, "the true selfhood of a person", is an idealized concept that cannot be realized. A person's complete self is a compound of all the selves that make up his or her identity. But all of one's selves, or all aspects of one's self, cannot be simultaneously active, because the mind cannot manage that kind of multiple concurrence. There is, too, the dilemma, possibly false: if all of one's selves or aspects of self were simultaneously active, what self or part of self would be aware of the activity? If one cannot realize one's complete self, then in what sense is one's incomplete self true? And if each of us has a true selfhood, do we also have a selfhood that is not true? There are no final answers to these metaphysical puzzles. Hill then quotes a sentence from Eliot's essay, 'Tradition and the Individual Talent': (Eliot 1955: 30) "Poetry is not a turning loose of emotion, but an escape from emotion; it is not the expression of personality, but an escape from personality".

'Tradition and the Individual Talent' is one of the main starting-points for current discussions of personality and impersonality in poetry; and Eliot's continuing influence is such that, even when we think he is wrong, we may feel required to refute his ideas rather than simply dismiss them. For these reasons, 'Tradition and the Individual Talent' is worth considering in some detail. Towards the end of section I, Eliot writes: (Eliot 1955: 26) "The progress of an artist is a continual self-sacrifice, a continual extinction of personality". The self the poet sacrifices cannot be the poetic self, the self who is realized in the act of writing. Or perhaps it is more appropriate to say the self who is activated rather than the self who is realized, because the poet in the act of creating is sometimes unaware of self; and it is surely this lack of self-awareness that Eliot means when he writes in 'Matthew Arnold' in *The Use Of Poetry And The Use Of Criticism* (Eliot 1933: 108) of that "joyful loss of self in the workmanship of art". What the poet sacrifices are all those selves that are irrelevant to or inconsistent with the poetic self. Poets might think that the poetic self is more important or more dominant than their other selves, but it is usually the case that, when poets are not involved in making a poem, their other selves become active again. Ambiguities can arise from the various concepts of personality, and so an attempt must be made to clarify some of these concepts.

For the poet as for the reader, it is no longer useful to think of fundamental personality types, or temperaments: the tender-minded and tough-minded types identified by William James (James 1975: 13) in the chapter, 'The Present Dilemma in Philosophy' in *Pragmatism*, and the extraverted and introverted types identified by Jung (Jung 946: 464-77) in *Psychological Types*. These types are not entirely consistent; the tender-minded person can occasionally be tough-minded. It is more relevant to think of personality as consisting of a wide range of behaviour, from personal manners and habits to modes of thinking and speaking, that makes a person a distinct individual. Some important forms of behaviour, for example, the poet's involvement in the creative process, and some values and beliefs, for example, a person's religious faith, are not usually considered to be aspects of personality, although they may be vital elements of the person's identity. When poets are involved in the making of poems, the main function of mind is the working of the poetic imagination and the sustaining of the poetic self; poets at work are not aware of their personalities. In the next paragraph of 'Tradition and the Individual Talent', when Eliot writes: (Eliot 1955: 26) "There remains to define this process of depersonalization and its relation to the sense of tradition", he is clearly using the word, "depersonalization", in the sense of a divesting of all features of everyday personality; the poet at work is still a person. In section II of the essay, Eliot contrasts the concept of the poet's personality with the poet's impressions and experiences: "for my meaning is, that the poet has, not a 'personality' to express, but a particular medium, which is only a medium and not a personality, in which impressions and experiences combine in peculiar and unexpected ways". (Eliot 1955: 28) The particular medium can only be the poetic self, the mind of the poet in the act of creating; and in that condition the poet's impressions and experiences are transformed by the poetic imagination, whose ways are peculiar; that is, they are both specific and strange. The ways are also unexpected because the largely conscious poetic imagination interacts with the largely nonconscious creative impulse to produce new combinations of thoughts and feelings that could not have been predicted. Section II of 'Tradition and the Individual Talent' ends with the sentence that has already been quoted, that "poetry is not the expression of personality, but an escape from personality".

We can agree with Eliot's conclusion, and yet among his early poems are exceptions to that general rule. In some of the poems in *Prufrock*, Eliot assumes a persona, and a poetic persona is partly a poetic self and partly a fictionalized personality. The persona of the poet has some features in common with what were once referred to as the *dramatis personae* of theatre, and with Jungian psychology. Behind the persona, or mask, the actor suspends his off-stage identity and adopts the identity of the person symbolized by the mask. In the twentieth century, Jung redesignated the word as a semi-technical term to denote a form of identity that people adopt in circumstances where their more intimately personal or habitual identity seems inappropriate. In *Psychological Types*, he writes: (Jung 1946: 59)

> Thus, the persona is a function-complex which has come into existence for reasons of adaptation or necessary convenience, but by no means is it identical with the individuality. The function-complex of the person is exclusively concerned with the relation to the object.

The persona is a form of identity that allows a person to adapt to external realities; the person casts himself, sometimes intuitively and sometimes more deliberately, in a social or professional role in order to meet the real or supposed demands of that role. And as Jung claims, the persona can be so powerful that the person is exclusively concerned with the immediate task.

In 'The Quest for Identity' in *The Dynamics of Creation* Anthony Storr says of the creative writer: (Storr 1972: 272) "His true identity is in his work, and what he presents to the world in social situations is either a false persona or less than half of himself". What Storr says is the writer's false persona is Storr's false dilemma. The writer's other identities – as husband, wife, parent, employee or employer, colleague, and friend – do not require him or her to assume false personas; their identities in these roles can be as true as their identities as writers. Storr is more convincing in his earlier work, *The Integrity of the Personality*. In the chapter, 'The Development of Personality', he states: (Storr 1960: 49) "a concept of maturity of personality and of interpersonal relationships is an ideal which is never wholly attained; for the development of personality seems to be a continuous process which is never completed". If this statement is true – and I believe it is – then Storr's phrase in *The Dynamics of Creation*, "less than half of himself", is unacceptable because we cannot know the whole self. In fact, we re-combine our sets of neural networks so as to re-group our selves into the appropriate composite self that produces the person's identity as husband, wife, parent, friend or poet. My concept of multiple selves is similar to Howard Gardner's in *Frames of Mind: The Theory of Multiple Intelligences* (Gardner s.l.: 1985) The creative artist with no self other than the artistic self and no identity other than the identity as an artist is a caricature.

A poet might create a persona to protect, or disguise, the essentially private, secret and sometimes vulnerable self. A persona can become false if the poet regards it as his or her whole poetic self instead of an expression that is only part of that self. The dilemma of the private poet may be that he or she is unable to reconcile the secret needs of poetry with the public needs; that is, unable to reconcile the need to discover truths so deeply hidden in the mind that, until the moment of their discovery, were secret even to the poet, with the need to disclose those secret truths in print or in a public performance. For whatever reason, some poets create personas: street-wise, shamanist, erudite, or the ironic and some-times self-mocking persona of the poet who seems surprised or embarrassed at partly revealing himself and then meeting himself in his own poems. The result can be the complex irony of Eliot's 'The Love Song of J. Alfred Prufrock', or the ironies in some of Louis MacNeice's poems, and in many of Roy Fuller's and Philip Larkin's. Larkin refers to his persona in an interview with Miriam Gross of *The Observer* in 1979, reprinted in Larkin's *Required Writing: Miscellaneous Pieces 1955-1982*. He notes that a poet can make a living by giving public readings, by lecturing, and as a poet in residence, and then, in that witty, ironic comparison of his public, or published, poetic identity and his private, personal identity, he adds: Larkin 1983; 47-56) "But I couldn't bear that: it would embarrass me very much. I don't want to go around pretending to be me".

Laura Riding and Robert Graves are among the first commentators on the new irony in early twentieth-century poetry. In the chapter, 'The

Humorous Element in Modernist Poetry', in *A Survey of Modernist Poetry* they write of the modernist poet: (Riding and Graves 2002: 113) "he is able to do what no generation of poets before him has been able to do – to make fun of himself when he is at his most serious". To illustrate the point, Riding and Graves quote the last stanza of John Crowe Ransom's 'Winter Remembered', which ends: (Ransom 1969: 37)

> Were ten poor idiot fingers not worth much,
> Ten frozen parsnips hanging in the weather.

Ransom's parsnips seem similar to Donne's carrots in Elegy VIII 'The Comparison': (Donne 1957: 33-4)

> And like a bunch of ragged carrets stand
> The short swolne fingers of thy gouty hand.

And in the same context Riding and Graves discuss Edith Sitwell's 'The Wind's Bastinado' and Eliot's 'Burbank with a Baedeker: Bleistein with a Cigar'. Later in the same chapter Riding and Graves add this reservation: "It is a question whether irony, as a means of self-mockery, does not fail, in overstepping the disrespect which the poet wishes to do himself. For it adds a pathetic element, a tearfulness, which rarely is entirely sincere". If the irony is excessive or ill-judged, it might suppress the poetic self; the poem would then be a misrepresentation or even an avoidance of inner realities, and there might be little or nothing behind the persona. When the poet finds the right form of words, then the reader senses a face beneath the mask and experiences the poet's simultaneous sense of anguish and the absurdity of the anguish.

Yeats was aware of the existence of a poetic self and a public persona. In an entry probably written in January 1909 in *Journal*, published in *Memoirs – Autobiography* he writes of his deliberate formation of a poetic identity. He uses the word, "personality", but the identity to which he refers is a poetic self: (Yeats 1972: 142)

> To oppose the new ill-breeding in Ireland, which may in a few years
> destroy all that has given Ireland a distinguished name in the world [...]
> I can only set up a secondary or interior personality created by me out

of the tradition of myself, and this personality (alas, to me only possible
in my writings) must always be gracious and simple.

Yeats' persona was his public identity. In a *Journal* entry for August
1910 he writes: (Yeats 1972: 254) "I see always this one thing, that
in practical life the mask is more than the face". Laurence Lerner in
'A Language within the Language' in *The Truest Poetry* states (Lerner
1960: 157) that the ironic mask is: "a characteristic modern way of cov-
ering an inner uncertainty, a form of insurance, a turning-off of some
criticism that the author cannot meet, and recognizes the justice of".
The criticism that the writer is trying to deflect is not only that of the
critic but also the self-criticism that is associated with what Lerner calls
the author's "inner uncertainty". In the same paragraph Lerner states:
"This is new, it is part of our new understanding of the uncertainty of
our own motives. As a creative instrument it has perhaps helped us to
become wiser than we were". The understanding is not entirely new;
Shakespeare, and Chaucer, too, clearly understood the uncertainty of
our motives. Even so, Lerner's distinction is important: what we have
gained, or regained, is not only an understanding of our motives but
also an understanding of their uncertainty. If the poetic persona is a con-
trivance, then the mask will impose constraints on the poet's voice and
vision. These constraints might also be expressions of poets' uneasiness
about their poetic selves as well as their everyday selves, and expres-
sions of their uncertainty about the role of the poet today. Auden's iro-
nies, by contrast, read like the expressions of a more assured poetic self
who seems untroubled by the question of role.

Eliot's poems of the ironic persona – 'The Love Song of J. Alfred
Prufrock', 'Preludes', 'Rhapsody on a Windy Night', and 'Sweeney
Among the Nightingales' – are intimately personal; the raw experience
of human suffering is transmuted by the poet's imagination into poetry
and is thus made imaginable, understandable, for the reader. Whether
the experiences are personal in the sense of autobiographical is less
important than the fact that they are intensely human; what makes these
poems unusual is that they adopt distinctive rhetorical, or narrative,
viewpoints in order to explore bewildering dimensions of the human
condition: a sense of absurdity, of emotional and spiritual disorienta-
tion, and of uncertainty about the poet's personal and poetic identity.
These are personal, not impersonal, matters; personal, but not of a par-

ticular personality. Other early poems, most obviously 'Gerontion', *The Waste Land*, and *The Hollow Men*, are impersonal in the sense that, although their vision of life is Eliot's personal creation, it is a vision not of the individual but of humanity.

A later commentator, Frank Lentricchia, captures the complexity of the self in Eliot's early work. In 'T. S. Eliot' in *Modernist Quartet* Lentricchia discusses Eliot's interest in the poetry of Jules Laforgue, and then he writes: (Lentricchia 1994: 243)

> The layered gestures of irony, indifference, and tiredness, the (self)-mock-heroics of the persona, the projected face of neurasthenia – all these Laforgian mannerisms are not ends but strategies for the slyer reclaiming of inward space, lyricism in the company of the relatively new science of anesthesiology.

Anesthesiology is the study of substances and methods for reducing pain, in this case the pain, mental rather than physical, of neurasthenia, that is, a state of disorientation or dislocation. Anesthesiology, then, is part of the persona; real pain is implicit in some of the poems, and these poems would be lesser achievements without their undercurrents of distress. Hughes in his centenary tribute to Eliot, 'The Poetic Self', suggests (Hughes 1994: 269) that Eliot's early poems are his response to "a universe that had, in primitive fashion, lost its soul" in the "stupefying shock" of the second and third decades of the twentieth century. Eliot expresses his sense of the shock in letters to his parents in *The Letters of T. S. Eliot: Volume I 1898-1922*. In his letter of 23 December 1917 to his father he writes: (Eliot 1988: 214) "Besides, everyone's individual lives are so swallowed up in the one great tragedy, that one almost ceases to have personal experiences or emotions". And in his letter of 28 April 1918 to his mother: (Eliot 1988: 230) "Your papers talk about the 'fight for civilization'; do they realize either what civilization means or what the fight for it means? We are all immeasurably and irremediably altered over here by the last three years".

Hughes notes the great paradox in Eliot's early poems. The poems are: "more privately personal at the one extreme and more powerfully public at the other". As Eliot's imagination evolves, so his poetic identity changes: the ironic personas that are the poet's presence in 'The Love

Song of J. Alfred Prufrock', 'Preludes', 'Rhapsody on a Windy Night', and 'Sweeney Among the Nightingales' develop into the presence that is the poetic self of *Four Quartets*. In some passages of *Four Quartets* the poet's presence is barely detectable because Eliot creates the superb artistic illusion of a rhetorical viewpoint that is sometimes outside and above the content of the poem.

In 'The Poetic Self' Hughes begins by describing the poetic self as it was in the past: (Hughes 1994: 268-9)

> The qualifications of the poetic self (apart from its inspiration) were: that it lived its own life separate from and for the most part hidden from the poet's ordinary personality; that it was not under his control, either in when it came and went or in what it said; and that it was supernatural. The most significant of these peculiarities was that it was supernatural. In ways that were sometimes less explicit than others, it emerged and was merged with a metaphysical Universe centred on God. And it did this happily throughout history, right up to the beginning of this [the twentieth] century.

Although some major poets, Burns, Byron and Arnold, for example, do not have a god-centred view of the universe, Hughes' generalization is largely true. The poetic self changed, Hughes states, because our consciousness changed: "In the twinkling of an eye, as Nostradamus would say, the whole metaphysical universe centred on God had vanished from its place. It had evaporated, with all its meanings". On an evolutionary time-scale the original emergence of human consciousness was a sudden development; and the emergence of the new, twentieth-century consciousness was even more sudden. But a God-centred universe survived into the twentieth century in the work of Eliot, Muir and, beneath her ambivalence, Anne Sexton. Systems of belief change over time, but they do not change in unison over time; old beliefs and new can co-exist for centuries, and when the new belief seems finally to prevail, it is sometimes because it has incorporated rather than displaced the old.

Hughes states that in losing our faith in a supernatural world, we lost the special terrors and cruelties, and also "the infinite consolation, and the infinite inner riches" of that world. In place of the supernatural, we "found merely a new terror: the meaningless". Belief and non-belief are never uniform in any society in any period, but we can accept the general truth of Hughes' claim that the new consciousness brought a new terror in the form of the feeling of the meaninglessness of existence that afflicted some artists in the early twentieth century. The new terror was probably different in kind, but not in degree, from that suffered by poets in earlier centuries; if poets in the past lived their lives in a God-centred universe, then those lives, however wretched, were not meaningless. Meaninglessness is more likely to be experienced by a poet without a God or gods, without myths, without faith.

These concepts, and the language in which they are expressed, are similar to those of I. A. Richards in *Science and Poetry*. In Chapter V, 'The Neutralisation of Nature', Richards writes: (Richards 1951: 752) "The central dominant change may be described as the *Neutralisation of Nature*, the transference from the Magical View of the world to the scientific". And in Chapter VI, 'Poetry and Beliefs', Richards writes of a great spiritual crisis in the first decades of the twentieth century: (Richards 1951: 759) "A sense of desolation, of uncertainty, of futility, of the groundlessness of aspirations, of the vanity of endeavour, and a thirst for a life-giving water which seems suddenly to have failed, are the signs in consciousness of this necessary reorganisation of our lives". At this point in his argument Richards writes of his indebtedness to Eliot's *The Waste Land*; it perfectly describes the state of mind of "all meditative people", says Richards, and it effects "a complete severance between his poetry and *all* beliefs, and this without any weakening of the poetry".

In later paragraphs of 'The Poetic Self', Hughes' argument begins to change in ways that undermine the earlier stages of the argument. He writes: (Hughes 1994: 274)

> We have no problem nowadays in seeing that the God-centred metaphysical universe of the religions suffered not so much an evaporation as a translation. It was interiorized. And translated. We live in the translation, where what had been religious and centred on God is psychological and centred on an idea of the self – albeit a self that remains a measureless if not infinite question mark.

To recreate the old universe within the human mind was a great achievement, and yet the transformation involved forms of personification that suggest modes of thought as old as Homer's. Homer projected his gods and heroes onto mountaintops and into the heavens; Freud's id, ego and superego, and Jung's anima, animus and shadow were introjected into the mind. One effect of the translation is that the poet now accepts responsibility for the working of his mind and the nature of his poetic self; what were once regarded by some poets as supernatural forces are now recognized as human. The self will probably remain a measureless and infinite question mark, because no finite measure can be made of the mind, including the nonconscious mind, in which the self exists. Hughes states (Hughes 1994: 274) that the old poetic self was transformed into the new through "the little mechanism of free-association" developed by Freud. Jung, too, developed techniques of free association in collaboration with Franz Riklin; their work, *Studies in Word Association*, was published from 1904 to 1906.

Psychoanalysts used word association as a diagnostic technique, but they did not know how words are stored in and retrieved from memory; even today these processes are little understood. Word association was, Hughes says: "the means of dismantling the old-style mystery of poetic inspiration and the poetic self – or rather, of translating them". And for Hughes, the translation is from the language of the superhuman and the divine to the language of Freudian psychoanalysis. But to shift responsibility in that way is still to evade personal responsibility for the state of one's poetic self. Freud neither dismantled nor translated the mysteries of poetic inspiration and the poetic self; he denied their existence except as aspects of sublimated sexuality.

Hughes' argument changes yet again. The modern poetic self, he claims, (Hughes 1994: 274) "turns out, in fact, to be very like the old poetic self". There are certainly similarities between the two. As an earlier paragraph suggested, the new consciousness is an extension, not a replacement, of the old, and the similarities in the task of poetry from one generation to another require similarities in the functioning of the poetic imagination. But the similarities that Hughes detects are those between psychoanalysis and religious faith. He treats psychoanalysis as a doctrine through which we can find: "the true self, the self at the source, that inmost core of the individual, which the Upanishads call the divine self, the most inaccessible self of all".

The *Upanishads* are a collection of Sanskrit teachings on how to attain communion with Brahma, the Hindu god of creation. Hughes does not use the word, 'Atman', but in Juan Mascaró's translation of and selection from the *Upanishads* the self is always identified as Atman; and in several of the *Upanishads* – the *Katha, Prasna, Mundaka, Mandukya, Svetasvatara, Chandogya,* and *Brihad-aranyaka* – the terms, "Atman", "Self" and "Spirit", are used in apposition, as if synonymously. The Atman of the *Upanishads* is a spiritual presence and metaphysical state of being that is comparable with the Christian Holy Spirit. The *Upanishads*, like the *Bible*, speak of eternity, of the immortal spirit or soul, and of ultimate truth. Hughes is surely mistaken in comparing these concepts with early psychoanalytical doctrine.

In the *Ten Principal Upanishads*, translated by the Swāmi, Shree Purohit, and 'Put into English' by W. B. Yeats in 1937, the translators do not use the term, "Atman", to identify the supreme being or supreme force. They use a variety of terms: in the *Eesha-Upanishad* the being is "Protector, Seer" and "Lord of all" (Yeats and Purohit 1970: 15-17); in the *Kena-Upanishad* the being is "a mysterious Person" who is "none but Spirit" (Yeats and Purohit 1970: 19-23); in the *Katha-Upanishad* it is "the undying Spirit", a "pure, powerful and immortal Spirit" who is "One, Governor, Self of all, Creator of many out of one" (Yeats and Purohit 1970: 25-38); in the *Mundaka-Upanishad* the being is "the Everlasting" (Yeats and Purohit 1970: 49-57).

Shree Purohit's and Yeats' translations of the *Upanishads*, like Juan Mascaró's, express concepts and principles that are similar to some tenets of Judaism and Christianity. The *Mundaka* states: "There is nothing in this world that is not God", and it refers to "the Kingdom of Heaven". The *Taittireeya* speaks of a god who "in the heat of his meditation created everything." The *Brihadāranyaka* states: "There is no hope of immortality through wealth"; it also states that man can attain the condition of "bright eternal Self", and in that condition he may become immortal. The Self in the *Ten Principal Upanishads* takes several forms, and in the *Māndooky-Upanishad* the Self eludes the very concept of form: (Yeats and Purohit 1970: 60) "He is not knowable by perception […] He is undefinable, unthinkable, indescribable".

Some of the similarities between concepts in the *Upanishads* and in Judaism and Christianity might have come about through the cross-fertilization and assimilation of cultures that follow migration. The

Biblical nomenclatures of *The Ten Principal Upanishads* is also Yeats' attempt to show that the *Upanishads* are not the expressions of an entirely alien religion and philosophy but instead express a holiness and sense of the sacred as powerful as those in the *Old* and *New Testaments*. In making the *Upanishads* more accessible to Western readers, Yeats might have misrepresented some of the concepts.

There is a universal and timeless wisdom in the *Upanishads*, but our only source of the universal and the timeless is our own mind. External sources of wisdom are effective only when a person has enough wisdom to recognize the wisdom in the external source; that is, we can learn from the *Upanishads* and other sources of wisdom and spirituality only when we ourselves have an equivalent potential for wisdom and spirituality. Hughes attributes to Freud and the *Upanishads* what are, in fact, qualities of his own poetic self. The *Upanishads* speak of a divine self, but a sense of divinity is a function of the mind's innate spirituality, as the earlier section of this work, 'A Biology of Religion', has shown. What makes Hughes' divine self "the most inaccessible self of all" is that, if it is really divine, then it is unattainable by humans, although other forms of spirituality are attainable. The divine self, like ultimate reality and truth, might always be beyond the limits of one's imagination, even when that imagination is extended in successive poems.

Psychoanalysis, writes Hughes, (Hughes 994: 275) re-established "the first law of psychodynamics, which states: any communion with that other personality, [the poetic self] especially when it does incorporate some form of the true self, is healing, and redeems the suffering life, and releases joy". Hughes is attributing to psychoanalysis those powers – of healing, redemption, and the release of joy – that are usually associated with Christianity. He does not use the Freudian terms for self or identity, "ego", "id", or "superego", perhaps because these terms seem inconsistent with the concept of a poetic self, a self that Freud in his hostility to literature would have found unacceptable; they are inconsistent, too, with the myths that Hughes creates in his poems and explores in his literary prose. The poetic self, as this chapter has claimed, emerges from the interaction of the creative imagination, which is a mainly conscious function of mind, with the creative impulse, which is mainly nonconscious but is brought to consciousness in the act of creating the poem. Such an interpretation is consistent with Hughes' conclusion that the poetic self must always be "some form of the true self".

William James expresses a similar concept. In 'The Consciousness of Self' in *The Principles of Psychology* he writes of the spiritual self: "it is felt by all men as a sort of innermost centre within the circle, of sanctuary within the citadel". Lionel Trilling, too, has a concept of an ultimate, original self. In 'Sincerity: Its Origin and Rise' in *Sincerity and Authenticity*, Trilling compares the modern use of the word, "role", with its original meaning, and he observes: (Trilling 1972: 9-10)

> But the old histrionic meaning is present whether or not we let ourselves be aware of it, and it brings with it the idea that somewhere, under all the roles there is Me, that poor old ultimate actuality, who, when all the roles have been played, would like to murmur 'Off, off, you lendings!' and settle down with his own original actual self.

King Lear's royal garments give him the superficial, the merely hierarchical identity of a king; beneath the borrowed identity, beneath the lendings, there is a different and a truer identity. But Trilling's extension of Shakespeare's metaphor implies that by shedding our superficial, or temporary, or occupational identities we can find our ultimate or original self. Such selves do not exist, and if they were to exist then they might be undesirable and might not even be recognizably human. We cannot know what our ultimate self will be unless we have a moment of metaconsciousness just before we die; and we cannot know what our original personal self was or what the original self of the species was because these things, like the origins of consciousness and mind, are beyond knowledge. Trilling is using the words, "ultimate" and "original", to express an idealized concept of a self that can never be fully realized.

Antonio Damasio explores the neurobiology of the self in *The Feeling of What Happens*. In the chapter, 'Extended Consciousness', he offers an account that is part-observation and part-conjecture: (Damasio 1999: 230) "The enchainment of precedences is most curious: the nonconscious neural signaling of an individual organism begets the *proto-self* which permits *core self* and *core consciousness*, which allows for an *autobiographical self*, which permits *extended consciousness*. At the end of the chain, *extended consciousness* permits *conscience*". In these words Damasio summarizes the evolution of brain, mind and self.

# 11

# A Fellowship of Poets

TOWARDS THE END OF BOOK XI of *The Prelude*, having expressed his sadness and anger at France's betrayal of the ideals of the Revolution, Wordsworth abruptly changes his narrative focus and writes: (Wordsworth 1956: 574)

> But indignation works where hope is not,
> And thou, O Friend! will be refreshed. There is
> One great society alone on earth:
> The noble Living and the noble Dead.

Even allowing for the ambiguity of the fourth line above – Are only some people noble, or is there nobility in all of us? – the lines affirm a community and continuity in life and death.

D. H. Lawrence confesses to a similar belief in community and continuity in a self-conscious passage in his Introduction to *Fantasia of the Unconscious,* first published in 1923: (Lawrence 1933: 18)

> How many dead souls, like swallows, twitter and breed thoughts and instincts under the thatch of my hair and the eaves of my forehead I don't know. I am almost ashamed to say, that I believe the souls of the dead in some way re-enter and pervade the souls of the living.

One can understand that Lawrence, careful of his reputation as a visceral critic of life and literature, should feel embarrassed at admitting his belief in metempsychosis; the fact that he feels impelled to make the admission shows the strength of his belief in the transmigration of the souls of the dead into the living.

Eliot writes of communion with the dead and the unborn in his discussion of the family in 'The Class and the Elite' in *Notes Towards the*

*Definition of Culture*. He refers to the immediate family, and he adds: (Eliot 948: 44) "But when I speak of the family, I have in mind a bond which embraces a longer period of time than this: a piety towards the dead, however obscure, and a solicitude for the unborn, however remote". He states the need for a spirit of reverence for past and future life, and he explains: "Such an interest in the past is different from the vanities and pretensions of genealogy; such a responsibility for the future is different from that of the builder of social programmes". In effect, Eliot is asking us to revere the wider human family, humanity itself; and his phrase, "the vanities and pretensions of genealogy", shows that his concern is unconditional, for human life and not for rank.

Human communion and continuity are recurring themes in the poetry and prose of Edwin Muir. In the lecture, 'Poetry and the Poet', in the posthumously published *The Estate of Poetry* Muir writes: (Muir 1962: 91)

> The past is a living past, and past and present coexist: that also the imagination tells us. It opens the past to us as part of our own life, a vast extension of our present. It cannot admit that anything that ever happened among the dead is dead for us, or that all that men and women have done and suffered was merely meant to bring us where we are.

The past comes alive and becomes part of the life of the living when it is revivified by the imagination, which is not constrained by the usual division of time into past and present. Muir's other claim, or rather, his denial, in the quotation above – that all that people in the past have done is to create a chain of life that extends into the present – is prompted by his Christianity and his belief in the immortality of the soul. For some non-Christian readers it is enough to be aware of the continuity of the earthly succession of generations of people.

In British society there is still a reluctance to speak openly about the dead. We allow a funeral oration for the individual, an annual Commemoration Day for those who died in war, and then there is silence. But the quotations above show poets speaking of the dead and the unborn as if they were members of the living community. Spender expresses the same kind of communion and continuity when he discusses the artist and the city in 'Inside the Cage' in *The Making of a Poem*: (Spender 1955b: 15)

A city should belong at the same time to the inhabitants, who use it, the dead who have invented forms which give pleasure to the eye, and the unborn in whom the delights enjoyed by the dead will live. In towns where the dead and the unborn are omitted, there are simply buildings and thoroughfares used by contemporaries.

That is not only a vision of the city but of the continuity and unity of successive generations of its inhabitants. Day Lewis in 'The Nature of the Image' in *The Poetic Image* extends the sense of community to every living thing as well as to the dead, and he states that the need for communion is an emotional need: (Day Lewis 1947: 32-3) "man, even at his most individual, still seeks emotional reassurance from the sense of community, not community with his fellow beings alone, but with whatever is living in the universe, and with the dead". The term, "emotional reassurance", suggests a kind of dependence, whereas what Day Lewis describes is an interdependence of the living and the dead; his reference to the universe implies a concept of community that is cosmic in scale. Kathleen Raine, too, feels an affinity with dead poets; in the chapter, 'The Lion's Mouth' in *Autobiographies* she writes of the community of poets: (Raine 1973: 329) "Not living poets only, or principally, but the dead also are, in that sense, our own people in a way that for the critic is not so". Anne Sexton has a similar concept. In her letter of June, 1974 to Erica Jong, Sexton writes: (Sexton 1977: 414)

I keep feeling that that there isn't one poem being written by any one of us – or a book or anything like that. The whole life of us writers, the whole product I guess I mean, is the one long poem – a community effort if you will. It's all the same poem. It doesn't belong to any one writer – it's God's poem perhaps.

These poets' experiences of communion with the anonymous dead seem wider and more conceptualized than the experience all of us feel about people we have known who are now dead. People whose lives are important to us, people alive and dead, are part of our identity in the most intimate way: they are represented in our minds as specifically encoded sets of neural networks. When a loved person dies, we feel the death as a lesion, a little death, in the designated set of networks. The networks that represent living people also represent them after their death; the fact of their death is encoded in the living network so that the dead continue to be represented, continue to live, in the mind of the survivor. Sometimes this inner representation is so vital that it is projected and seems to correspond momentarily with outer reality, as when a woman sees her dead husband alive and walking in the street. But this experience is clearly different from the sense of communion with the dead expressed by Wordsworth, Lawrence, Eliot, Muir, Spender, Day Lewis, Raine and Sexton.

A sense of communion with the dead extends into the twenty-first century. Muriel Spark in an interview with Robert Hosmer published in *The London Magazine* in the August/September issue in 2005, was asked: "How do you perceive your relationship to great writers of the past?" She replied: "Well, I think if I was writing for anybody, I would be quite happy to write for the great past, for the great dead". And in her Foreword to *All the Poems* Spark identifies herself as a poet: (Spark 2004: xii) "Although most of my life has been devoted to fiction, I have always thought of myself as a poet. [...] my outlook on life and my perceptions of events are those of a poet". Spark is one of the most recent in a long line of poets who have written about a sense of continuity and community with the dead.

Margaret Atwood expresses the same kind of affinity. In the title lecture in her Empson Lectures, *Negotiating with the Dead*, she states that dead people persist in the minds of the living, and then she adds: (Atwood 2002: 159) "All writers learn from the dead. As long as you continue to write, you continue to explore the work of writers who have preceded you; you also feel judged and held to account by them". There is a particular continuity from dead to living writers, and the living writer is accountable to the dead. In 'Nine Beginnings' in *Curious Pursuits* Atwood states (Atwood 2005: 146) that the writer is one of "the community of writers, the community of storytellers that stretches back through time to the beginning of human society".

Poets take account of the anonymous dead in something like the way in which a nation takes account of its Unknown Soldier, who represents the mass of dead soldiers. Poets know that we must not only take account of the dead but also listen to them; and when the dead speak to us we must respond. Indeed, Auden writes of communion with the dead as a sacrament without which we cannot be fully human. In 'Words and the Word' in *Secondary Worlds* he writes: (Auden 1968: 141)

> Further, let us remember that, though the great artists of the past could
> not change the course of history, it is only through their work that we
> are able to break bread with the dead, and without communion with the
> dead a fully human life is impossible.

Listening and responding to the dead are such natural acts that a capacity for an inner dialogue with the dead must be part of the mind's design; and in that sense, hearing voices inside our head is not an aberration. We should feel that we are free to converse silently with the dead and even, in private places, to speak to them aloud. The cultural constraints against such dialogues have the effect of distorting the natural response into a shameful act; the constraints also have the effect of breaking one's sense of the natural continuity of generations.

Community and continuity of a different kind have been discovered by molecular biologists and other scientists working in the field of genetics. In *The Language of the Genes*, Steve Jones stresses the genetic similarity of humans of all races; the genetic differences between European and African peoples are little more than the differences between Europeans in neighbouring countries. Genetic diversity, Jones states, occurs at the level of the individual, whose genetic material, DNA, has around three thousand million markers, or letters, in unique combinations. Jones writes: (Jones, S. 1993: 24) "There is so much variety that everyone alive today is different, not only from everyone else, but from everyone who has ever lived or will live". A loose comparison can be made between the human genetic system and the brain: each brain has the same structure and the same faculties but has a unique combination of neural networks. Genetic continuity in humans, Jones states, began with the beginning of life on earth around three thousand million years ago; primates and anthropoids evolved around fifty to sixty million years ago; Homo sapiens, our most immediate ancestor, evolved around half a million years ago. These time-scales could change as new discoveries are made, but the genetic continuity from the beginning of life to the present is unbroken. As long as our species survives, each person in each succeeding generation will have a genetic configuration that is at once unique and also a recombination of pre-existing genes. Each person's genes and neurons decay, but the genetic and neural condition of the species is continually renewed through unique combinations, or re-combinations, of genetic material and neural networks. Our earthly genetic succession and our diversity-in-unity, stretching from the beginning of life into the indeterminable future, are facts. Could the experience of poetic communion and continuity also be factual?

Shelley overstates the case for poetic communion to such an extent that the modern reader might dismiss as hyperbole the reference in *A Defence of Poetry*: (Shelley 1956: 119-20) "that great poem, which all poets, like the co-operating thoughts of one great mind, have built up since the beginning of the world". A remarkably similar idea is expressed by Eliot, whose poetic views and values often differ from Shelley's. In 'Tradition and the Individual Talent' Eliot writes: (Eliot 1950: 4)

> No poet, no artist of any art, has his complete meaning alone. His significance, his appreciation is the appreciation of his relation to the dead poets and artists. You cannot value him alone; you must set him, for contrast and comparison, among the dead.

Virginia Woolf discusses a similar concept in 'A Letter to a Young Poet' in *The Death of the Moth*. Woolf warns the young poet of the danger of adopting a false persona and of becoming (Woolf 1942: 134-5) "a self-conscious, biting, and scratching little animal whose work is not of the slightest value or importance to anybody." And then she adds: "Think of yourself rather as something much humbler and less spectacular, but to my mind far more interesting – a poet in whom live all the poets of the past, from whom all poets in time to come will spring". The concepts are attractive: all poems are part of a great universal poem, a living force that is continuously revitalized and extended by new poems. Equally attractive is the idea of a succession of poets whose unity of purpose is like one great talent or one great poetic self, continuously evolving but never losing sight of the original talent or self.

Robert Nye discusses just such a succession in his Introduction to *A Selection of the Poems of Laura Riding*. He recalls his meetings with Riding in 1991: (Nye 1996: 7)

> I shall never forget how at one point, after we had been talking of the ancient idea of the Great Chain of Being, she called me back urgently

into her room to tell me that the Great Chain of Being consisted of po-
ets. 'Poets inspire poets,' she said. 'From here in this room to Homer
the Great Chain of Being stretches back.'

Nye's and Riding's words remind one of the doctrine of Apostolic Suc-
cession, the belief that there is a continuity of spiritual authority that
begins with Christ and his Apostles and has been transmitted continu-
ously by popes and bishops ever since. Genetically, continuity is a fact
of the human condition; poetically, the continuity is, like Apostolic Suc-
cession, a doctrine, a faith in a truth that is essentially imaginative or
mystical but could also have a basis in fact. Establishing that basis,
however, might prove impossible. No one reader could possibly trace
the chain from its beginning to the present, because no one could read
all the poetry that has survived from the time of the Homer poets.

Riding, Nye and the other poets quoted above are referring to a spiri-
tual or metaphysical community. Richards is hostile to the concept. In
the final paragraph of the chapter, 'Four Kinds of Meaning' in *Practical
Criticism*, he repeats his complaint that too much of what passes for
criticism of poetry is merely a projection of the critic's personal feel-
ings. Richards states: (Richards 1960: 188) "eminent examples" of this
kind of false reading are: "Dr Bradley's remark that Poetry is a spirit,
and Dr Mackail's that it is a continuous substance or energy whose
progress is immortal". Andrew Cecil Bradley (1851-1935) was Profes-
sor of Poetry at Oxford University from 1901 to 1906, when he was
succeeded by John William Mackail (1859-1945). Some of Bradley's
views in his *Oxford Lectures on Poetry* – on meaning in poetry, the
experience of a poem, the reader's presuppositions, and on poetry as
discovery – are so similar to Richard's views in *The Principles of Liter-
ary Criticism* and *Practical Criticism* that one wonders why Richards
complains about Bradley. Perhaps it is partly a matter of anthropology:
a younger generation tries to establish itself by attacking the preceding
generation. The words Richards objects to appear at the end of 'Po-
etry for Poetry's Sake' in *Oxford Lectures on Poetry*, where Bradley
writes of poetry: (Bradley 1909: 27) "It is a spirit. It comes we know not
whence. It will not speak at our bidding, nor answer in our language. It
is not our servant; it is our master". If Bradley is wrong, then it follows
that others who have made similar claims – Wordsworth, Shelley, Law-
rence, Eliot, Muir, Day Lewis, Spender, Raine, Riding, Sexton and Nye

– are also wrong. Clearly, the weight of opinion is against Richards. But what if it is merely received opinion?

Few poets today would claim that poetry has divine or supernatural origins, but most would accept that the words, "spirit" and "spiritual", can be applied to those functions of mind that include the religious and creative impulses and their interaction with the creative imagination. And it is there, in the working of the poet's mind, that community and continuity are found, because most poets in most periods exercise the same properties of mind as they engage in the same task, which is the realization of the creative and religious impulses through the creative imagination and language. Unless humanity destroys itself or is destroyed in some minor cosmic accident, poets will continue to respond to the same spiritual impulses; they will write in the same spirit, and poetry as an expression of that spirit will continue to renew itself into the future. We can argue, then, that poetry, as the natural and inevitable outcome of mind and language, the natural and inevitable expression of the human spirit, has a kind of immortality.

Auden in 'Making, Knowing and Judging' in *The Dyer's Hand* perfectly captures the triumph of poetry over mortality when he writes: (Auden 1963: 42) "a vision of a kind of literary All Souls Night in which the dead, the living and the unborn writers of every age and in every tongue were seen as engaged upon a common, noble and civilizing task". Denise Levertov, like Auden, a British-born poet who settled in the United States, writes with a similar religious intensity in 'Some Duncan Letters – A Memoir and a Critical Tribute' in *New & Selected Essays*, where she imagines a sacred fellowship of poets: (Levertov 1992: 206)

> If Poetry, the Art of Poetry, is a Mystery, and poets the servers of that Mystery, they are bound together in a fellowship under its laws, obedient to its power.

Heaney refers to the concept in familial terms when he says in *Stepping Stones*: (Heaney 2008: 206) "But you're espoused to poetry too, after all, and other poets, dead and alive, attain the status of in-laws".

The art of poetry is, indeed, a mystery, because language and mind are mysterious and because poetry is the celebration of and participation in mystery. When poets believe that in the making of a poem they have participated in a mystery, then they know that they have been admitted to a truth. And when, in reading dead poets' work, they see that the dead, too, have participated in mysteries and have been admitted to their truths, then the living might feel part of a great fellowship of poets.

# 12

# Language

## The Language of Poetry

THE ORIGINS OF LANGUAGE ARE the origins of poetry, but we cannot know when language originated. We may accept that we are descended from a matriarchal prototype, the near-mythological African Eve, and that we began to take our human form and those determining features of our humanity – consciousness and speech –around the time of the great exodus from Africa. Even if the exodus occurred over centuries rather than decades, we do not know when the exodus took place.

The geneticist, Luigi Luca Cavalli-Sforza, in *Genes, People and Languages* writes: (Cavalli-Sforza 2000: 93) "the late palaeolithic expansion out of Africa was greatly served by the development of language". The Palaeolithic age spans millennia. Cavalli-Sforza adds: "Our most distant human ancestors might have had some primitive linguistic ability, but the complexity characteristic of all contemporary languages probably wasn't attained until around 100,000 years ago". Such time-estimates change as palaeontological dating techniques become more precise and as palaeontologists make chance discoveries of human and pre-human remains. The British geneticist, Steve Jones, gives a different estimate. In *The Language of the Genes* he writes: (Jones, S. 1994: 124) "Around a hundred and thirty thousand years ago, the first humans of distinctly modern appearance (light build, thin skull, large brain and small jaw) appear in Africa". The existence of a large brain is probable but not certain; the brain size is an estimate based on the capacity of the skull.

In *Grooming, Gossip and the Evolution of Language* the psychologist, Robin Dunbar, gives a different kind of estimate. He refers to the claim by his fellow-psychologist, Julian Jaynes, that the authors of the Homeric poems written between c9000 to c8000 BC were not fully conscious. Dunbar adds: (Dunbar 1996: 139) "My own feeling is that

Jaynes is on the right lines". A more appropriate assessment than "not fully conscious" is that the writers were conscious but not fully conscious of their identifiable, authorial selves and to that extent not self-conscious. That kind of explicit awareness does not appear in English literature until the age of Chaucer, whose *Canterbury Tales*, written around 1387, is a great revolutionary work; it marks the end of the dominance of some forms of oral poetry and the new dominance of the written word. The act of writing is a self-conscious process.

There can be no language without consciousness but it is not possible to date the emergence of consciousness. Even now we do not know the full extent of our conscious and nonconscious minds. Noam Chomsky is less conjectural than the geneticists and psychologists quoted above. In *Reflections on Language* he writes: (Chomsky 1976: 4) "It [language] is a product of human intelligence, created anew in each individual by operations that lie far beyond the reach of will or consciousness". Later in the same work he states that the origin of language is unknowable and mysterious: "What I have called 'the creative aspect of language use' remains as much a mystery to us as it was to the Cartesians who discussed it, in part, in the context of the problem of 'other minds'". When Chomsky returns to the question of the origins of language in the Third Edition of *Language and Mind* he is even more emphatic. In the chapter, 'Form and meaning in natural languages' he asserts: (Chomsky 2006: 88-9) "We do not understand, and, for all we know, we may never come to understand what makes it possible for a normal human intelligence to use language as an instrument for the free expression of thought or feeling". Like Chomsky, the British linguist, David Crystal, thinks that questions about the origins of language can never be answered. In *How Language Works* Crystal writes: (Crystal 2005: 350)

> Each generation asks the same questions, and reaches the same impasse
> – the absence of any evidence relating to the matter, given the vast,
> distant time-scale involved. We have no direct knowledge of the origins
> and early development of language, nor is it easy to imagine how such
> knowledge might ever be attained.

We are ignorant of the origins of language but as poets and readers of poetry we can note Chomsky's observation and rejoice: language is a mysterious instrument for the free expression of thought and feeling.

# Poetic Diction

The debate about the most appropriate language for poetry has been running for more than two thousand years. Aristotle in his *Poetics*, which was written around 330 BC, makes observations that are still relevant today. Towards the end of Chapter XXVI in Part II he suggests a mix of the plain, the formal and the metaphorical in order to create a colloquial mode: (Aristotle 1955: 45) "but to iambic verse, which is, as much as may be, an imitation of common speech, those words which are used in common speech are best adapted, and such are the common, the metaphorical, and the ornamental". Aristotle relates the language of poetry to common speech, but the relationship is "an imitation" in which words are "adapted" from common speech. Concepts of this relationship are central to any discussion of the subject.

Our current concepts of the most appropriate language for poetry stem from Wordsworth's Preface to the second edition of *Lyrical Ballads*, first published in 1800. In the opening paragraph of the Preface he refers to the first edition of *Lyrical Ballads* in these terms: (Wordsworth 956: 734)

> It was published, as an experiment, which, I hoped might be of some use to ascertain, how far, by fitting to metrical arrangement a selection of the real language of men in a state of vivid sensation, that sort of pleasure and that quantity of pleasure may be imparted, which a Poet may rationally endeavour to impart.

These aims, to use the real language of men in order to give pleasure, are stated repeatedly, almost repetitiously, throughout the Preface. Statements on language (Wordsworth 1956: 734, 735, 736, 739) are sometimes linked to statements on pleasure (Wordsworth 1956: 734, 736, 737, 738, 739, 741). In repeating these aims, Wordsworth is saying that plain language can be used in poetry and can give as much pleasure as poems written in poetic diction. Wordsworth uses the phrase, "poetic diction", (Wordsworth 1956: 736) and states that in the *Lyrical Ballads* "as much pains has [sic] been taken to avoid it as ordinarily taken to produce it". His aim in this, he says, is "to bring my language near to the language of men"; and his underlying purpose is to give pleasure "of a kind very different from that which is supposed by many persons to be the proper object of poetry". The experiment was a daring attempt to transform the language of poetry from the conventional artifice of late eighteenth-century poetic diction to something plainer and more vital.

In his Introduction to the *Use of Poetry and the Use of Criticism*, Eliot states (Eliot 1933: 26) that Wordsworth was not simply occupied with the reform of language but with the revolution of language. The revolution was more than linguistic: in changing the language of poetry Wordsworth also changed the kinds of experience than can be the subject matter and themes of poetry and the modes of thought in which the experience can be mediated. He changed the concept of what a poem is and what it does.

In discussing the language of *Lyrical Ballads*, Wordsworth shows some of the connections between a variety of language and the kinds of thought and emotion, the kinds of truth, that can be expressed in the language. In the third paragraph of the Preface, in the words, (Wordsworth 1956: 734) "in what manner language and the human mind act and re-act upon each other", he not only makes it clear that poetry is a product of language and the human, not the divine, mind; in his understanding of the interplay of language and mind he also shows a new understanding of the poetic imagination. Wordsworth's combination of topics, their forceful and systematic presentation, and their continuing relevance today make the Preface, despite its convoluted prose style, one of the great essays in poetics. At the same time, the Preface is effective as a credo and manifesto in which Wordsworth repeatedly states his aim: (Wordsworth 1956: 734) "The principal object, then, proposed in these poems was to choose incidents and situations from common life, and to relate or describe them, throughout, as far as was possible, in a selection of language really used by men".

But here and elsewhere in the Preface his bold assertions are counterbalanced by reservations and by a mode of argument that is either self-deluding or disingenuous: (Wordsworth 1956: 734)

> and, at the same time, to throw over them a certain colouring of imagination, whereby ordinary things should be presented to the mind in an unusual aspect; and further, and above all, to make these incidents and situations interesting by tracing in them, truly though not ostentatiously,

the primary laws of our nature: chiefly, as far as regards the manner in which we associate ideas in a state of excitement.

The "language really used by men" was adopted only "as far as was possible"; and just as Wordsworth transforms the real language of men, so he transforms the "incidents and situations of common life" by throwing over them "a certain colouring of imagination"; his imagination transmutes the ordinary to the archetypal. The association of ideas and the state of excitement to which Wordsworth refers are features of his poetic imagination. And when he argues that the essential passions of the heart attain their maturity only in "humble and rustic life" because "in that condition the passions of men are incorporated with the beautiful and permanent forms of nature", then one knows that he is speaking as a poet, and not for the hill farmers and tenant farmers in Cumberland and Westmorland at the end of the eighteenth century. Wordsworth is mistaken when he writes: (Wordsworth 1956: 735)

> The language, too, of these men has been adopted (purified indeed from what appears to be its real defects, from all lasting and rational causes of dislike or disgust) because such men hourly communicate with the best objects from which the best part of language is originally derived.

Any claim that a particular speech community has special access to "the best part of language" is a false claim to linguistic superiority; no dialect of a language is linguistically superior to another. And if Wordsworth's parenthesis, "(purified indeed from what appears to be its real defects, from all lasting and rational causes of dislike or disgust)", means that he expurgated the people's language, then it confirms that the language of the poems is his, not theirs.

In December 1799, shortly after he went to live in Grasmere, Wordsworth wrote to Coleridge and said of the manners of his neighbours: (Wordsworth 1984: 34) "They seem little adulterated; indeed as far as we have seen not at all". These manners must have included speech. As members of an isolated rural community, Wordsworth's neighbours must have spoken the regional dialect because it was the only mode of speech available to them, but few dialect words appear in *Lyrical Ballads*. Cumbrian dialect – 'He's oop rek behint intek wi tethera yows', that is, 'He's up the fell track behind the enclosure with three ewes'

– was still being spoken in the middle of the twentieth century. The people in Wordsworth's poems do not use regional dialect and folk grammar; when they speak, they use their individual forms of Words-worthian. Even so, in dialogue poems in *Lyrical Ballads* – 'The Broth-ers', (Wordsworth 1956: 75-80) 'We Are Seven', (Wordsworth 1956: 66) the Matthew conversations, and the intensifying anxiety of Betty Fox and Susan Gale in 'The Idiot Boy' (Wordsworth 1956: 100-104) – the characters are subtly differentiated by their speech. Johnny, the idiot boy, is given the two lines:

> The Cocks did crow to-whoo, to-whoo,
> And the Sun did shine so cold.

And in the three great monologues or portrait monologues – 'The Last of the Flock', 'The Female Vagrant' and 'The Mad Mother' – in these poems the characters' speech reveals extreme, wholly convincing states of mind.

Wordsworth must have known, if only intuitively, that he was not writing in the language of the common people. He must have known that he was writing his own variety of English, a variety that he alone created, a language that at its best has a seemingly natural dignity and a firmly controlled eloquence that can sometimes be mistaken for plain speaking. Wordsworth's plainness of speech in *Lyrical Ballads* is his own poetic voice rather than the voices or the collective voice of the ordinary people. Even so, *Lyrical Ballads* was a great liberating, revivi-fying force in English poetry: Wordsworth restored the truth of poetry by relating it to the language of a living speech community and by freeing it from the falsehoods of poetic diction. As an illustration of poetic diction, Wordsworth quotes in full the sonnet, 'On the Death of Mr. Richard West' by Thomas Gray, but without giving the title of the sonnet or the name of the poet: (Wordsworth 1956: 736)

> In vain to me the smiling mornings shine,
> And redd'ning Phoebus lifts his golden fire:
> The birds in vain their amorous descant join;
> Or cheerful fields resume their green attire:
> These ears, alas! for other notes repine;
> A different object do these eyes require:

My lonely anguish melts no heart but mine;

And in my breast the imperfect joys expire.

Yet morning smiles the busy race to cheer,

And new-born pleasure brings to happier men:

The fields to all their wonted tribute bear:

To warm their little loves the birds complain:

I fruitless mourn to him that cannot hear,

And weep the more, because I weep in vain.

Artifice becomes artificiality, and sentiment sentimentality. Language is falsified not only by the diction but by repeated syntactical distortions in order to maintain the rhyme; the false language falsifies the thought and emotion in the poem. A poet's use of language becomes poetic diction when its vocabulary and syntax are remote from or consistently different from, the use of language by most people in a language community.

Wordsworth could not have been alone in seeing the artificiality, but he was almost alone in exposing it; and by exposing it, he exposed himself to the anger of readers and critics who had grown to enjoy the comfort, the consolation, the reassuring sentimentality of Gray and some of his contemporaries. One can say these things and yet admit that comfort, consolation, and reassurance are legitimate functions of poetry. Some ten years later Wordsworth relents, and equivocates. In the third section of *Upon Epitaphs,* first published in 1810, (Wordsworth 1925: 132) he commends Gray's poem, 'Epitaph on Mrs. Clark' ("Lo! Where the silent marble weeps"), as a poem that is "pure from vicious diction", but 'Epitaph on Mrs. Clark' is as sentimental, syntactically distorted and linguistically decadent as 'On the Death of Mr. Richard West'.

## Poetry and Contemporary Speech

In the two centuries since the Preface appeared, and especially since the second decade of the twentieth century, the language of English poetry has been closer to Wordsworth's ideal than to Gray's. And in the second half of the twentieth century there emerged the received opinion that a poem is more vital and true to life the closer it is to the language of ordinary speech. As the previous chapter has shown, if the language of poetry were the same as ordinary speech, then ordinary speech would be poetry; and we know that in ordinary speech almost every speaker is sometimes vague, self-contradictory, hesitant, elliptic, repetitive.

Poetry, whether it is read silently or aloud, is clearly different from ordinary speech; it is a fallacy to assume that only one mode of speech or one dialect is ordinary. Anyone who listens to the speech of people from different English-speaking countries, or to the speech of people from different parts of the British Isles, can hear that ordinary speech varies from country to country and region to region. And within a single region of Britain, speech varies from one language community to another. Received pronunciation, the standardized prestige dialect in Britain, cannot be considered ordinary because it is the dialect of a small minority but, as the earlier chapter poetic voice has shown, received pronunciation is widely understood. If no single dialect can be identified as ordinary, how did the view originate that poetry should be written in the language of ordinary speech?

Fluent, premeditated speech, even if the premeditation is only an instant before the moment of utterance, can have a semantic content and rhythmic and syntactic structures that are similar to some kinds of poetry. But the question of an appropriate language for poetry can never be answered finally, because the concept of appropriateness, and the concepts of what poetry is and what it does, vary over time, as do all living languages and dialects. Wordsworth's answers in the Preface and the poems are right for most of his own work, but when his ear and imagination fail him, his language is occasionally flat and false; and this suggests that poets cannot answer the question once and for all but must find different answers to the question of appropriateness for different poems and at different stages in their career. The dilemma is this: if poets' language is too remote from the fluent and premeditated speech of their own and other speech communities, then their poems might seem remote from people's lives; but if the language becomes too colloquial it could become unoriginal and inadequate to express some forms of experience.

Auden is aware of this dilemma when he states in 'Writing' in *The Dyer's Hand*: (Auden 1963: 24)

> The English-speaking peoples have always felt that the difference between poetic speech and the conversational speech of everyday should

be kept small, and, whenever English poets have felt that the gap be-
tween poetic and ordinary speech was growing too wide, there has been
a stylistic revolution to bring them closer again.

Auden writes as if the two styles occur in alternating cycles when, in
fact, they co-exist in every age. Both varieties of English, the formal
and the informal – or more precisely, innumerable varieties on a gra-
dience from formal to informal – have been used in most periods of
English poetry: the deliberate, elegant symmetries of the *Gawain* poet
and the urbane modernism of Chaucer; the metaconscious intricacies of
Donne's sonnets and the achieved simplicity of the King James *Bible*;
the measured resonance of Tennyson and the differently measured, dif-
ferently resonant poetry of Hopkins; the expansiveness of Whitman and
the compression and ellipsis of Dickinson. Varieties even co-exist in
the work of a single poet: Auden's own use of language ranges from
the grimly ironic colloquial ballads, 'Miss Gee' and 'Victor', to the
linguistic and structural formality of *Horae Canonicae*. Auden seems
to make the false assumption that there is a single form of ordinary
speech, whereas Wordsworth, although he misrepresents the relation-
ship between ordinary speech and the language of poetry, nevertheless
refers to an actual speech community.

In 'Making, Knowing and Judging' in *The Dyer's Hand* Auden
presents this strikingly different observation on the language of poetry:
(Auden 1963: 58)

> A poem is a rite; hence its formal and ritualistic character.
>
> Its use of language is deliberately and ostentatiously different from
> talk. Even when it employs the diction and rhythms of conversation, it
> employs them as a deliberate informality, presupposing the norm with
> which they are intended to contrast.

We can readily agree that a poem is a rite and that in any literary period
there are norms of language, but we cannot agree with Auden's implicit
claim that there is a norm for the language of poetry, or with his explicit
claim that poetry must be "ostentatiously different from talk". In mak-
ing such a claim Auden contradicts himself, and makes mischief at the
expense of the literal-minded academic critic.

In the course of his career as a critic and poet, Eliot changed his view of the poet's relationship with language. Over a period of several decades, as a writer's knowledge and imagination develop, changes of critical viewpoints and values, like changes of poetic voice and vision, are almost inevitable. Eliot writes in the early essay, 'The Metaphysical Poets', first published in 1921: (Eliot 1955: 118-9) "The poet must become more and more comprehensive, more allusive, more indirect, in order to force, to dislocate if necessary, language into his meaning". Here he writes as if a poem's meaning can be known before the poem is written, but even at the time his experience as a poet must have told him that a poem evolves in unpredictable ways.

By 1950, in 'A Talk on Dante', Eliot's forcefulness has become attentiveness: (Eliot 1955: 99-100) "The whole study and practice of Dante seems to me to teach that the poet should be the servant of his language, rather than the master of it". Perhaps this later view is too submissive. The poet is always at the service of language, but it can be the service of the suitor, in which case the relationship is neither mastery nor servitude but courtship. Courtship seems the right relationship, because a true poem is, among other things, a love poem to the language in which it is written. The poet must, as Auden insists in 'Writing', "woo Dame Philology."

A more convincing comment on the language of poetry is Wallace Stevens' in 'The Noble Rider and the Sound of Words': (Stevens 1971: 978)

> The deepening need for words to express our thoughts and feelings, which, we are sure, are all the truth that we shall ever experience, having no illusions, makes us listen to words when we hear them, for a finality, a perfection, an unalterable vibration, which it is only within the power of the acutest poet to give.

The poet hears the sounds of words not in a particular speech community but in his auditory imagination. The auditory is part of the creative imagination, and it is only through imagination that the poet can be admitted to the mysteries of language and truths of human experience.

Implicit in Stevens' statement is the idea that the poet creates his language rather than finds it. This concept is not an escape from the realities of language but a quest for a vision of reality that can be expressed through language. Perhaps the quest, and the experience of "a finality, a perfection", are less rare than Stevens allows; it is in the power not only of "the acutest poet" but good poets at their most acute. There are moments of perfection, of revelation, in the work of minor poets.

Use of language is one of the subjects of every poem, no matter what the ostensible subject of the poem might be. The poet's relationship with language is never one of mastery; no poet can have a complete understanding of language and the interplay of language and mind, and no poet can master the language to the extent that he or she can command all its resources or all its artistic possibilities. And because poets can never be greater than the language in which they write, they must respect that language. Some poets feel that in the making of a poem their relationship is not that of a user but a discoverer of language. And some poets feel that in creating the poem they also create, or re-create, the words in which it is written; the delusion is understandable, because every original poem is a unique combination of words.

Coleridge disagrees with Wordsworth on the question of the appropriate language for poetry. In Chapter XVIII of *Biographia Literaria* he writes: (Coleridge 1956: 217-8) "But if it be asked by what principles the poet is to regulate his own style, if he do not adhere closely to the sort and order of words which he hears in the market, wake, high-road and plough-field?" Unlike Wordsworth, Coleridge thinks that the language of the market, the wake, which was an annual festival or fair in a rural parish, the street or the farm – that is, the real language of the common people, men and women – is not appropriate for poetry. In the same paragraph he continues: (Coleridge 1956: 218) "I reply: by the principles, the ignorance or neglect of which would convict him of being no poet, but a silly, presumptuous usurper of the name! By the principles of grammar, logic, psychology". Psychology for Coleridge included the soul as well as the mind. In the temperate prose of *Biographia Literaria* the phrase, "a silly, presumptuous usurper of the name!" is a fierce denunciation. Why is Coleridge so emphatic? Not because of an unquestioning obedience to authority, but because he knows that without a common agreement on the meanings, sounds, forms and ordering of words, one writer would have difficulty in understanding another writer of the same language. A standardized grammar allows the poet to represent reality with some precision and consistency.

Some poets are troubled by the principles of grammar. Philip Sidney in *An Apology for Poetry* writes of (Sidney 1947: 59) "those cumbersome differences of Cases, Genders, Moods, and Tenses, which I think was a piece of the Tower of Babylon's curse". More recently Charles Olson in 'Projective Verse', first published in 'Poetry New York' 3 in 1950 and reprinted in *Modern Poets on Modern Poetry*, states that the elements of a poem must be allowed "their proper confusion". And he adds: (Olson 1966: 277) "Which brings us up, immediately, bang, against tenses, in fact against syntax, in fact against grammar generally, that is, as we have inherited it". Shelley, like Coleridge, accepts the need for grammar. In *A Defence of Poetry* he writes: (Shelley 1956: 106) "The grammatical forms which express the moods of tense, and the difference of persons, and the distinction of place, are convertible with respect to the highest poetry without injuring it as poetry". In all languages, written and spoken, there are conventions about how the language is used; that is, all languages have a grammar. Most languages have two or more grammars, or rather a variety of grammars from the formally standardized to the informal and folk. All languages change over time – Old English or Anglo-Saxon is now incomprehensible unless it is studied as a foreign language – and these changes are reflected in new conventions about how the language is used. Poets can, independently, establish new conventions, as Chaucer and Wordsworth do; or they can defy contemporary conventions, as Eliot, Pound, Williams and Cummings do.

The grammar of spoken English is less firmly codified than the grammar of written English, and because poetry partly reflects speech, so the grammar of poetry is less firmly codified than the grammar of prose. Modern poetry, for example, tolerates verbless sentences and other forms of elliptical syntax more readily than prose:

> Asleep, or drunk, or dead,
> that figure in the doorway?

And

Blood. A mink among the chickens.

Blood. And a blizzard of feathers.

Grammar can be regarded not as a set of rigid rules but as taxonomy, a principle of organization that brings order to what would otherwise be confusion. If poets do not have a working knowledge of the main grammatical properties of their language, how can they edit or proof-read their work, or write about other poets' work? More fundamentally: how can a writer who is ignorant of grammar be fully literate?

Muir and Spender make interesting observations on the idiomatic use of language. In 'The Public and the Poet' in *The Estate of Poetry*, Muir notes that a younger generation of poets uses language more idiomatically than older generations: (Muir 1962: 109)

> So far as I can judge from their work, young poets now find themselves free to write in a natural tongue. What their mentors do not realize is that to write naturally, especially in verse, is one of the most difficult things in the world; naturalness does not come easily to the awkward human race, and is an achievement of art.

In effect, the "natural tongue" is not entirely natural but is a dialect created by the poet. Seamus Heaney recognizes this when he says in *Stepping Stones*: (Heaney 2008: 192) "sounding natural is a stylistic achievement."

Spender in 'Tradition-Bound Literature and Traditionless Painting' in *The Struggle of the Modern* briefly argues a case that is similar to Wordsworth's in the Preface to *Lyrical Ballads*: (Spender 1963: 194)

> It seems to me that the idiomatic is a language in which it should, ideally, be possible to conduct a dialogue with the people from whom the idiom is borrowed. It should be recognizable by those from whom it is derived as being about them, and not seem to be their involuntary contribution to an elite speech which they cannot understand.

Clearly, Spender is not referring to people in general but to people of a particular language community with whom it should be possible to conduct a dialogue. But there is a sense in which poets create their own speech community; that is, they appeal to readers irrespective of the readers' social or geographical language communities.

Poets and linguists disagree about the properties of a language: linguists are observers and analysts; poets sometimes see themselves as the guardians of language. The notion that a poet battles against degradation in a language is a fairly widespread delusion among poets. In the article, 'A Georgian History of Victorian Literature' written in 1917, A. E. Housman states (Housman 1961: 118) that the language continues "to deteriorate in fibre". The poet and critic, Donald Davie, in 'The Diction of English Verse' in *Purity of Diction in English Verse* says of the poet: (Davie 1976: 16) "He is responsible to the community in which he writes, for purifying and correcting the spoken language". Day Lewis in the title chapter of *The Lyric Impulse* states: (Day Lewis 1965: 24) "It would be difficult to over-estimate the harm done to language by modern advertisement". (The accomplished minor poet, Norman Cameron, was an advertising copywriter.) Day Lewis' contemporary, Stephen Spender, makes a similar observation in *Love-Hate Relations: A Study of Anglo-American Sensibilities* when he states (Spender 1974: 241-2) that, at the beginning of the twentieth century: "In Ireland the English language had still the down-to-earth pithiness of that used by peasants. It had not been corrupted by the vulgar abstractions of journalism, commerce and advertising to the same degree as in England". These activities, journalism, commerce and to a lesser extent advertising have been practised for centuries in Britain. The practices are vulgar in the early sense the word: of the common people, or vernacular speech; and the language, or languages, of these three pursuits are more concrete than abstract. In the chapter, 'Case Histories' in *Professing Poetry* John Wain, an Oxford Professor of Poetry, writes: (Wain 1977: 279) "poetry, in our century, [the twentieth] is under unprecedented difficulties". And he adds: "But in our time language is sick, debilitated". Douglas Dunn, in interview with John Haffenden in *Viewpoints*, (Dunn 1981: 32) speaks of "the various pressures on the language, which leaves it very corrupt for exact literary use". Speakers and writers may use language corruptly, for example, as political propaganda but the language itself is not corrupt.

Eliot once again presents an interesting case study; or rather, studies: at all stages in his career, in his poems, critical studies and plays he is acutely aware of his use of language. In 'The Music of Poetry' he refers (Eliot 1955: 60) to the "ill-breeding" of some words and he gives "television" as an example. He assumes that his readers will know that the word is ill-bred because it is a compound derived from two languages, "tele" from Greek and "vision" from Latin. But this kind of compounding is a standard method of forming new words in English; for example "antibody", "cinemagoer", "cyberspace", "hinterland", "megaton", "salesman", "subsea", "troublemaker" and many others. Later in the essay he writes (Eliot 1955: 66) of the "deterioration" of a language and of the poet's "battle against degradation" in a language.

When Eliot writes about language in general or when he generalizes about language in poetry, he sometimes writes in terms of received opinion, discussing how he thinks language ought to function rather than how it actually functions in poetry and speech. In 'The Music of Poetry', for example, he writes as if the poet were the guardian or even the purifier of language: (Eliot 1955: 66)

> He in turn has the privilege of contributing to the development and maintaining the quality, the capacity of a language to express a wide range, and subtle gradation, of feeling and emotion; his task is both to respond to change and make it conscious, and to battle against degradation below the standards he has learned from the past.

But the poet is not always the best guardian of language. Some eighteenth-century English poets preserved a false language; and a language cannot be guarded by writers whose unpunctuated, asyntactic, arrhythmic free verse reveals that they do not know the properties of language. Eliot uses the words, "quality" and "degradation", as value judgments rather than as descriptions of the properties of language; such judgments are social and, in a confused way, moral rather than linguistic: we sometimes feel that a rule of language – on split infinitives, for example, or double negatives – has the force of a moral law. Part of the poet's task is, as Eliot says, to express feeling and emotion, but the poet should note that all social, national and regional dialects of English allow the users of these dialects to express a wide range of feeling and emotion.

Eliot's assumed role as guardian and purifier of the language appears again in 'The Unity of European Culture', an Appendix to *Notes towards the Definition of Culture*, where he writes: (Eliot 1948: 111-2) "a great poet is one who makes the most of the language that is given him. The truly great poet makes his language a great language". By contrast, when Eliot writes about language in *Four Quartets*, he writes as a poet who has learned over many years how language actually functions, how it can be made to function differently, and how it sometimes refuses to function, during the making of a poem. Apart from the line, "To purify the dialect of the tribe", in section II of 'Little Gidding', Eliot's references to language convince the reader that these are the ways in which the poet actually experiences language. The references include the opening sequence of section V of 'Burnt Norton'; "the intolerable wrestle/With words and feelings" in section II of 'East Coker'; the first half of section V of 'East Coker', which includes the much quoted phrase, "a raid on the inarticulate"; the lines, "So I find words ... on a distant shore", in section II of 'Little Gidding'; and the opening sequence of section V of 'Little Gidding'.

On the question of the corruptibility of language, linguists and poets disagree. A recurring theme in the collection, *Language Myths*, edited by Laurie Bauer and Peter Trudgill is that languages change over time and place but they do not decay. In 'The Meanings of Words Should Not Be Allowed to Vary or Change' Trudgill writes: (Trudgill 1998: 8) "Languages are self-regulating systems which can be left to take care of themselves". In the same collection Jean Aitchison writes (Aitchison b 1998: 19) in 'The Media are Ruining English': "English, like any tongue, maintains its own patterns and keeps itself organized". [...] And then she adds: "Some inbuilt property in the human mind maintains all languages, everywhere". That is, language maintenance, like language processing, is innate. David Crystal summarizes the linguists' view succinctly in *How Language Works*. He writes: (Crystal 2005: 459) "Languages do not develop, progress, decay, evolve, or act according to any of the metaphors which imply a specific endpoint and level of excellence. They simply change as society changes". As a writer of poems and a student of language, I agree with the linguists. Language is an innate faculty of mind. A language cannot decay unless an individual mind, or the collective mind of a whole speech community, decays.

The debate about the appropriate language for poetry is ancient, but our knowledge of how the brain generates and processes language is recent, and incomplete. Speaking, listening, reading and writing are conscious acts, but the processing of language during those acts is largely nonconscious, as earlier chapters of this work have shown. We are not aware of the neural activity that transduces electrochemical energy into the sound symbols of speech, or the graphic symbols of writing, or the mainly spontaneous, involuntary activity involved in attaching meaning to writing and speech. This unawareness is part of the mind's design; awareness of all these processes would overwhelm the mind. In the course of writing a poem, then, poets are not conscious of most of the language-generating and language-processing activities in the brain, although they are sometimes aware of a neural agitation when the creative impulse begins to stir, or when they have difficulty in finding the right words for a poem; and they might be aware of a different kind of agitation when the creative imagination becomes more fully active or when they are in a state of inspiration and the words flow freely.

# 13

# Poetry and Music

WHEN WALTER PATER WRITES IN 'The School of Giorgione' in *The Renaissance*, first published in 1873: (Pater 1907: 135) *"All art constantly aspires towards the condition of music"*, he uses italic type to emphasize his concept of an absolute aesthetic that is realized through a union of form and matter. Lyrical poetry, Pater states, is "the highest and most complete form of poetry" because in lyrical poetry "mere intelligence" is "reduced to its *minimum*". And he adds: (Pater 1907: 138) "Art, then, is thus always striving to be independent of mere intelligence, to become a matter of pure perception, to get rid of its responsibilities to its subject or material". Intelligence, of course, is not enough, but an artist's particular mode of intelligence in the making of a work of art will have a vital influence on the nature of the finished work. Artists' responsibilities to their subjects and materials are equally vital. The meanings in any painting include the painter's subject matter and use of materials: paints, brushes and palette knives to create colours, textures, thicknesses. And the meanings in any poem include its subject matter, its theme and the poet's use of and respect for language. To get rid of these responsibilities, as Pater recommends, is to deny not only the particular nature of an individual work of art but also the nature of an entire art form.

Our capacity for music, like our capacity for language, is innate. In *Musicophilia* Oliver Sacks writes: (Sacks 2011: 101) "There is clearly a wide range of musical talent, but there is much to suggest there is an innate musicality in virtually everyone". Children from the age of six months can bob and sway to the rhythms of music, and when children begin to speak at about the age of two they can be heard uttering original combinations of words and non-words in the melodies and rhythms of song as well as speech. In the adult mind, songs, melodies, and melodic fragments often play and replay themselves spontaneously.

Anthony Storr discusses this experience in the chapter, 'Music, Brain and Body' in *Music and the Mind*: (Storr 1992: 124) "Whenever my attention is not fully engaged, music 'runs in my head' involuntarily. [...] I do not understand why some music is so persistent that it is hard to rid oneself of it". In *Musicophilia* Oliver Sacks discusses the same experience and concludes: (Sacks 2011: 49) "the automatic or compulsive internal repetition of musical phrases is almost universal – the clearest sign of the overwhelming, and at times helpless, sensitivity of our brains to music". Storr suggests that this kind of spontaneous replay is purposeful: (Storr 1992: 125) "If I am engaged in any occupation not requiring intense concentration, the music which comes unbidden to my mind usually has physical and emotional effects of a positive kind". And then, in a persuasive insight, he adds: "It alleviates boredom, makes my movements more rhythmical, and reduces fatigue. A routine trudge can be transformed into an enjoyable exercise". It is as if the music in one's head is private work song, a musical accompaniment to a task; this metaphysical sense of companionship is something that music does supremely well.

We recognize and reproduce melody so readily that we must conclude that our mind is designed for music as well as for rhythm and language. The innateness of a mental capacity usually indicates that it emerged at an early stage in our evolution, as Charles Darwin observes in Chapter XIX of *The Descent of Man,* first published in 1871. He discusses the production and recognition of musical notes, and then he adds: (Darwin 1981: 334)

> Whether or not the half-human progenitors of man possessed [...] the capacity of producing, and no doubt of appreciating, musical notes, we have every reason to believe that man possessed these faculties at a very remote period, for singing and music are extremely ancient arts.

In the same paragraph Darwin adds that poetry can be considered as the offspring of song. What Darwin discovers through reflection, Oliver Sacks discovers through direct observation. In his Introduction to *Mu-*

*sicophilia* Sacks writes: (Sacks 2011: xii) "Our auditory systems, our nervous systems, are indeed exquisitely tuned for music".

There are other similarities between language and music. The grouping of words in speech is similar to the grouping of notes in a musical phrase. In speech, the pauses do not usually occur between individual words but between clusters of words. Music is similar in that the pauses occur between phrases rather than between single notes. In speech, the length of a word-cluster or a sequence of word-clusters is often determined by the number of words the speaker can utter in one breath; a similar limitation applies to singers and players of wind instruments, although some wind instrumentalists use a technique that allows them to inhale while they are playing. (When I asked a musician in the Royal Scottish National Orchestra how this was done, his reply was "Through the anus".) There are similarities, too, between the rising and falling pitch in the intonation contours of speech and the intonation contours of musical phrases. And there are further similarities between the stress, rhythm, tempo, and loudness of speech and music; the stress-timed nature of English speech is roughly comparable to the beats in a musical bar. The overall structure of a long poem can be compared to the structure of a musical work; a closer structural comparison is probably that of a poem sequence such as a sonnet cycle and a set of musical variations on a theme.

Perhaps it was these similarities, along with the emotional power of music, that led F. S. Flint and Williams, two of the founders of the Imagist movement in poetry, to associate poetry so closely with music that they mistakenly defined poetry in musical terms. Ezra Pound makes a similar identification in *ABC of Reading*. In the prefatory 'Warning' he states his conviction: (Pound 1951: 14) "that music begins to atrophy when it departs too far from the dance; that poetry begins to atrophy when it gets too far from music". And he repeats the conviction in Chapter Six: (Pound 1951: 61) "Music rots when it gets too far from the dance. Poetry atrophies when it gets too far from music". In *ABC of Reading* Pound is unconvincing on the subject of music. In the final chapter, 'Treatise on Metre', he states: (Pound 1951: 200) "Music in the past century [1850 to 1950] of shame and human degradation slumped in large quantities down into a soggy mass of tone". But in Chapter One he commends the music of Debussy and Ravel. In the section,

'Exercise' he writes: (Pound 1951: 151) "Dowland, Lawes, Young, Jenkins, the period of England's musicianship". John Dowland was a composer, singer and lutantist. William Lawes composed songs, madrigals and music for the stage; his older brother, Henry, wrote the music for Milton's masque, *Comus*, in 1634. William Young was a composer, viol player and flautist. John Jenkins wrote over eight hundred instrumental works. Pound might have heard enough of seventeenth-century English music to make an informed judgement, but that seems unlikely.

H. D. (Hilda Doolittle) comments on Pound's knowledge of music in *End to Torment: a Memoir of Ezra Pound by H. D.* The Memoir is in the form of a journal from March 7 to July 13, 1958, the year Pound was released from a mental hospital. In her entry for May 17, H. D. refers to Pound's opera, *Villon*, and she states (Doolittle 1980: 49) that the music "must have been transcribed by some musical expert", clearly implying that Pound himself could not read or write music. Pound's one-act opera, *Le Testament de François Villon*, was written in 1920-1921; the music was transcribed by the American composer, George Antheil, who was then twenty-one years old.

In the same journal entry, H. D. says of Pound: "He seemed unintimidated by the fact that (to my mind) he had no ear for music and, alas, I suffered excruciatingly from his clumsy dancing". Edith Sitwell met Antheil at a party in London. In her letter of circa January 17, 1925 to the English poet, John Freeman, she writes (Sitwell 1998: 52) of "the young pianist and composer George Antheil, so much admired by Mr. Ezra Pound (who knows nothing about music)".

Sitwell's witty sequence, *Façade*, first published in 1922, plays with the poetic resources of prosody and relates them to musical properties of pitch, syncopation and counterpoint. *Façade* was set to music by William Walton, but even without the music the poems – for example, 'Trio for Two Cats and a Trombone', (Sitwell 1982: 120-1) 'Fox Trot', (137-8) and 'I Do Like to Be Beside the Seaside', (Sitwell 1982: 153-4) – still dance on the page in entertaining, sometimes nonsensical, ways. In 'Notes on the Nature of Poetry' in *A Poet's Notebook* Sitwell states (Sitwell 1943: 16) that in two poems in *Façade*, 'By the Lake' and 'Four in the Morning', along with 'Daphne' in *Five Songs*: "the rhythmical element has produced the music".

But a sustained comparison of poetry and music will uncover more differences than similarities. Music, like language, is an abstract symbolic system of expression and communication that can be realized in sound and in writing. Music is the more abstract of the two. Most words in a language have extra-linguistic referents; that is, words usually refer to things other than language itself and often denote external physical realities. In music, by contrast, there are no such links, not even in song, opera, or oratorio, because in these musical forms it is the words and not the music that convey referential meaning. The sounds and the written notations of instrumental music have no agreed referents. Music can be written, performed, and heard without reference to any order of reality other than music itself.

Most forms of music proceed by repetition, only one form of which, variations on a theme, is found in modern poetry. The refrain, that is, one or more lines repeated at the end of each stanza or second stanza of a poem, is seldom used in poetry today, mainly because it is seen as an artificial, needlessly repetitive device. Music routinely uses the immediate repetition of phrases and melodies, and the structured or delayed repetition of a major theme in a later movement of the work.

Repetition in music is conventional: composers accept that it is the way in which music is composed. But it is also functional: if there were no repetition, then the listener, and perhaps some performers, would be unable to detect the internal figures that are essential in developing the overall structure of the work. One reason why listeners have difficulty in enjoying some modern music is the lack of repetition, especially of recognizable melodies and rhythms.

The writing system of musical notation is roughly comparable to an alphabetical writing system in that each proceeds horizontally by linear progression, bar by bar and line by line. But musical notation also proceeds vertically, or simultaneously, by chords and harmonies. A keyboard instrument, for example, can produce ten notes simultaneously; a group of instruments, say, a string quartet, can produce a variety of musical effects simultaneously: two or more chords, harmonies, melodies, rhythms, and even tempos. Language has no such simultaneous functions; the nature of our writing system makes it impossible to achieve the simultaneity of music. Poetry can partly escape from linearity through typography and layout, but few poets write good poems by contradicting the linear nature of the writing system and the natural rhythms of the language.

Music can produce a more immediate and intense emotional response than poetry, and this suggests that there is a close relationship between music and emotion, both of which were formerly thought to be functions of the right hemisphere of the brain but are now known to be functions of both hemispheres. Weeping in response to music is a mainly adult experience;  young people up to and beyond the age of adolescence are often excited by music but seldom moved to tears by it. Perhaps music exerts its emotional influence only on people who have neural networks that have already been shaped by emotion, that is, people whose minds have been affected by the joys and sorrows of life.

Steven Pinker in the chapter provocatively entitled 'The Meaning of Life' in *How the Mind Works* suggests that we are conditioned to react in certain ways to certain kinds of music: (Pinker 1998: 532) "A person merely has to listen to melodies in a particular idiom over time, absorbing the patterns and contrasts among the intervals, and the emotional connotations develop automatically". When the idiom changes, for example, from Russian romanticism to the music of Prokofiev and Stravinsky; or, in the work of a single composer, from Copland's *Piano Variations* in 1930 to his popular ballets, *Billy the Kid*  and *Rodeo* – when the idiom changes, the new music may seem challenging or, if there is nothing in our experience to which the new work can be related, it may seem alien. The neuroscientist, Daniel Levitin, is more specific than Pinker. In 'Anticipation' in *This Is Your Brain on Music* Levitin writes: (Levitin 2007: 117) "By the age of five, infants have learned to recognize chord progressions in the music of their culture".

An example of this in British culture is – or was until the late twentieth century – the seemingly spontaneous reaction to the emotional power of English hymns. In fact, the reaction was conditioned, mainly through seasonal rehearsals of the hymns in British primary and secondary schools and daily performances at morning assembly. The repetition became a form of imprinting in the young person's mind, and when the adult mind recognized the imprint, then the adult felt the emotional reassurance, the sense of community, and perhaps a sense of innocent childhood, that came with that kind of recognition.

Music enters the listener's mind as a series of auditory sensory impressions that are sometimes closely related to emotion, whereas the auditory sensory impressions of the words of a poem are instantly trans-duced to the various kinds of poetic meaning: connotative, figurative, experiential, aesthetic. Poetry and music come together in song, and neuroscientists report that some patients whose speech is patholectic as a result of a stroke or a brain injury can sometimes pronounce words clearly when they sing. In *Musicophilia* Oliver Sacks reports (Sacks 2011: 239) that after six weeks of melodic intonation therapy a patient who had been speechless, aphasic, for eighteen months was able to have short conversations. And in *This Is Your Brain on Music* Daniel Levitin writes: (Levitin 2007: 127) "The brain's music system appears to oper-ate with functional independence from the language system". And he concludes: "This told us that attending to structure in music requires both halves of the brain, while attending to structure in language only requires the left half".

When the language areas of the patients' brains are damaged, some patients can recall the song's words as musical notes rather than as words. These clinical studies confirm what poets have known for cen-turies: the two systems, the auditory and the semantic, can be activated simultaneously by rhyme and other literary sound effects, and that our auditory memory of the sounds of words is distinct from our semantic memory of the meanings of words.

Another measure of the unequal emotional relationship of words and music is that the words of popular songs, hymns, operatic arias, and lieder-like songs from the concert repertoire are often acceptable when they are sung but sound trite if they are uttered without the music or are read as texts. As Philip Hobsbaum notes in 'Verse Forms' in *Metre, Rhythm and Verse Form*: (Hobsbaum 1996: 184) "It is possible for an entertainer such as Frank Sinatra to impart to a trivial love song a great measure of intensity. This does not make the love song any the less trivial. The intensity is in the performance". Professional singers some-times perform works in languages that they cannot speak and, apart from the pieces in their repertoire, cannot understand. In rehearsing a new work in a foreign language, the singer concentrates primarily on the words' musical notations, their phonetic values, and the phonology of the intonation contours, that is, the characteristic recurring patterns of pitch, or tone, created by clusters of words in a language.

That claim is confirmed in almost every performance of Joseph Canteloube's *Chants d'Auvergne*, written between 1923 and 1930. The work includes a sequence of nine songs for soprano and orchestra, and an alternative version for soprano and piano. The words of the songs are in a regional, rural dialect of Auvergne in the Central Plateau in France. That dialect is unlikely to be the first language of the singer. In song, poetry and music are not equal partners. When instrumentalists or singers are presented with new and challenging pieces of music, they may be struck by works' emotional quality and they will wish to express that quality in performance, but in the course of learning the new work they must partly suspend their emotional responses in order to master the sequence of sounds.

Cinema offers different illustrations of music's emotional power. From the viewpoint of the film director, the main purpose of the music is to influence the cinema audience's emotional response to and involvement in the drama on the screen. For the director, then, film music is most effective when, irrespective of its loudness, it operates at the threshold of the audience's consciousness, a level at which the music is not heard as sounds and rhythms and figures issuing from an external source but is experienced as internal emotional cues in the minds of the viewers. In effect, what some members of the audience experience is not music but a sequence of seemingly spontaneous emotions. Film music can be as complex and challenging as contemporaneous orchestral music, and there is an irony in the fact that countless millions of cinema-goers have enjoyed, if only subliminally, music they would not have chosen to listen to in the concert hall, on radio, or on record.

Later in *Musicophilia* Sacks makes an even greater claim for the power of music when he writes: (Sacks 2011: 332) "As music seems to resist or survive the distortion of dreams or parkinsonism, or the losses of amnesia or Alzheimer's, so it may resist the distortion of psychosis and be able to penetrate the deepest states of melancholia or madness, sometimes when nothing else can". The powers of music lead Geoffrey Hill to speak of his envy of the composer. In an interview with John Haffenden published in *Viewpoints* Hill says of the composer: (Hill 1981: 91) "he unites solitary meditation with direct, sensuous communication to a degree greater than the poet". Music is more direct because its sounds go straight to the emotional centres of the brain whereas the reader of a poem has to decode the words for meanings before the poem can make its emotional and intellectual appeal. Hill adds:

> In the first instance musical composition is the scratching of pen upon paper but then these signs are translated into the immediate sensuous configurations of sound, the actual iconic presence of brazen instrument and shaken air, in a way that poets can only envy.

Although the emotional impact of music can be powerful and lasting, emotion is not the only response to music. An instrumentalist playing in a group – a string quartet, a chamber or symphony orchestra, a big band – is simultaneously aware of the sound of his own instrument and the sounds of all or most of the others. These kinds of awareness, which are intellectual as well as emotional, are not available to the poet. The player, like the conductor, may also be aware of the structure of each musical figure within the wider structure of the movement, and of the structure of the movement within the whole work. The creative impulse is essentially an emotional force, but the creative imagination must combine emotion and intellect, feeling and thought, in order to create a coherent work of art. When composers orchestrate large-scale instrumental works such as a symphony or concerto, or when they write the parts for solo voices, chorus, and orchestra for an opera or an oratorio, the composers must think logically and analytically in order to achieve the extraordinary precision required. Few poets today are capable of that kind of sustained, intricate creativity.

Geoffrey Hill expresses envy but poetry can express thoughts and feelings that are beyond the power of music. Poetry, that is, can express almost all forms of human experience.

# 14

# Technique

## Poetry: Craft and Art

DYLAN THOMAS WRITES ENGAGINGLY on the craft and art of the creative process in advice he gave in reply to a student in 1951. In his reply, published as 'Notes on the Art of Poetry' in *Modern Poets on Modern Poetry* he states: (Thomas, D. 1966: 93-4)

> What I like to do is treat words as a craftsman does his wood or stone or what-have-you, to hew, carve, mould, coil, polish and plane them into patterns, sequences, sculptures, fugues of sound expressing some lyrical impulse, some spiritual doubt or conviction, some dimly-realized truth I must try to reach and realize.

What Thomas is recommending is a lifelong apprenticeship in poetry, and poets' apprenticeships as artists and wordsmiths (the epicene term is used instead of the words, "craftsman" and "craftsmanship") continue until death or until the professional death that is their abandonment of poetry or abandonment by poetry. Even the great artist-wordsmith can never command all the resources of language and thus can never have a complete command of poetry.

Thomas perfectly captures a gradience from craft to artistry, from hewing and polishing to the realization of an emotional or spiritual truth. When the gradience is expressed in a well-made poem, a reader may be unable to distinguish the craft from the art, but poets, editors and critics should have a sense of the two sets of properties. Craft workers can often predict the outcome of their work because they follow a pattern in the form of a sketch, a mental image, or an object they have previously made; they know in advance what the finished work should look like: a wrought-iron screen, a silver brooch, a wooden rocking-horse. The poet seldom knows in advance what the finished poem will be, because it develops in unpredictable ways under the motive force of the creative impulse and the transforming power of the poetic imagination. The craft worker often makes several versions of the same item; the poet may write several variations on a theme, but each variation must be original, unique.

The criterion of utility can sometimes be used to distinguish a work of craft from a work of art, but the aim of some craft workers – the potter, for example, or the glass-blower or silversmith – is to produce something that is decorative and beautiful as well as, or rather than, useful. In poetry, craft and art combine in a continuum in which the craft flows into the art, and for the poet who is an artist-wordsmith the two kinds of creativity are inseparable. If a poet is a wordsmith as well as an artist, as distinct from a writer who claims to be an artist but neglects the craft, the poet can rightly claim that the finished work is a more complex achievement that offers a fuller experience, because it includes the aesthetic experience of poetic skills and of the thing well made in addition to the experience that is a subject in the poem.

## Form and Content

Received opinion on form and content assumes that their integration is natural and organic. Coleridge, for example, states in 'Shakespeare, a Poet Generally' in *Essays and Lectures on Shakespeare*: (Coleridge 1951: 46-7)

> The form is mechanic, when on any given material we impress a pre-ordained form, not necessarily arising out of the properties of the material; – as when to a mass of wet clay we give whatever shape we wish it to retain when hardened. The organic form, on the other hand, is innate; it shapes, as it develops, itself from within, and the fullness of its development is one and the same with the perfection of its outward form.

Coleridge states the ideal; in practice, integration of form and content is sometimes achieved through craft and art.

Denise Levertov challenges received opinion when she discusses form and content in 'Some Affinities of Content' in *New & Selected Essays*: (Levertov 1992: 2)

We have long assumed that it is an aesthetic truism to assert the indivisibility of form and content – but there is a certain amount of hypocrisy in that statement, after all. Perhaps it needs to be reformulated, to say that although inadequate formal expression always diminishes or distorts content, yet form itself can be perceived, admired and experienced as pleasure or stimulus even when the reader's attention is not held by content.

Levertov's account is more pragmatic, and more convincing, than Coleridge's. What is understood by the word, "content", in most discussions of poetry is the poem's subject and theme, the experience in the poem and the meaning of that experience. And what is usually understood by the word, "form", is a number of features: the regularity or irregularity of rhythm, the presence or absence of rhyme and other musical features, the lengths of lines and stanzas if the poem is in stanzaic form, and the internal figures and overall structure of the poem. Clearly, the content of a poem can be accommodated in a variety of forms; a single form, for example, the sonnet or the ballad, can accommodate a variety of subjects and themes. Levertov is less convincing when she writes in the same paragraph: "Thus, while content cannot be apprehended without a fusion with form equal to its task, form can be apprehended and absorbed in and of itself." A poet's formal craft and artistry can be enjoyed in their own right and can partly compensate for a slightness of subject or theme. But when a poem is amorphous, its subject can and must be apprehended with little or no regard for form. A legacy of the Imagists is a poetry that disregards form or subjugates form to content; lacking any of the properties of form outlined above, such poems offer content alone. Without form, Coleridge states in his lecture on Shakespeare, the spirit of a poem might be lost. And of that spirit, he writes: (Coleridge 1951: 45-6 "It must embody in order to reveal itself; but a living body is of necessity an organized one; and what is organization but the connection of parts in and for a whole so that each part is at once end and means?"

What complicates the question of form and content is the fact that another important element of form is a poem's ideational, or semantic, structure, that is, the patterns of images, ideas and feelings that develop throughout the poem until the patterns and the poem are complete. And because ideation is also the experience in, and thus the content of, the poem, form and content are to that extend coincidental. An amorphous poem, then, has some form in that the sequence of ideation shapes the semantic structure, while the lengths of lines and stanzas, however ill-considered they may be, give the poem a physical form; but if that form is achieved through ideation only and not through any linear, stanzaic, rhythmic, or musical principle of structure, then the poem is technically and artistically amorphous. The craftless poet writes amorphous poems that concentrate on imagery.

# 15

# Imagery

IMAGERY IN POEMS IS MAINLY VISUAL, auditory, and kinesthetic, and is so closely related to sensory perception that the images in a poem are often, in effect, sensory perceptions transduced to cognition. Images that capture the particularity of a thing – its shape, colour, and texture, or its sound or motion – are, in the absence of other features of artistry and craft, the focal points in an amorphous poem and can engage our attention in such a way that we, like the poet, may fail to notice the poem's arbitrariness of structure. Arbitrarily, craftless poets vary the lengths of lines and stanzas in order to avoid regularity and they use a high proportion of short lines in the belief that they create tension. Irregularities of line and stanza, the craftless poet argues, reflect the irregularities of thought or spontaneous speech. An asyntactic, arrhythmic statement might well seem like spontaneous speech, but if poetry were the same as speech then every speaker would be a poet. Intensity of feeling and being true to one's feelings, the craftless poet argues, are more important than craft and artistry; but if poets do not have the skill to give shape to their feelings, then these feelings remain only partly articulated; and without a principle of structure, feeling might outstrip thought and overwhelm the poem. Such poets do not think to ask: If I do not create a structure and form for the poem, how will the content be expressed? The answer is, of course, that the content will be expressed arbitrarily and amorphously.

Some findings in neuroscience help us to understand some of the mental mechanisms involved in image-making. Imagination in its simplest form is the ability to make images in response to sensory stimuli, but even the simplest form is highly complex. The psychiatrist, John Ratey, discusses links between perception and cognition in *A User's Guide to the Brain*. He states (Ratey 2001: 99) that a visual image on the retina is transformed into 126 million pieces, every one of which is transmitted to an information-processing centre, the thalamus, which then fires neuronal networks in the visual cortex; the information is then transferred to, and transduced in, the frontal cortex, where the information becomes conscious. Ratey states that in addition to these pathways there are distinct perception-to-cognition visual routes for shape, colour, movement and location. A visual image is decoded, re-encoded and decoded several times before we become conscious of it.

Although poets' various impressions of time are different from sensory stimuli, they often treat time as if it, too, were a sensory impression. Poets write of time as if it were a substance, of the passing of time as a metaphysical as well as a physical process, and of the imagined juxtaposition of time states, especially the past and the present, as a physical encounter. The ability to simulate perception is an essential function of the artistic imagination. No adult artist can view the world as innocently as a child but, for some of the purposes of their art, artists try to maintain an unconditional mode of perception, a way of looking that does not assign new experience, new images, too quickly to existing schemas but instead allows the artist to see things in their own right and as if for the first time. It is a way of looking that sometimes produces eidetic imagery, images that are so vivid, precise, and persistent that poets feel they are transcribing existing sequences of images rather than creating original sequences, and painters might feel that they are copying pictures in the mind.

The mind of the creative artist is designed to create and enjoy images, to store them in memory, and to combine them in new associations. In effect, the artist's mind is designed to disregard the commandment in the Ten Commandments in *Exodus* chapter 20, verse 4: "Thou shalt not make unto thee any graven image, or any likeness of any thing that is in the heaven above, or that is in the earth beneath, or that is in the water under the earth". The commandment is impossible to observe because it demands the suppression of the natural functions of perception and cognition. Moses and the elders of the tribe must have thought that artistic creation, the making of images of the world and its creatures, was not a celebration but a usurpation of the power of their God. The early Hebrew lawmakers might also have feared that the divergent imagination of the creative artist was a threat to the unity of the tribe. Lawmakers in subsequent civilizations have felt the same kind of fear.

Although the ability to form images is innate, it is neither uniform nor universal. As early as 1890 William James in the chapter, 'Imagination', in *The Principles of Psychology* wrote (the italics are his): (James 1983: 704)

> A person whose visual imagination is strong finds it hard to understand how those without the faculty can think at all. *Some people undoubtedly have no visual images at all worthy of the name*, and instead of *seeing* their breakfast-table, they tell you that they *remember* it or *know* what was on it.

And in 1929, I. A. Richards in Introductory in *Practical Criticism* discusses the difficulties some readers have in responding to the imagery in a poem: (Richards 1960: 14)

> They [the difficulties] arise in part from the incurable fact that we differ immensely in our capacity to visualize, and to produce imagery of the other senses. Also the importance of our imagery as a whole, [...] in our mental lives varies surprisingly.

At the time of writing, Richards' conclusion was based mainly on the evidence of students' interpretations of poems; since then, neuroscientists have confirmed that the ability to form mental images varies from one person to another, and that some people lack the ability to form some kinds of sensory images. This inability to form mental images could be a result of a deficit in sensory receptor cells or in the sensory cortices. If we cannot form the image then, at a simple level, we cannot imagine the object or event, although we should still be able to understand its significance. These deficits could partly explain why some people are unable to enjoy some kinds of poetry. To people who think habitually in images, these findings might be hard to accept, but perhaps the difference is illustrated by the common expression: some people have perfect musical pitch while others are tone deaf.

Because they are associated with sensory perceptions and not with words, images are modified when they are transduced into language; and because images in the mind can seem more particular and more diverse than words, some poets may feel that the images are not only transduced but also reduced into words. A possible dilemma for the poet, then, is whether to try to be true to the images or to the language in which the images must be expressed. Imagery, or some expression of sensory perception, is an essential element in a poem but, with the exception of Imagist and sub-imagist poetry, imagery is not so much an end in itself as a means of illustrating the subject matter and theme of a poem, and revealing the nature of the experience in a poem and the experience of a poem as a work of art.

A poem that expresses its meaning entirely or mainly through images makes a different, probably lesser, demand on the reader. The poetic imagination delights in image-making, but its deeper concern is to explore those faculties of mind, especially emotion and thought, that confirm our humanity. Although the two sets of mental activities, emotion and thought, or feeling and intellect, are sometimes discussed as if they were mutually exclusive, one of the main functions of the poetic imagination is to relate the two faculties so as to achieve levels of understanding that cannot be attained through emotion alone or thought alone, as the earlier chapters on emotion and thought have shown.

# 16

# Rhyme

EVERY POEM CONTAINS ELEMENTS of music, mainly in the phonetic values of syllables and in the phonologies produced by the intonation contours of a language; these effects can be supplemented by various other phonic devices to produce a complex music. Rhyme is the most obvious of these devices, and the commonest form of rhyme is end-rhyme, in which the rhyming words appear at the ends of lines; additional effects can be gained through the use of internal rhymes within lines. Half-rhymes, for example, "large", "surge", "emerge" or "fail", "fall", "fool", are widely used by poets and accepted by readers; so too are eye-rhymes, that is, words with similar clusters of letters but with different pronunciations: "four", "hour", "tour", or "love", "move", "drove". A half-rhyme or an eye-rhyme that gives continuity of meaning is usually more acceptable than a full rhyme that distorts the meaning or the syntax at a particular point in the poem, because a variation in sound is often heard or read as part of a poem's changing pattern of sounds, whereas a full rhyme with an inappropriate meaning could introduce a distracting ambiguity or even an obscurity; and an inversion of syntax in order to have a full rhyme at the end of a line will always disrupt the continuity of that line and the next. This simple example illustrates the use of end-rhyme, internal rhyme and half-rhyme: (Aitchison a 2009: 169)

> Another April and another day
> with all the seasons in it, with lapwings
> stalling on a squall and then tumbling
> over the collapsing wall of air
> to float in zones of weightlessness again.

In his prefatory letter of November 1666 to Robert Howard, John Dryden comments on his poem, 'Annus Mirabilis', first published in

1667. He discusses  rhyme in some detail and then states three princi-
ples of rhyme that are still observed today: (Dryden 1956: 20) "Neither
can we give ourselves the liberty of making any part of a verse for the
sake of rhyme, or concluding with a word which is not current English,
or using the variety of female rhymes". A female, or feminine, rhyme
is an end-rhyme of two or more syllables. Most end-rhymes in Eng-
lish-language poetry are single syllables and are sometimes known as
masculine rhymes: "joy" and "destroy", "brake" and "overtake", "fact"
and "abstract"; the full word may have more than one syllable but mas-
culine rhyme appears only in the final syllable. Feminine rhymes, in-
cluding half-rhymes and eye-rhymes, are acceptable if they meet the
requirements of meaning, stress, and pitch. These rhymes, for example,
"nourish", "cherish", "perish", and "vanity", "sanity", "humanity",
could be effective in the right contexts. But poets are cautious in their
use of feminine rhymes because such rhymes are a major element in
comic and satirical verse. Coleridge in Chapter XVIII of *Biographia
Literaria* notes this effect of feminine rhymes: (Coleridge 1956: 207)
"Double and trisyllable rhymes, indeed, form a lower species of wit
and attended to exclusively for their own sake may become a source of
momentary amusement".

Towards the end of his career, in his dedication letter to his tragicom-
edy, *The Rival Ladies*, first performed in 1694, Dryden again discusses
the techniques and effects of rhyme in detail and then he leavens the
lesson by saying that rhyme controls the poet's over-heated imagina-
tion. In playful metaphors he adds: (Dryden 1950: 187-8) "For imagi-
nation in a poet is a faculty so wild and lawless that, like a high-ranging
spaniel, it must have clogs tied to it, lest it outrun the judgment". In his
hyperbole of the poet's wild and lawless imagination, Dryden is imply-
ing that if the creative impulse and the creative imagination are not
disciplined by the artistry and craft of rhyme, then the resulting poetry
might be wayward and diffuse. The discipline of rhyme, Dryden adds:
(Dryden 1950: 188)

> requires the poet to use his judgement, that is, his discriminating intel-
> lect, and to clarify his thoughts. But certainly, that which most regulates
> the fancy, and gives the judgment its busiest employment, is like to
> bring forth the richest and clearest thoughts.

The most perplexing comment on the use of rhyme in English-language poetry is Milton's Preface to *Paradise Lost*. Milton, a contemporary of Dryden, states that he is following the examples of Homer in Greek and Virgil in Latin, and he adds: (Milton 1862: 2) "Italian and Spanish Poets of prime note, have rejected Rime". He does not mention Shakespeare or any other Elizabethan or Jacobean dramatist by name, but he commends the absence of rhyme in "our best English Tragedies". What puzzles this reader is the intensity of Milton's denunciation – "the jingling sound of like endings" is "a fault" – when he himself was a master of rhyme. *Paradise Lost* was published 1667, the same year as Dryden's *Annus Mirabilis: the Year of Wonders*, which is composed in the simple a b a b rhyme scheme. There is irony in the fact that two major English poets of the seventeenth century make such contradictory claims about rhyme.

Milton died in 1674. Three years later Dryden paid tribute to Milton by writing an opera, *The State of Innocence and Fall of Man*, prompted by *Paradise Lost*. The opera, in rhyming couplets, was published in 1677 and published as a Google eBook in 2009 but it was never performed. It opens with the words of Lucifer rising from a lake: (Dryden 2009: 18 of transcript)

> 'Is this the Seat our Conqueror has given?
> And this the climate we must change for Heaven?'

It ends with the words of the archangel Raphael: (Dryden 2009: 45)

> For now the war of nature is begun:
> But, part you hence in peace, and having mourned your sin,
> For outward Eden lost, find Paradise within.'

Dryden is a wise and witty commentator on the practice of poetry, but his tribute is as ill-judged as Eliot's observations on Milton in 'The Music of Poetry': (Eliot 1958: 64) "We may think that Milton, in expressing the orchestral music of language, sometimes ceases to talk a social idiom at all". We can of course offer the counter-argument that the language of *Paradise Lost* is necessarily oratorical, the language of oratory and of oratorio, rather than conversational. Richards supports this view of Milton in his interview with B. A. Boucher and J. P. Russo in *Complementarities: Uncollected Essays*, where Richards states: (Richards 1977: 265) "What most people need, though, with Milton more than anything else is to hear him really well read aloud. He's the most readable-aloud there is, magnificent beyond description". Milton's mighty music is reduced by Dryden's rhyming couplets, and by giving his opera a happy ending, or the promise of happiness: "find Paradise within", Dryden contradicts Milton's conclusion to *Paradise Lost*, which ends with the spiritual exile of Adam and Eve: (Milton 1862: 312)

> They, hand in hand, with wandering steps and slow,
> Through Eden took their solitary way.

One of Eliot's most interesting comments on rhyme appears in 'Reflections on *Vers Libre*', first published in 1917, where he writes: (Eliot 1955: 91) "When the comforting echo of rhyme is removed, success or failure in the choice of words, in the sentence structure, in the order, is at once more apparent". Some poets might argue that their use of language in blank verse or other non-rhyming poems is as meticulous as it is in rhyming poetry, but Eliot is probably right in claiming that the poet's use of language is more exposed when it does not have the little aural focal points that rhyme can provide. The "echo of rhyme", is more comforting for the reader than for the poet, just as a recognizable melody in music is more comforting for the listener than for the composer.

For Philip Larkin, rhyme is a normal component of a poem. In his interview with Robert Phillips for *Paris Review*, reprinted in Larkin's *Required Writing*, Larkin states: (Larkin 1983: 71) "Writing poetry is playing off the natural rhythms and word-order of speech against the artificialities of rhyme and metre". The subtlety of Larkin's virtuosity creates the artistic illusion that his use of rhyme and metre is as natural as speech. On the specific question of rhyme, Larkin's reply suggests that rhyme is not only a normal but a necessary component of his poems: "Normally one does rhyme. Deciding *not* to is much harder".

Rhyme can give a poem an encompassing and integrated structure. The visible structure of the poem is determined by its overall length

and the lengths of lines and stanzas; a poem's semantic structure is de-
termined by the expression of thought and feeling. But a poem is also
a structure of sounds, a configuration in which the recurrence of the
same or similar phonemes creates a phonic framework in addition to the
poem's visible and semantic frameworks. Rhyme can unify a poem in
this way even when the lines are of unequal length and the rhythm is ir-
regular, as in this extract from a sequence on Thomas Hardy: (Aitchison
a 2009: 110)

> The trees, sir, in this arch
> that stands between the graveyard and the church;
> these yews are seeded from
> parent plants older by far than Christendom.
> And all our christenings
> will not wash away our knowledge of these things.

Rhyme delineates; it defines and redefines the poetic line whether the
line is end-stopped or run-on. Two or more rhyming words from simi-
lar semantic fields, for example, "suspense" and "intense", or "trance"
and "deliverance", can extend or clarify that part of the meaning of the
poem. Two or more rhyming words from different semantic fields, say,
"thrill" and "still", can produce the double effect of the similarity of
sounds and the contrast of meanings as the rhymes act on the mind's
auditory and semantic networks. An unexpected but appropriate rhyme
can give a slight shock of delight, but the element of surprise is not a
necessity; delight can also be found in rhyming words that strike the
reader as being natural and inevitable.

Poets know that when they choose to create rhymes, the demands on
their use of language will be more exacting than the demands in a non-
rhyming poem, because the choice of a rhyming word is determined by
its meaning and stress as well as its pitch; that is, when poets decide
to use rhyme, they know that their lexical options are greatly reduced.
Rhyme can be so difficult to sustain that some poets use it inconsis-
tently. Intermittent rhyme can be effective, but if rhymes are used in one
part of a poem and are then abandoned for no artistic reason, the reader
has the right to be suspicious. Readers respond, if only intuitively, to
recurring sound patterns in a poem; if the pattern arbitrarily ceases,

readers may feel a discrepancy between the rhyming and non-rhyming passages. Some readers will conclude that the poet was unable to sustain the rhyme, or unable or unwilling to sustain the mental effort required to sustain the rhyme.

For poets, part of the appeal of rhyme is the linguistic challenge of the search for the perfect rhyming word and the satisfaction they feel when they think they have found it, or the lesser satisfaction when they find a match that is less than perfect and yet still effective. But the main appeal of rhyme, for the reader as well as the poet, is the double pleasure, linguistic and extra-linguistic, of hearing patterns of similar sounds. The experience is both phonetic and phonic; that is, we hear the sounds as speech sounds that have lexical and connotative meanings, and also as auditory stimuli that are partly divorced from words and the meanings of words. Within the overall artistic experience of the poem we can distinguish the intellectual experience of sound as language and meaning, and the sensory, often emotional, experience of sound as music.

# 17

# Rhythm

## Some Misconceptions

POETS AND CRITICS ATTRIBUTE TO RHYTHM powers that it cannot possibly have. Ezra Pound in 'Credo', written in 1917 and included in *Modern Poets on Modern Poetry* states: (Pound 1966: 37) "Rhythm. – I believe in 'absolute rhythm', a rhythm, that is, in poetry which corresponds exactly to the emotion or shade of emotion to be expressed". Rhythm can express emotion to a limited extent: the rhythm of an elegy, for example, is slower than that of a joyful lyric, but rhythm cannot express exact shades of emotion. Absolute rhythm as Pound defines it is unattainable. Eliot also makes exaggerated claims for the power of rhythm. In the chapter on Matthew Arnold in *The Use of Poetry and the Use of Criticism* Eliot writes: (Eliot 1933: 118-9)

> What I call the 'auditory imagination' is the feeling for syllable and rhythm, penetrating far below the conscious levels of thought and feeling, invigorating every word; sinking to the most primitive and forgotten, returning to the origins and bringing something back, seeking the beginning and end.

Heaney quotes that sentence in 'Englands of the Mind' in *Finders Keepers* and describes it as: (Heaney 2002: 77) "One of the most precise and suggestive of Eliot's critical formulations". But when poets penetrate "far below the conscious levels of thought and feeling", what they discover cannot be used in a poem until it has been transduced into consciousness and language. The innateness of a mental capacity, in this instance the capacity for rhythm, is usually an indication that the capacity appeared at an early, perhaps prelinguistic, stage in human evolution. But Eliot is discussing the rhythmic use of language in poetry; and a poet who is as conscious, even self-conscious, of his craft as Eliot knows that the rhythms of poetry are not achieved by "sinking to the most primitive and forgotten" but through acquired technique. The auditory imagination is partly dependent on the language-processing functions of the brain, which operate largely nonconsciously; but in poetry the auditory imagination is a function of the auditory cortex and the poetic imagination, a condition of mind that has some access to the nonconscious but is essentially a heightened state of consciousness. Eliot's quest for origins and ends is expressed more convincingly in the near-mysticism in some passages of *Four Quartets* than in the uncharacteristically psychoanalytic and melodramatic quotation above.

Maud Bodkin presents a more reasoned case in *Archetypal Patterns in Poetry: Psychological Studies of Imagination*, first published in 1934, in which she adopts a Jungian approach to literature. In section V of chapter VI she writes: (Bodkin 1951: 321-2)

> The body's enactment, through changes of speech-rhythm and intonation, of changes in the dramatic content of poetry, is the factor that links the reading of verse – even though silent, reduced to sub-articulation – with the ritual dance, concerned as the prototype of the arts. As the wild rhythms of the ancient dance tended to annul the participants' consciousness of separate personality, exalting him to union with his group and with its God, so, in fainter degree, the rhythms of poetry still serve to hold the reader apart from his everyday self and cares, caught up into the thought and feeling communicated.

The ritual dance, says Bodkin, was the prototype of the arts, but we have no way of knowing if dance was more prototypical than the shaman's visions, sacrificial killings of humans and animals, initiation rites, fire ceremonies, body painting, chants or some forms of totemism. In *A Defence of Poetry* Shelley assumes that dance was only one of several rhythmic ritual activities among early human societies. Others, he states, (Shelley 1956: 104) were the melodies of songs, combinations of language and imitations of natural objects.

Oliver Sacks writes of the millennial and elemental power of rhythm and dance. In *Musicophilia* he states: (Sacks 2011: 106) "forms of rhythm deafness are rarely total, because rhythm is represented widely in the brain". Later in *Musicophilia* Sacks states: (Sacks 2011: 381-2)

"We bond when we sing together, sharing the specific affects and connections of a song; but bonding is deeper, more primal, if we dance together, coordinating our bodies and not just our voices". Primitive forces persist in the modern brain.

Although the ritual dance probably had the effects that Bodkin suggests, that is, the promotion of a collective, tribal consciousness and union with the tribe's god or gods, these effects are different from the effects of reading and enjoying poetry. When readers are caught up in the thought and feeling of a poem, they might be temporarily released from their everyday self and cares, and the experience they recognize in the poem might be a shared experience. But that experience, and the reader's experience of the poem as a work of literature, and the very act of reading, are solitary, conscious and interpretative. Bodkin states: (Bodkin 1951: 322) "It would seem to be the relation to the dance, the experienced presence of motor schemata, wraiths of gesture and action, that constitutes, even more than sound, the link between the arts of poetry and music". Perhaps that is the test: if the particular reader of a particular poem finds that her motor schemas are activated, that is, if her motor neurons are activated and produce a physical response or even the mental sensation of a physical response, then for that particular reader there could be a link between the poem and dance. But a physical response that was not accompanied by an imaginative response would be inadequate. When we are moved by a poem, we are more likely to be moved emotionally and intellectually than physically.

James Craig La Drière, like Maud Bodkin, associates the rhythms of poetry to the rhythms of dance. In 'Prosody' in *The Princeton Encyclopedia of Poetry and Poetics*, La Drière writes: (La Drière 1975: 669-677)

> It is with the rhythmic structure of the dance that the verbal rhythms typical of verse have most direct affinity; this is not strange, since speech like the dance is an organization of bodily movements, including those of the specialized 'vocal' organs, and it is an ordering of the physical movements and pressures which produce sounds, even more than of the physical motion or vibration which constitutes the sound, that is the basis of rhythm in speech.

When a chant accompanies a dance, then the two must have a similar rhythm, but the physiology and dynamics of the vocal tract are unlike those of the body in dancing; and when poetry is independent of dancing it does not follow the rhythms of dance.

Emerson relates metre, or rhythm, to pulse-rate and breathing in his essay, 'Poetry and Imagination': (Emerson s.d.: 584) "Metre begins with pulse-beat, and the length of lines in songs and poems is determined by the inhalation and exhalation of the lungs". William Empson in the first chapter of *Seven Types of Ambiguity*, first published in 1930, makes a similar comparison of the rhythms of poetry and the reader's pulse-rate: (Empson 1984: 30)

> a rhythmic beat taken faster than the pulse seems controllable, exhilarating, and not to demand intimate sympathy; a rhythmic beat almost synchronous with the pulse seems sincere and to demand intimate sympathy; while a rhythmic beat slower than the pulse, like a funeral bell, seems portentous and uncontrollable.

Charles Olson, too, relates breath and breathing to the making of poems. His 'Projective Verse', first published in 'Poetry New York' 3 in 1950 and reprinted in *Modern Poets on Modern Poetry*, begins as a manifesto: (Olson 1966: 271)

> Verse now, 1950, if it is to go ahead, if it is to be of *essential* use, must, I take it, catch up and put into itself certain laws and possibilities of the breath, of the breathing of the man who writes as well as of his listenings.

Olson then stresses the kinetics of poetry: "A poem is energy transferred from where the poet got it [...] by way of the poem itself to, all the way over to, the reader". He explains this in mechanistic terms; the poem, he insists, "must, at all points, be a high energy-construct and, at all points, an energy-discharge". He then relates breath and breathing to the syllable, and he says of the syllable: "It is the king and pin of versification", but he does not discuss the beats and sounds, the rhythms and phonetics of syllables.

As Olson proceeds, 'Projective Verse' becomes less a manifesto and more an exploration of aspects of the creative process and of the art and craft of poetry. He gives the syllable its context: it is born "from the union of the mind and the ear". He seems to lapse into the language of manifesto with the formulas: (Olson 1966: 275)

> the HEAD by way of the Ear, to the SYLLABLE
> the HEART, by way of the BREATH, to the LINE

But his formulas introduce new concepts: hearing is now as important as breathing, and the line as important as the syllable: "it is the LINE that's the baby that gets, as the poem is getting made, the attention, the control, that it is right here, in the line, that the shaping takes place, each moment of the going". The control and shaping are "The dance of the intellect", the acts of a mind engaged in serious play. Alternating from assertions to questions, Olson asks: "So, is it not the PLAY of a mind we are after?" "And the threshing floor for the dance? Is it anything but the LINE?" (Olson 1966: 275) Later in 'Projective Verse' he makes the assertion: "the LAW OF THE LINE, which projective verse creates, must be hewn to, obeyed". (Olson 1966: 277)

Olson's and Empson's analogies seem to have a common-sense plausibility, but the rhythms of poetry are not derived from or influenced by the physiological rhythm of pulse, heart, or breathing; they are related to the rhythms of speech, which are determined by the pronunciations of words, especially the patterns of stressed and unstressed syllables, and the pitch of intonation contours. Pulse-rate, heartbeat, and rate of breathing are controlled by the autonomic nervous system, which usually functions autonomously – hence the name – and nonconsciously. All three – pulse-rate, heartbeat and breathing – differ from each other and are individually variable rhythms; our pulse-rate, heartbeat and breathing vary according to our state of body and mind. Rhythm in poetry is a product of the poet's craft and artistry; it is shaped and re-shaped by the poet until it is an integral part of the finished poem. Readers may be unaware of this; indeed, some poets are not fully aware of the ways in which they create rhythm, but neither poets nor readers relate their pulse-rate, heartbeat, or rate of breathing to the rhythm of the poem.

Richards makes an exaggerated claim for the power of rhythm in 'The Command of Life', Chapter IV of *Science and Poetry* in *The Great Critics*, when he states that a false or inferior poem can be iden-

tified by a poet's use of rhythm: (Richards 1951: 750) "Characteristi-
cally its rhythm will give it away. For rhythm is no matter of tricks
with syllables, but directly reflects personality." Spender, too, makes an
exaggerated claim for the power of rhythm. In 'The Seminal Image' in
*The Struggle of the Modern*, he writes: (Spender 1963: 112) "Rhythm
carries the tone of the inner personality". The concept of an inner per-
sonality is similar to the concept of the poetic self, but the idea of the
inner personality having a tone, and the associated idea of the power
of rhythm to express that tone, are hard to accept. Spender adds: "It
[rhythm] is the least analysable element in a poem: the invisible quality
in which the poet exists". But rhythm can often be analyzed, measured;
and one could argue that other elements in a poem – meanings, music,
imagination, and vision – are less analyzable than rhythm. There is little
to be gained from dismantling a poem to try to show that the poet's
presence is stronger in one element of the poem than another; but if we
were to make such an attempt, then we would argue that the poet exists
as much in the other elements of a poem as in the rhythm.

Graham Dunstan Martin offers an original, precisely reasoned, but
ultimately unconvincing comparison of the rhythms of poetry and jazz.
In 'Some Varieties of Oddness' in *Language Truth and Poetry* Martin
writes: (Martin 975: 171)

> If verse is a music, it is certainly more like jazz than classical music, in
> that it presupposes a basic underlying rhythm (audible in verse only in
> the mind's ear; whereas the drums or the double bass keep it steadily
> audible in jazz), above which the actual verbal or melodic line moves
> in syncopation.

Syncopation exists in poetry when, even within a regular rhythm, there
is an irregular occurrence of beats from line to line. But the music of
poetry is not the same as music itself; and the rhythms of poetry are
related not to the rhythms of music but to the rhythms of speech, and
are thus related to the pronunciation of words and word-clusters. In
his carefully detailed comparison of the rhythms of poetry and jazz,
Martin names only one musician, the tenor saxophonist, Lester Young
(1909-59), who represents only one style, sometimes known as main-
stream, of the many contrasting styles of jazz. Rhythm in poetry could
be compared to rhythm in music, but the tempos in jazz, from the blues

to the racing tempos introduced by the founders of the bop movement, Charlie Parker and Dizzy (John Birks) Gillespie, are more varied and extreme than the tempos at which one reads poetry. Martin illustrates his case by quoting in full Cummings' poem, 'ygUDuh' but, as the chapter on poetic voice has shown, the lurching, irregular rhythms of that satirical monologue are designed to echo the speech of a drunken, uneducated racist.

The claims made by Pound, by Eliot in his essay on Arnold, by Olson, Empson, Spender, and Martin are sometimes daring but they are mistaken. Rhythm cannot express precise shades of emotion; it does not operate only at a nonconscious level; it cannot express the poet's inner personality; and it is not similar to the rhythms of jazz. How, then, does the poet create rhythm, and what can rhythm actually do in a poem? I shall identify the properties of rhythm as precisely as possible, because the subject is widely misunderstood.

## Fixity and Flux

Coleridge reveals part of the secret of rhythm in poetry when he writes in Chapter XVIII of *Biographia Literaria*: (Coleridge 1956: 207)

> As far as metre acts in and for itself, it tends to increase the vivacity and susceptibility both of the general feelings and the attention. This effect it produces by the continued excitement of surprise, and by the quick reciprocations of curiosity still gratified and still excited, which are too slight indeed to be at any one moment objects of distinct consciousness, yet become considerable in their aggregate influence.

His use of the word, "metre", clearly includes the idea of rhythm generally, and not only strictly metrical poetry. The reader may not be conscious of the rhythm at any one point in a poem but he feels the cumulative effect, an effect Coleridge identifies not as repetition but an alternating satisfaction and expectancy. His phrase, "quick reciprocations", gives the impression of rhythm and counter-rhythm; and that, of course, is how rhythm works in English-language poetry. No two lines in a poem can have exactly the same rhythm unless they have the same number of stressed and unstressed syllables in exactly the same sequence. Such reduplication is possible in strictly metrical poetry, but a more common experience is to find that, in a poem in which the rhythm is regular, most lines offer slight variations on the basic rhythm.

Eliot in 'Reflections on *Vers Libre*' emphasizes the importance of this kind of rhythmic variation: (Eliot 1955: 88-9)

> But the most interesting verse which has yet been written in our lan-
> guage has been done either by taking a very simple form, like iambic
> pentameter, and constantly withdrawing from it, or by taking no form at
> all, and constantly approximating to a very simple one. It is this contrast
> between fixity and flux, this unperceived evasion of monotony, which
> is the very life of verse.

The critic, Lascelles Abercrombie, makes a similar observation in the chapter, 'The Sound of Words' in *The Theory of Poetry*, when he writes: (Abercrombie 1926: 164) "Rhythm is the alternation, at recognizable though not necessarily uniform intervals, of any variations in a sound or succession of sounds". And then he identifies the three main sources of rhythm in a language: "alternation of long or short syllables, of stressed and unstressed syllable, of syllables high or low in tone". Later in the same chapter he quotes the first three stanzas of John Clare's (Clare 1973: 316) 'The Invitation' ("Come hither, my fair one, my choice one, and rare one") and says of its rhythm: (Abercrombie 1926: 171-2) "We feel a constant pattern maintaining itself through many variations. These two things, constancy and variation, are the essential things not merely in this metre, but in the very idea of metre". And in the chapter, 'Technique', Abercrombie identifies the real basis of rhythm in poetry: (Abercrombie 1926: 100) "*syllabic sound* – the quality of vowels and consonants in combination". By "*syllabic sound*" Abercrombie does not, of course, mean a syllabic mode of composition but the pitch and stress of each syllable in a poem. Roy Fuller reaches the same conclusion in the chapter, 'Fascinating Rhythm', in *Professors and Gods: Last Oxford Lectures on Poetry* when he writes: (Fuller 1973 88-9)

> Poets do not possess the rhythmic freedom of the composer, nor can
> they take the prolix and irregular liberties of prose to tease out their

meanings. They work – all too conscious of the paths nevertheless of-
fered – in the area bounded by syntactical sense, conversational accents
and the stress patterns of the medium.

Fuller states that the sound of a poem must be tested aloud, and he
makes the subtle distinction: "And a most important part of the testing
out is to appreciate the conflicts and accords of the poem's notional
rhythm and its spoken rhythm". (Fuller 1973: 90)

When Pound returns to the question of rhythm in 'Treatise on Metre'
in *ABC of Reading* he, too, notes that the rhythms of poetry are related
to the rhythms of speech: (Pound 1951: 199)

> The writer of bad verse is a bore because he does not perceive time and
> time relations, and cannot therefore delimit them in an interesting man-
> ner, by means of longer and shorter, heavier and lighter syllables, and the
> varying qualities of sound inseparable from the words of his speech.

Robert Graves also writes of the need for rhythmic variation. In
'Harp, Anvil, Oar' in *The Crowning Privilege* he states that poetry can
be "soporific unless frequent changes occur in the metre". And Denise
Levertov in 'Some Notes on Organic Form' in *New & Selected Essays*
finds the same feature: (Levertov 1992: 72) "some rhythmic norm pecu-
liar to a particular poem, from which the individual lines depart and to
which they return". Graves is less convincing when he extends the idea
from the poem to the poet. In 'Poets And Gleemen' in *The White God-
dess* he states (Graves 1948: 17) that twentieth-century poets would
agree that there is a metrical norm to which a poet relates his personal
rhythm, and that the norm serves to define a poet's rhythmic idiosyncra-
sies. Perhaps what Graves calls personal rhythm overlaps with personal
poetic voice; it would take an exceptionally sensitive ear to identify
twentieth-century poets by their use of rhythm alone.

We usually read poetry, whether silently or aloud, at a slower pace
than we read prose, and at this slower pace we can be more aware of
the word, its sound, echoes, and connotations. But rhythm can also be
used to quicken the pace of a poem. I. A. Richards notes in 'Poem XI' in
*Practical Criticism*: (Richards 1960: 137) "A poet may imitate the mo-
tion of his subject by the motion of his verse." Levertov, too, discusses
the extent to which rhythm can reflect the subject of a poem. In 'Some

Notes on Organic Form', she states: (Levertov 1992: 71) "In organic
poetry the metric movement, the measure, is the direct expression of the
movement of perception". At first thought the claim seems excessive.
Surely poetic perception can be expressed only through words. But
when one notes that Levertov is not referring to the content or substance
of perception but to its movement, that is, the fluctuating flow of ide-
ation in a poem, then one sees that rhythm can be directly related to that
flow. Levertov gives clearer expression to the link between rhythm and
the flow of ideation when she adds: "The varying speed and gait of the
different strands of perception within an experience (I think of strands
of seaweed moving within a wave) result in counterpointed measures".
When rhythm is adapted to reflect changes in the tempo and the mode
of transition from one image or idea to another, then a counterpointing
of rhythm, and of ideation, can be achieved. Coleridge's "quick recip-
rocations", Eliot's "fixity and flux", and Levertov's "counterpointed
measures" express what rhythm actually does in poetry.

There are occasions when rhythm seems more complex and subtle than
the linguistic properties from which it is formed; even so, in a study
such as this an attempt must be made to show how these properties in-
teract to produce rhythm. The linguistic properties are these: the lengths
and pronunciations of words, the structures of phrases, clauses, and
sentences, and the punctuation that divides these syntactic units. And,
as Levertov notes, rhythm is also influenced by the pace of the flow of
ideation, that is, the sequential patterns of images and ideas that give a
poem a rhythmic as well as a semantic structure; and is influenced, too,
by the lengths of the lines of a poem, the use of stanzas, and by internal
structures or figures within the complete poem.

The lengths and pronunciations of words have an obvious effect
on rhythm: every syllable of every word in English is a stressed or
unstressed beat, and the patterns of beats from line to line in a poem
are the basic components of rhythm. A syllable usually has a vowel
as its nucleus and one or more consonants before or after the vowel.
In speech, the audible stress that is placed on a particular syllable is
determined by the vocal force produced by the speaker, that is, the rate
and pressure of air flowing through the vocal tract. Changes in stress

are usually accompanied by changes in the loudness, the pitch, and the length of time, or duration, taken to utter the syllable. Stressed vowels are usually pronounced louder, for a longer duration, and at a different pitch from unstressed sounds; the change of pitch, higher or lower, varies from one dialect to another and from one speaker to another.

Every syllable has a pitch, a sound that can range from high to low on a tonal scale. Exceptions appear in oratorio and occasionally opera when a single syllable is repeated as different notes on a musical scale. Although pitch is essentially a musical, or tonal, rather than a rhythmic effect, it is inseparable from rhythm because it is produced by the same linguistic units as rhythm. In spoken English, each syllable and most alphabetical characters in every word are speech sounds, or phonemes, with an agreed sound value, or phonetic value, in standard spoken English. The spoken standard varies from one country to another: Britain, America, Australia. Every line in a poem, or a syntactic unit within a line, or a unit that runs from one line to the next, produces a sequence of pitches that is sometimes known as an intonation contour. The combined sounds of the phonemes and the intonation contours produce the rhythm and the music of a poem; they also reflect the phonology, that is, the characteristic sounds of a language and its dialects.

Human awareness of rhythm and phonology is probably older than speech, as the chapter, 'Poetry and Music', has shown. The fact that our minds are programmed for rhythm and phonology could explain why strictly rhyming metrical poetry, or rhyming poetry with a regular rhythm, can be so insinuative. Even when such poetry is not memorable, it can be memorizable, lodging in the reader's mind more readily and lastingly than poetry that has no clear pattern of rhythm or rhyme. The experience is so widespread that one must conclude that the language areas of the brain, along with memory and the auditory imagination, are more receptive to rhyme and regular rhythm than to free verse and amorphous poetry. It is the auditory imagination that allows the silent reader to experience the rhythm and music of a poem by relating the sound system of the language to the writing system.

A line or sequence of lines consisting only or mainly of monosyllabic words is likely to have a firmer, slower and more insistent beat than a sequence of lines containing several polysyllabic words, because a line of monosyllables is likely to have a greater number of stressed syllables, whereas most polysyllabic words have only one stressed syllable and two or more unstressed syllables. Musically, a line with a high proportion of monosyllables will have a more level intonation contour, that is, fewer fluctuations of pitch, than lines with polysyllabic words. A line consisting mainly of monosyllables is more likely than a line containing polysyllables to end with a stressed beat; the final syllable of a polysyllabic word is not usually stressed.

Monosyllabism is so obvious a feature of the language that it seems unremarkable, but it affects the rhythms of all English-language poetry. The point is not that there are more monosyllabic words than disyllabic and polysyllabic words in English, but that most forms of English speech and writing must include a high proportion of monosyllabic words. Examples are the present tense and simple past tense of the most frequently used verbs in English; colloquial fusions such as "can't" and "they're"; the standard non-medical nouns for most parts of the anatomy; all pronouns except the reflexives such as "himself" and "themselves"; the most frequently used adjectives; some prepositions and prepositional adverbs such as "in" and "down"; the simpler conjunctions; determiners such as "each" and "few".

The rhythmic unit and the intonation contour often coincide with the phrase, clause, or sentence that forms the syntactic unit. A syntactic unit can occasionally be a single word, for example, an imperative verb, "Jump!", but a rhythmic unit usually consists of two or more beats, and an intonation contour usually spans several words. A monosyllabic word, then, is seldom a complete rhythmic unit and cannot be an intonation contour. A polysyllabic word, by contrast, is itself a rhythmic unit because it has three or more syllables, including at least one stressed syllable; and because two or more of its syllables are likely to vary in pitch, a polysyllabic word is also an intonation contour in miniature. Monosyllabic and polysyllabic words also influence the length of a line, or what is sometimes called eye-rhythm, for this simple reason: if a line consisting mainly of monosyllabic words has the same number of beats, either stressed or unstressed, as a line that includes one or more polysyllables, the line of monosyllables will usually be longer because of the spaces between each word.

# Arrhythmia and Free Verse

Knowledge of rhythm is essential for the poet. A poet who is unaware of the real properties of rhythm might also be unaware of how to achieve, and how to avoid, some of the effects discussed in this chapter. The rhythm of a poem can be created intuitively, and intuition plays an important part in the making of a poem; but rhythm should also be part of the poet's conscious knowledge, because it is the conscious mind that is responsible for the final version of the poem. Knowledge and understanding are not the enemies but the allies of intuitive creativity.

The poet who fails to cultivate the craft of rhythm runs the risk of arrhythmia, that is, arbitrary sequences of beats that might be irrelevant to the thought and feeling, the diction and imagery, the true experience in the poem. Arrhythmia can be effective in poems that speak of breakdown, chaos, hysteria; effective, for example, in representing the terrified flailings of a drowning man or the fragmented strands of thought and feeling in the mind of someone stricken by grief. In other contexts, arrhythmia might be seen as incompetence or negligence. If the poet disregards the rhythms of the language, the rhythms that are present in every syntactic structure, every intonation contour and every polysyllabic word; if the rhythms of the poem's lines and stanzas do not support the central experience in the poem; if there is no rhythmic recurrence, then essential elements of the poem will be missing. The result is often an amorphous structure that defies the rhythms of the English language. Amorphous poems are typeset so that groups of words that form semantic, syntactic, or rhythmic structures are broken across two or more lines and sometimes across two or more stanzas; but no artistic purpose is served by breaking a unit across two stanzas when the stanzas are already irregular.

These tricks of typesetting compound the irregularity to produce absurdly breathless statements. As Levertov writes in 'Technique and Tune-Up' in *New & Selected Essays*: (Levertov 1992: 100) "If you are not consistent in your use of any device, the reader will not know if something is merely a typographical error or is meant to contribute – as everything, down to the last hyphen, should – to the poem". A poetry that is so divorced from the naturally occurring rhythms and the standard syntax of the language is partly divorced from language itself and is as distorted and artificial a use of language as a poetry of rigid, alien meters. Every original poem makes its own unique impression in the mind of the reader. If a poet rejects some of the main features of poetry – rhyme and other musical effects, recurring rhythm, syntactic structures and intonation contours that are natural to a language – then the poem is likely to make a narrower impression in the reader's mind. In these respects, Imagist poetry makes a lesser demand and offers a lesser reward.

Some of the Imagists deluded themselves into thinking that they had solved the mystery of poetry, or had at least mastered its essential principles, as the chapter, 'Poetry and Music', has shown. The same delusion occurs in the minds of members of Symbolist, Surrealist, Vorticist, Apocalyptist, and other ideological schools and movements of poetry. But as Laura Riding and Robert Graves state in 'The Problem of Form and Subject-matter' in *A Survey of Modernist Poetry*: (Riding and Graves 2002: 22) "No genuine poet or artist ever called himself after a theory or invented a name for a theory".

In the March 1913 issue of the journal, *Poetry*, and quoted in *Imagist Poetry*, F. S. Flint, one of the founders of Imagism, claimed that part of the secret of poetry was this: (Flint 1972: 18) "As regarding rhythm: to compose in sequence of the musical phrase, not in sequence of a metronome". Similar claims about music and poetry are made by Pound and Williams, but the musical effects of poetry, based as they are in language, are different from the melodies and harmonies of music. The Imagists and their followers abandoned the natural rhythms and some of the natural musical properties of poetry in the mistaken belief that they were investing their poems with the properties of music itself.

Williams is an original, daringly innovative poet whose daring and innovation become conventionalized and threaten his originality, partly because of his idiosyncratic attitudes to poetic form. His views on poetic content reflect his search for authenticity and individuality. In 'Notes in Diary Form' in his *Selected Essays* he states: (Williams 1969: 71) "The only human value of anything, writing included, is intense vision of the facts". In 'Kenneth Burke' Williams states: (Williams 1969: 132)

"The local is the only thing that is universal", a statement he repeats in 'Against the Weather: A Study of The Artist', where he insists on "the universality of the local"; and in the same essay he writes: (Williams 1969: 217) "And what is a man saying of moment as an artist when he neglects his major opportunity, to build his living, complex day into the body of his poem?" Williams regards traditional English measures of rhythm, line and stanza as poetic imperialism, but his idiosyncratic views on poetic form are restricting. In 'The Tortuous Straightness of Chas Henri Ford' in *Selected Essays* he writes: (Williams 1969: 236) "To me the sonnet form is thoroughly banal because it is a word in itself whose meaning is definitely fascistic". His view is illustrated by the poems in his sequence, *Three Sonnets* in (Williams 1988 volume 2: 73) they are not in sonnet form.

Williams regards the sonnet form as a product of an alien, tyrannical culture; for some poets the appeal of the sonnet is the opportunity for original disciplined play. In the first sonnet in *Miscellaneous Sonnets I* Wordsworth writes: (Wordsworth 1956: 199)

> In sundry moods, 'twas pastime to be bound
> Within the Sonnet's scanty plot of ground.

And in the first sonnet in *Miscellaneous Sonnets II* he defends the sonnet form in the lines: (Wordsworth 1956: 206)

> Scorn not the Sonnet, Critic, you have frowned
> Mindless of its just honours; with this key
> Shakespeare unlocked his heart.

Williams dismisses the sonnet form again in the essay, 'Author's Introduction': "To me all sonnets say the same thing of no importance". And in the next paragraph he writes: (Williams 1969: 257)

> There is no poetry of distinction without formal invention, for it is in the intimate form that works of art achieve their exact meaning, in which they most resemble the machine, to give language its highest dignity, its illumination in the environment to which it is native.

A writer who believes that works of art achieve their exact meaning when they most resemble a machine might well lead himself into a mechanistic concept of poetic rhythm and form.

Williams tries to establish a poetic identity not only through poetic voice and vision but also through the visual pattern of the poem on the page; and like F. S. Flint, he believed that he could replace some linguistic features of poetry with the features of music. In a letter written in 1954 to his fellow-poet, Richard Eberhart, and published as 'A New Measure' in *Modern Poets on Modern Poetry*, Williams writes: (Williams 1966: 71)

> By its *music* shall the best of modern verse be known and the resources
> of music. The refinement of the poem, its subtlety, is not to be known
> by the elevation of words but – the words don't so much matter – by the
> resources of the music.

But as the chapter on poetry and music has shown, the resources of music are not available to the poet. Much of Williams' poetry is a fascinating but sometimes mistaken attempt to escape from the natural rhythms and music of the English language, in his case, American English. The attempt is mistaken because, as this chapter has emphasized, a poetry that rejects the natural properties of a language is not entirely of that language, and in rejecting the properties of language the poet also rejects the resources of language. No poet is cleverer or wiser than the language in which he writes. A few poets – Chaucer, Shakespeare, and Wordsworth certainly, and Eliot to a lesser extent – can influence the language and the modes of thought that are possible in it, but no writer is greater than the language.

Two of Williams' collections, *The Desert Music* and *Journey to Love* are typeset in such a way – the second line indented by six to ten spaces, or ems, from the first, and the third line indented from the second by the same amount of space – that the visual rhythm is stepped like a staircase. For example, in 'To Daphne and Virginia' in *The Desert Music*, Williams writes of poetry: (Williams 1988: 346-7)

The mind
    lives there. It is uncertain,

can trick and leave us
agonized. But for resources
what can equal it?
There is nothing. We
should be lost
without its wings to
fly off upon.

Williams presents the reader with the dilemma: to follow the rhythm of the typesetting, or to follow the meanings that emerge from the linguistic rhythms of the stressed and unstressed syllables of the words, from the syntax and the punctuation, and from the semantics. The typesetting produces linguistic novelty; the more natural linear way of reading reveals eloquent and impassioned speech. In the title sequence of his late collection, *Pictures from Brueghel*, published in 1962, a year before he died, the effect of the short lines, the broken syntax, and the absence of punctuation is to give a fragmented quality to all sections of the sequence, including sections that speak not of fragmentation but of wholeness. In 'The Poem as a Field of Action' in *Selected Essays,* Williams discusses Auden's poetry and concludes: (Williams 1969: 289) "I am sure the attack must be concentrated on the *rigidity of the poetic foot*". The evidence clearly shows that Williams' foot grew more rigid than Auden's.

Levertov in 'On Williams' Triadic Line, Or How to Dance on Variable Feet' in *New & Selected Essays*, discusses rhythm in Williams' poetry: (Levertov 1992: 24) "But whether or not Williams' concept and practice of the variable foot are of vital importance for modern poets and poetry in general, their significance is not 'spatial' (and thus visual) but temporal and auditory". All poetry is auditory because it is directly related to speech, and it follows that, whether the poetry is written in stress-timed or syllable-timed units, all poetry is temporal. Levertov is surely correct in saying that the significance of Williams' poetry is not spatial; that is, the visual effect of the typesetting of his lines is less important than his subjects and themes. The linear nature of our writing system gives all printed poems a spatial and visual quality; Williams sometimes tries to defy that linearity. Levertov's implicit point is that if we read a poem by Williams as a sequence of syntactic and semantic units, which is our normal way of reading any text, then we learn to see and yet ignore the idiosyncratic typesetting and enjoy the experience in the poem.

Received opinion states that poets hear, sometimes nonconsciously, the appropriate rhythm as they compose the poem, and that the rhythm evolves with the evolving poem. In fact, the creation of rhythm is often a conscious exercise in which the poet adapts the rhythm to suit the words or changes the wording of a phrase, a line, or even several lines in order to suit the rhythm. If the resulting rhythmic patterns seem natural and inevitable, that effect is as likely to have been achieved through deliberate craft and artistry as through intuition.

Arrhythmic poetry takes the form of free verse. At the beginning of the twentieth century, with the arrival of Imagism and free verse in English-language poetry, there was abrupt and fundamental change in the concept of what constitutes a poem. The popularity of arrhythmic and amorphous poetry owes much to the influence of some American experimenters with rhythm and form, notably Williams, Moore and Cummings. Their work, in turn, owes something to the small group of American and British poets who formed the Imagist school in the second decade of the twentieth century; a few of Williams' early poems appeared in the Imagist anthology, *Des Imagistes* in 1914. The Imagists associated their work with vers libre of late nineteenth-century France, even to the extent of using the French spelling, "Imagiste", to identify their work. Eliot detects an influence on the vers libre poets; in 'The Unity of European Culture' in *Notes towards the Definition of Culture* he writes: (Eliot 1948: 112) "this French movement itself owed a great deal to an American of Irish extraction: Edgar Allan Poe".

In the Preface to *Some Imagist Poetry*, first published in 1916 and reprinted as an appendix to *Imagist Poetry*, the editors identify Imagist poetry with vers libre, and they state: (Jones, P 1972: 139)

> The unit in vers libre is not the foot, the number of syllables, the quantity, [duration of the sound of a syllable] or the line. The unit is the strophe, which may be the whole poem, or may be only a part. Each strophe is a complete circle: in fact, the meaning of the Greek word 'strophe' is

simply that part of the poem which was recited while the chorus were making a turn around the altar set up in the centre of the theatre. The simile of the circle is more than a simile, therefore; it is a fact.

The editors are deluded or deceitful. In 1916 the principal meaning of the word, "strophe", in poetry was a number of lines forming an internal figure within the overall structure of the poem; but the editors deny that the poetic line is a unit, and so they make the ludicrous comparison of an Imagist poem and the performance of the chorus in classical Greek theatre.

The conclusion in the quotation above, that the simile of the circle is not a simile but a fact, is clearly false; no poem that uses a linear writing system, not even a poem that is typeset to look like a circle on the page, is an actual circle. A poem with a circular train of ideation, a poem, that is, that begins and ends with the same image or idea, could be described as a semantic and metaphorical circle. But that is not the argument of the editors of *Some Imagist Poetry;* the 1916 Preface is an attempt to give Imagist poetry an authority and a provenance that it does not have.

Visual effects in poetry can be achieved legitimately through the typographical patterns produced by the lengths of lines and stanzas. Poems that assume recognizable visual patterns – they are variously known as pattern poetry, visual poetry or concrete poetry – are usually the result of the poet's serious professional play. An example from the early seventeenth century is George Herbert's short poem, 'Easter Wings', (Herbert 1863: 36) in which the two pairs of stanzas resemble two angels' wings, or what one imagines angels' wings to be, flying from right to left across the page. Herbert's 'The Altar' (Herbert 1863: 17) has a base, or pedestal, a column and a top; his 'Confusion' (Herbert 1863: 283) has four lucid lines at its centre, with short, abruptly broken confused lines above and below. An example from the mid-twentieth century is Dylan Thomas's twelve-poem sequence, *Vision and Prayer*, (Thomas, D. 1956: 137-48) where the first six poems are diamond-shaped and the last six are cruciform. The language of *Vision and Prayer* might strike the modern reader as rather bombastic, but the sequence is an effective declaration, or protestation, of faith.

Edwin Morgan plays witty games with language and poetic form in 'French Persian Cats Having a Ball' (Morgan 1968: 27), 'The Chaffinch

Map of Scotland' (Morgan 1968: 52), 'Construction for I. K. Brunel' (Morgan 1968: 70) and other poems in *The Second Life*. One of the most ingeniously playful sequences of visual poems in English is John Hollander's *Types of Shape* with its skeleton key (Hollander 1991: 2), electric light bulb, (Hollander 1991:4) umbrella, (Hollander 1991:12) and the intricate elegance of a swan sailing on its reflection, (Hollander 1991:36) as well the more obvious, but no less technically demanding, figures of a bell, a heart, a star, and a Christmas tree. All these poems are semantic as well as visual structures; they include patterns of thought and emotion as well as imagery. They also demonstrate the resources of the typewriter and the inventiveness of the poet-typist.

Eliot was one of the earliest objectors to the vers libre of Imagism. In 'Reflections on Vers Libre' he writes: (Eliot 1955: 87-8) "If vers libre is a genuine verse form it will have a positive definition. And I can define it only in negatives: (1) absence of pattern, (2) absence of rhythm, (3) absence of metre". The English term, "free verse", a literal translation of "vers libre", began to be applied to Imagist poetry. When Eliot returns to the question of free verse in 'The Music of Poetry', he recalls his essay of 1917, and he adds: (Eliot 1958: 65)

> No one has better cause to know than I, that a great deal of bad prose has been written under the name of free verse: though whether its authors wrote bad prose or bad verse, or bad verse in one style or in another, seems to me a matter of indifference. But only a bad poet would welcome free verse as a liberation from form.

For some of the original Imagists and for most of their followers, the attraction of free verse is exactly that: it invites a liberation from form. Eliot regards free-verse poets as bad poets not only because of their technical incompetence, whether that incompetence is wilful or the result of a lack of craft, but also because the incompetence prevents them from writing a well made poem; and a poem that is not well made, a poem that does not respect the properties of the language in which it is written, cannot be honest or truthful.

Laura Riding and Robert Graves also reject the false liberation of free verse. In the chapter, 'The Problem of Form and Subject-Matter' in *A Survey of Modernist Poetry*, they write: (Riding and Graves 2002: 22) "Modern poetry, that is, is groping for some principle of self-determination to be applied to the making of the poem – not lack of government, but government from within". Riding and Graves add: "Free verse was one of the largest movements towards this end. But it has too often meant not self-government but complete laissez-faire on the part of the poet, a licence to metrical anarchy instead of a harmonious enjoyment of liberty". They refer to free verse in the past tense, "was", but amorphous poetry is more popular than ever. And in the chapter, 'Modernist Poetry and Dead Movements' in *A Survey of Modernist Poetry*, Riding and Graves write as if Imagism, too, were in the past: (Riding and Graves 2002: 56) "Imagism is one of the earliest and the most typical of these twentieth-century dead movements". But Imagist, or sub-imagist, poetry is still with us.

Although Williams was a founder of the Imagist movement he writes of the need for some kind of discipline in poetry; his discipline, as earlier paragraphs have shown, becomes too rigid. In the essay, 'Against the Weather – A Study of the Artist', he writes: (Williams 1969: 212) "Verse is measure, there is no free verse". Williams returns to the question in 'On Measure – Statement for Cid Corman', where he writes: (Williams 1969: 339) "No verse can be free, it must be governed by some measure, but not by the old measure. [...] We have to return to some measure but a measure consonant with our time and not a mode so rotten that it stinks". Williams did not, of course, "return" to a measure; he devised measures of his own. In the final paragraph of 'On Measure' he states: "Without measure we are lost". Williams also objects to the illusory freedom of syllabic verse. In 'Caviar and Bread Again – A Warning to the New Writer' he writes ironically: (Williams 1969: 103) "Let's play tiddly-winks with the syllable".

Conrad Aitken also objects to syllabic verse. In 'Poetry and the Mind of Modern Man' in *Poets on Poetry* he writes: (Aitken 1966: 6)

> As for form, here again I have always maintained that, as poetry is an art, and perhaps the highest, it should use every prosodic and linguistic device at its disposal; I cannot subscribe to the theory that a mere counting of syllables can be substituted for verse.

Muir, like Eliot, Riding, Graves, Williams and Aitken, deplores the abandonment of form in free verse. In 'Poetry and the Poet' in *The Estate of Poetry,* Muir writes: (Muir 1962: 78-9)

> The main defect of free verse is monotony; it can be used apparently for any subject and any mood; there is no escape for the writer of free verse except into free verse. The whole world of forms, the whole variety of poetic expression, lie outside. The poet, it seems to me, attains his freedom through some given form or set of forms.

The importance of form lies, of course, not only in the rhythmic and visual patterns it produces but also in the ways in which it shapes and structures, that is, gives form to, the thought and emotion in the poem. The formless expression of thought and emotion, along with the rejection of the genuine rhythmic and musical properties of the English language, inevitably results in amorphous poetry.

Spender, too, rejects Imagism and free verse. In the chapter, 'Poetic Moderns and Prose Contemporaries' in *The Struggle of the Modern*, he notes the disproportionate influence of Imagism: (Spender 1963: 116)

> One reason why imagism remains historically important, despite the slight production of the imagists, may be that as a method, a modus operandi, it demolished a frontier between poetry and prose. For if nothing except the image matters, and form, music, rhythm, rhyme are of secondary importance, then there is no boundary dividing imagist prose and imagist poetry, except perhaps the degree of concentration of the imagery.

What is perhaps more important than the boundary between poetry and prose, which can be bridged legitimately by the prose poem and by rhythmic and melodic prose, is that a written statement that lacks form, rhythm and music is likely to be so deficient in craft and artistry that it cannot be regarded as a work of literature but merely as a piece of writing. Auden makes a more robust and colourful rejection of free verse, but his objection is essentially the same as those already noted: an absence of the order that is created by artistry and craft. In 'Writing' in *The Dyer's Hand* Auden states: (Auden 1963: 22)

> The poet who writes 'free verse' is like Robinson Crusoe on his desert island: he must do all his cooking, laundry and darning for himself. In a few exceptional cases, this manly independence produces something original and impressive, but more often the result is squalor – dirty sheets on the unmade bed and empty bottles on the unswept floor.

Levertov makes an absolute distinction between a poetry of form and an amorphous poetry. In 'On the Need for New Terms' in *New & Selected Essays*, she writes: (Levertov 1992: 77) "My passion is for the vertebrate and cohesive in all art. I believe any distinction between form and that which lacks form can only be a distinction of art from non-art, not kinds of art". There is no escape from art and craft except into amorphous, or invertebrate, statements that are sometimes not only escapes from form but from poetry itself. Despite that body of hostile opinion, from the middle of the twentieth century a growing number of English-language poets adopted free verse as their main mode of expression.

The Imagists' greatest influence lies in their abandonment of the poetic line and their attack on the very concept of the line; but the line is an inexhaustible, and inexhaustibly variable, resource.

## Punctuating Rhythm

Punctuation has an obvious effect on rhythm because every punctuation mark except the hyphen indicates a pause or division in a text. When the ends of two or more syntactic units coincide with the ends of two or more lines, when the lines have the same or a similar number of syllables, and when the lines are end-stopped, that is, with punctuation marks at the ends, then the rhythm will be regular, as in this sequence: (Aitchison a 1998: 43)

> The willow man, the keeper of the songs,
> The healer, the astronomer and the priest –
> The Indian told me how his kinsmen died:
> One taken by wolves and one crushed by a tree;
> "Eaten by tree" was what the Indian said.

> Another entered the river and was drowned,
> And one was seized by a thunderbolt, he said.

The lines are not rhythmically identical because, as an earlier chapter has shown, no two lines can have exactly the same pattern of rhythm unless they have exactly the same sequence of stressed and unstressed syllables; the seven-line sequence above has that measured quality of repetition with variations. The underlying pattern is iambic pentameter, the ten-syllable, or decasyllabic, line, but each line has a slightly different pattern of beats, and four of the lines have eleven syllables. Each of the seven lines above is mid-stopped as well as end-stopped: the pause, or caesura, within the line is the result of punctuation in lines 1, 2, 5, and 7, whereas lines 3, 4, and 6 have caesuras that are produced by syntactic structures. The rhythmic pattern produced by the end-stops and the caesuras, which are indicated by vertical lines, is this:

> The willow man,| the keeper of the songs,
> The healer,| the astronomer| and the priest -
> The Indian told me| how his kinsmen died:
> One taken by wolves| and one crushed by a tree;
> "Eaten by tree"| was what the Indian said.
> Another entered the river| and was drowned,
> And one was seized by a thunderbolt,| he said.

The rhythms of the groups of words separated by vertical lines are similar to the rhythms produced by word-clusters in speech; that is, there are fused sequences of words, with pauses between the clusters rather than between individual words.

When two or more lines are not end-stopped but run-on, a technique sometimes known as enjambment, or when the syntactic unit and thus the meaning it contains also runs on from the end of one line into the next, and when the poem is read according to the syntax and punctuation, then an undulating or even an irregular rhythm can be produced, especially if the lines have unequal numbers of syllables, as in this sequence: (Aitchison a 1990: 5)

> Year after year the rains and the freezings and thawings
> wash away layers of soil.

Gravel goes rattling down the flooded gullies.
When the land dries out at the end of May
more stone has been laid bare,
more knuckles and shoulder blades of stone
have broken through the hill
like bones from a hundred shallow graves.

The alternating length of line creates a slightly contrapuntal tension, but the run-on lines produce a continuity of meaning that unifies the lines, in contrast to the kind of unity produced by regular rhythm and end-stopped lines. Rhythm is a vital part of a poem's effect and thus a vital part of its meaning.

# 18

# Poetry and Reality

CONCEPTS OF REALITY AND POETRY VARY over time. At the beginning of the twentieth century A. C. Bradley in 'Poetry for Poetry's Sake' in *Oxford Lectures on Poetry* wrote of the reality of poetry in these terms: (Bradley 1909: 5)

> For its nature is not to be a part, nor yet a copy, of the real world (as we commonly understand that phrase), but to be a world by itself, independent, complete, autonomous: and to possess it fully you must enter that world, conform to its laws, and ignore for the time being the beliefs, aims, and particular conditions which belong to you in the other world of reality.

Bradley is saying that poetry exists in areas of mind and modes of thought that are separate from everyday life. He is also saying that poetry is to some extent an escape from the world of external physical reality, an attitude that remains attractive to some poets, critics and readers even today. But within ten years of the publication of the *Oxford Lectures*, the new poets, Siegfried Sassoon, Wilfred Owen, Isaac Rosenberg and others, had made external physical realities – the intimacies and monstrosities of war – the main subjects of their poems, and since that time British and American poetry has seldom strayed far from the physically real world. When that world is represented in poetry, then it is a product of the mind of the poet, and we now know with certainty what Bradley could not have known: the mind is directly related to the neurophysiology of the brain, and so the mind has its basis in physical reality. Knowing these things, we also know that what occurs inside the mind is as real as what occurs outside it. The real world, real life, includes the world and the life of the mind.

One of the achievements of neuroscience of particular interest to the poet is the confirmation that external physical reality can have no significance for humans until it has been processed by the human brain. In the chapter, 'Do Martians See Red?' in *Phantoms in the Brain* – the title of the book is a playful comment on Gilbert Ryle's 'the dogma of the ghost in the machine' (Ryle 1990: 17) in the chapter, 'Descartes' Myth' in Ryle's *The Concept of Mind*, first published in 1949 – the neurologist, V. S. Ramachandran, writes: (Ramachandran 1999: 227-8)

> Everything I have learned from the intensive study of both normal people and patients who have sustained damage to various parts of their brains points to an unsettling notion: that you create your own 'reality' from mere fragments of information, that what you 'see' is a reliable – but not always accurate – representation of what exists in the world

Writing from a different scientific viewpoint, Richard Dawkins reaches a similar conclusion. In the chapter, 'A Much Needed Gap' in *The God Delusion*, Dawkins states: (Dawkins 2006: 371) "What we see of the real world is not the unvarnished real world but a *model* of the real world, regulated and adjusted by sense data – a model that is constructed so that it is useful for dealing with the real world". The reality we make is reliable because of its consistency from day to day and from one person to another; the reality may not be wholly accurate because our sense perceptions, and our interpretations of these perceptions, are limited.

In confirming the neurophysiological basis of language, neuroscience has exposed the irrelevance of that ancient theory of reality, material dualism, which states that reality consists only of physical, material things, and that the mind and its functions are outside the bounds of that reality. Dualism is so persistent a mental condition and takes so many forms that it must reflect a dichotomy of mind that leads to categorical, either-or, right- or- wrong, modes of thought. But if we accept that language processing and all other functions of mind have a neurophysiological substrate, then material dualism becomes a redundant concept because mind, too, has its basis in matter. If, on the other hand, we reject the wider concept of reality and insist on dualism, then we are faced with the old dilemma:  If mind has no basis in physical reality, where and how does it exist? Because of our possession of mind, human nature is partly detached from the natural world; but if we argue that the mind does not exist in the natural world, then we are led to attribute a supernatural existence to the mind. Neuroscience has partly resolved the dilemma by showing us that, although the external world might seem the more substantial, we can know that world only through our mental representations of it.

Questions about external physical reality and the inner physical reality of the mind that seemed unanswerable a generation ago, and unaskable to the generation before that, are being answered as scientists and technologists devise new machines that can measure what was once immeasurable: planets almost infinitely remote in space and time, neurons almost infinitely numerous in the brain. But even if all physical questions were answered, the debate about the nature of reality would continue and the same questions would continue to be asked by succeeding generations because we are ineluctably drawn to relate inner realities of mind to outer realities. And now that some questions have been answered, we find that human perception of reality is limited. We know, for example, that dogs have a more acute sense of hearing and smell than humans, that hawks have a more acute sense of sight, that owls and other nocturnal creatures can see in the dark, that migratory birds have an unerring sense of direction, and that bats have a natural form of radar. Since human sensory perception in ordinary circumstances is limited in these and perhaps other ways, how much of external physical reality do we fail to perceive? Since human perception is so closely linked to cognition, and since there are limits to the power of the human brain and mind, how much reality are we incapable of conceiving? There is also a natural process of mind that could be called dematerialization, a tendency to convert physical reality into abstractions and then to interpret new experience through these abstractions. These questions are metaphysical as well as physical, and in ordinary human circumstances each generation is impelled to ask the same questions about the nature of reality. Much is already known about our perception of physical reality.

As the chapter, 'Imagery', has shown, when our sensory receptors detect a stimulus, they make the first of a series of transductions through which the original signal is successively decoded and re-encoded as it travels along the neural pathways to the appropriate cortex, where the representation of external reality is formed and where we become conscious of that representation. The correspondence between the reality in the mind and the external reality of the physical world is usually close and consistent; we could not survive as a species otherwise. When we add a third order of reality, the abstract symbolism of language, then we require another kind of correspondence, one that relates language to inner and outer realities. The processing of sensory stimuli is nonconscious; the writing of a poem, by contrast, is mainly a conscious effort to create a linguistic structure that represents inner and outer realities. In writing poems, poets usually find that their mental impression of external reality, although adequate for ordinary, everyday cognition, is not an adequate model for the poem; the model might have to be reformulated several times before there is a correspondence between inner and outer reality and the representation of these two orders of reality in the linguistic structure, the poem, which is itself an order of reality.

Keats had some understanding of the complexity of the process. In his letter of 8 April 1818 to Benjamin Robert Haydon he writes: (Keats 1952: 128) "The innumerable compositions and decompositions which take place between the intellect and its thousand materials before it arrives at that trembling delicate and snail-horn perception of Beauty".

In 'Words and Experience' in *Poetry in the Making*, first published in 1967, Hughes argues that the reality of some forms of experience cannot be expressed in words. He takes the example of a crow in flight – his collection, *Crow*, appeared in 1970 – and he claims: (Hughes 1994: 20) "There are no words to capture the infinite depth of crowiness in the crow's flight". To express in words the visual, spatial, and kinetic experience of a bird in flight is, indeed, a difficult task. Hughes concludes: "In a way, words are continually trying to displace our experience. And insofar as they are stronger than the raw life of our experience, and full of themselves, and all the dictionaries they have digested, they do displace it". Between these two denials, in a short flight of delightful wit, the poet creates a superb impression not only of a crow in flight but of a crow in flight as seen by Ted Hughes: (Hughes 1994: 20)

> But the ominous thing in the crow's flight, the barefaced, bandit thing,
>
> the tattered beggarly gipsy thing, the caressing and shaping yet slightly
>
> clumsy gesture of the down-stroke, as if the wings were both too heavy

and too powerful, and the headlong sort of merriment, the macabre pantomime ghoulishness and the undertaker sleekness – you could go on for a very long time with phrases of that sort and still have completely missed your instant, glimpsed knowledge of the world of the crow's wingbeat.

He offers a dazzling exception to his own rule about the power of the poet to express in words the reality of some kinds of experience. And yet the rule remains valid: there are kinds of experience that cannot be expressed fully in words; but although some kinds of reality defy the most painstaking linguistic exactitude, there are few kinds of reality that cannot be expressed effectively or adequately in words. That is, although poets cannot create the verisimilitude of all kinds of reality, they can create a recognizable impression of most kinds of reality. And there are occasions when poets achieve what Hughes says is impossible.

A poet's subject is often an aspect of external physical reality – Shelley's skylark, Keats' nightingale, Hardy's thrush, Hughes' first hawk in *The Hawk in the Rain* (Hughes 1957: 11) and his later sparrow hawk in *Wolfwatching* (Hughes 1989: 1); Heaney's sedge-warbler in 'Serenades' (Heaney 1998: 72); and the great aviary in the work of the most observant of British bird-watching poets, John Clare, notably in the sequence grouped as *Poems about Birds* in (Clare 1975: 211-17). Perching, nesting, fluttering and singing through Clare's poems are blackcap, crane, crow, cuckoo, fern-owl (nightjar), jay, skylark, missel-thrush (mistle thrush) and song thrush, nightingale, pewit (peewit or lapwing), reedbird (reed-warbler), robin, snipe, starnell (starling), teal, widgeon, wild duck and wren.

Birds fly equally brightly through twentieth-century American poetry. Among the best known are Wallace Stevens' 'Thirteen Ways of Looking at a Blackbird' (Stevens 1965: 43-6) and his parakeets in 'The Bird with the Coppery, Keen Claws' (Stevens 1965: 37); Robert Frost's whippoorwills in 'Ghost House' (Frost 1951: 25) and 'A Nature Note'(Frost 1951: 396); Marianne Moore's three fledgling mockingbirds in 'Bird-Witted' (Moore 1981: 105-6). Other distinctive bird poems include Theodore Roethke's 'The Heron' and 'The Siskins' (Roethke 1968: 14, 146); Elizabeth Bishop's 'Roosters' and 'Sandpiper' (Bishop 1991: 35, 131); Richard Wilbur's caged birds in 'Marché aux Oiseaux' and his mixed flock in 'All These Birds', (Wilbur 1988: 269,

296); Richard Eberhart's 'Ospreys in Cry', 'Tree Swallows' and 'Hoot Owls' (Eberhart 1960: 218, 205-6, 206-9). Randall Jarrell's bright birds include his surrealist fantasy, 'The Black Swan', the ventriloquial 'The Mockingbird', the owls in 'The Bird of Night' and the Aesopic 'The Owl's Bedtime Story.' (Jarrell 1971: 54, 281 313 348)

This little survey is clearly incomplete; its aim is to summarize ways in which poets can realize, make real, the subject with such particularity of detail and luminosity of vision that the reality represented in the poem can, for the reader, be more imaginable and more intelligible than the same reality in its natural context. A sighting in a poem can be clearer than a sighting in the field. Heaney recognizes this experience when he writes in the title essay in *Government of the Tongue* (Heaney 1988: 93): "The poet is credited with a power to open unexpected and unedited communications between our nature and the nature of the reality we inhabit". Poets have an even greater power: the power to create the artistic illusion that they see into the life of things, the power, that is, of imaginative participation, or what psychologists sometimes call projective identification. And because a poem is also a work of artistry and craft, the reality in a poem can seem superordinate to the reality it represents. Reality is transmuted, intensified and clarified by the poet's imagination and then encapsulated in the finished poem.

Howard Nemerov expresses these poetic faculties in his essay, 'Attentiveness and Obedience' in *Poets on Poetry*. He writes of changes in his concepts of language, poetry and reality, and he concludes: (Nemerov 1966: 241) "The second change is harder to speak of; it involves a growing consciousness of nature as responsive to language or, to put it the other way, of imagination as the agent of reality". That observation is similar to two of Wallace Stevens' many aphorisms in 'Adagia' that relate the outer world of nature with the inner world of mind: (Stevens 1982: 170) "In the world of words, the imagination is one of the forces of nature" and (Stevens 1982: 179) "The imagination is the liberty of the mind and hence the liberty of reality".

Modern poets' understanding of the working of the mind is certainly no deeper than Shakespeare's and no keener than Donne's, but our concept of mind is different. Apart from what they might take from the findings of neuroscience, poets know that mind is the source of all emotion, thought and language, and that their poems are composed in the human mind and not the mind of a God or gods. Knowledge of the reality of the mind allows poets to discuss the two orders of reality, the inner and the outer, with a new confidence.

Wallace Stevens' knowledge takes the form of belief based on his own understanding of the workings of mind. In 'The Noble Rider and the Sound of Words' he writes: (Stevens 1971: 976) "The subject matter of poetry is not 'that collection of solid, static objects extended in space' but the life that is lived in the scene that it composes; and so reality is not that external scene but the life that is lived in it". In order to write a poem, the poet must reject the claims that true reality exists only in the external world, and that the world of the mind is either unreal or is a secondary, lesser reality. We know that mind is the source of poetry, and that external reality cannot be represented in a poem, cannot even be known, until it has been recognized by the mind. The life that is lived in the external scene is the poet's interpretation or re-creation of that scene; that is, it is the life of the poet's imagination. Stevens goes on to express the interaction of inner and outer reality in these terms: "It is an interdependence of the imagination and reality as equals". (Stevens 1971: 977) By "reality" Stevens means external reality. He adds: "It is not only that the imagination adheres to reality, but, also, that reality adheres to the imagination and that the interdependence is essential". The interdependence is also the inner interdependence and interaction of the poet's creative impulse and creative imagination; his imagination gathers real people, real places, real events and allows him to understand them and then to express his understanding of these realities in poetry.

Hughes, a celebrant of the natural living forms of external reality, writes in 'Learning to Think' in *Poetry in the Making* of the primacy of the inner world of the mind: (Hughes 1994: 16) "There is the inner life, which is the world of final reality, the world of memory, emotion, imagination, intelligence, and natural common sense, and which goes on all the time, consciously or unconsciously, like the heart beat". But to argue the primacy of mind over external reality or the primacy of mind over body is pointless; and in a later discussion, 'Myth and Education', also published in *Winter Pollen*, Hughes recognizes that the mind is not, as he previously claimed, "the world of final reality" and that it is essential for the poet to reconcile inner and outer reality. He writes: (Hughes 1994: 51)

> The inner world, separated from the outer world, is a place of demons.
> The outer world, separated from the inner world, is a place of meaning-
> less objects and machines. The faculty that makes the human being out
> of these two worlds is called divine.

The word, "divine", leads the reader to think momentarily that Hughes
is suggesting a theistic force, but in his next sentence he explains:

> That is only a way of saying that it is the faculty without which hu-
> manity cannot really exist. It can be called religious or visionary. More
> essentially, it is the imagination which embraces both outer and inner
> worlds in a creative spirit.

Most poems, of course, take account of the outer world of physical real-
ity and the inner world of the poet's thoughts and feelings; most poems,
then, are representations of both orders of reality. In addition, a poem as
a work of art and a linguistic structure is a reality in its own right.

# 19

# Reading Poetry

## Poetry and the Reader

A POEM IS, AMONG OTHER THINGS, A RECORD of some of the answers poets hear when they interrogate the poetic self. When they submit the poem for publication, poets know that the editor and any subsequent readers will pass some kind of judgment on the poem and may also, if only fleetingly and intuitively, judge the self it reveals. Some young poets, and older poets at a crisis in their career, fear the risk of exposure; if their poems are rejected, or if a published collection receives hostile reviews, or no reviews, the poets might feel a deep sense of personal rejection. For these reasons some poets almost involuntarily assume an attitude of anxious resentment towards the uncertainties of publication and reviews.

Writing to John Hamilton Reynolds in April 1818, Keats declares: (Keats 1952: 129) "I have not the slightest feel of humility towards the Public – or to anything in existence, – but the eternal Being, the Principle of Beauty, and the Memory of great Men". For Keats, the eternal being is not God or Christ but the spirit of poetry, traces of which, he dares to think, he finds in himself. The principle of beauty, too, is eternal, a sacred ideal. He feels that he is a participant in that ideal when he reads the poetry of great men, especially his intellectual and spiritual companions, Shakespeare and Chatterton; and sometimes when he writes, Keats himself is the presence. In the same paragraph in the letter to Reynolds, Keats continues: "but a Preface [to *Endymion*] is written to the Public; a thing I cannot help looking upon as an Enemy, and which I cannot address without feelings of Hostility".

The function of a preface is to allow writers to introduce themselves as well as their work. For Keats, the poetic self is a sublime but not a theistic state of being, and a poem is a record of an experience of a sublime order of reality. He knows that if he is to write a truthful poem, he must reveal his innermost self and his sacred ideals, but to say these things in prose to what he sees as an unregenerate public would be so stark an exposure of his poetic self that it might feel like self-betrayal. In the same paragraph in the same letter to Reynolds Keats continues:

> If I write a Preface in a supple and subdued style, it will not be in character with me as a public speaker – [a published poet] I would be subdued before my friends, and thank them for subduing me – but among Multitudes of Men – I have no feel of stooping, I hate the idea of humility to them.

Although Keats might have been subdued when he met his friends in person, when he speaks to them in his letters he reveals the most intimate workings of his creative imagination. To say intimate things in a letter to a friend is to share a confidence; to say intimate things in public might seem mawkishly confessional. Keats is not an innately or habitually hateful man; the hostility he expresses in the letter to Reynolds is a defensive persona he assumes for some of the reasons outlined above. A more specific reason emerges indirectly from the Preface he was so reluctant to write. The third paragraph reads: "About a twelvemonth since, I published a little book of verses; it was read by some dozen of my friends who lik'd it; and some dozen whom I was unacquainted with, who did not". That is, his collection, *Poems by John Keats*, published in 1817, did not catch the public's attention and was a commercial failure. *Endymion*, he feared, might suffer the same fate.

Writing in August 1819 to his friend and publisher, John Taylor, Keats redirects his hostility. He feels humility when confronted by genius but expresses contempt for the contemporary literary scene: (Keats 1952: 372)

> Just so much as I am humbled by the genius above my grasp, am I exalted and look with hate and contempt upon the literary world – [...] Who would wish to be among the commonplace crowd of the little-famous – who are each individually lost in a throng made up of themselves?

And then, as if sensing that his words might seem like self-pity, he adds: "This is not wise – I am not a wise man – Tis Pride". He is aware of the great gulf between the grandeur of his cause, part of which is to win a place among the writers of genius, and the indignity, the near-futility, of the struggle for recognition, a struggle that is perfectly expressed in words as valid today as they were in 1819: "the commonplace crowd of the little-famous – who are each individually lost in a throng made up of themselves". There is, perhaps, an element of self-disgust in his hate and contempt: he longs for fame, and is ashamed of the ambition; he longs for fame but fears he is one of the lost among the little-famous.

Keats' hostility can again be partly explained by events. When *Endymion* was published in 1818, both poem and poet were ridiculed by John Gibson Lockhart in the August edition of *Blackwood's Edinburgh Magazine*, reprinted in *Critics on Keats*: (Keats 1967: 9) "His Endymion is not a Greek shepherd, loved by a Grecian goddess; he is merely a young Cockney rhymester, dreaming a phantastic dream at the full of the moon". Fame and the little famous – today, Lockhart is remembered mainly as the man who wrote that review of Keats. "Tis Pride," Keats says apologetically to Taylor, and there is an element of injured vanity in the letter; but a public humiliation, however unjust, can leave a deep hurt in the mind of the young aspiring poet, or any poet whose aspiration is unrealized. A day after his angry letter to Taylor, Keats writes again to Reynolds and says: (Keats 1952: 374)

> The more I know what my diligence may in time probably effect; the more does my heart distend with Pride and Obstinacy – I feel it is in my power to become a popular writer – I feel it is in my strength to refuse the poisonous suffrage of a public. [...] The Soul is a world of itself and has enough to do in its own home.

The wounded vanity of the previous day has been replaced by a proper pride; he writes with a renewed self-confidence and new awareness of the need for obstinacy, that is, a persistence that defies the ridicule of reviewers and the indifference of the public. And what he says about the sufficiency of the soul sounds like his reconciliation with himself and his re-affirmation of the cause. But his belief that he can become a popular writer contradicts his rejection of the public, because he cannot, of course, become popular unless he attracts large numbers of readers. Here and elsewhere in his letters Keats is thinking of a future readership and a posthumous fame. Writing to his brother and his sister-in-law, George and Georgiana Keats in October 1818, he says: (Keats 1952: 231) "I think I shall be among the English poets after my death".

## The Poet as Reader

Keats was so attentive and receptive a reader that sections of the poems he read became imprinted in his memory and were quoted spontaneously in his letters. He was so receptive, in fact, that he temporarily abandoned *Hyperion* because, he wrote in a letter to Reynolds, (Keats 1952: 384) "there were too many Miltonic inversions in it". It was the intensity of his response as a reader that impelled him to write the poems in celebration of Homer, Chaucer, Spenser, Shakespeare, Burns, Chatterton, and Byron. There is poetic justice, then, in the fact that Keats himself is the subject of one of the great formal elegies in English poetry, Shelley's 'Adonais'. Keats' poems on poets are, of course, eulogistic; he shows a more balanced and independent critical judgement in his letters when he briefly discusses Chaucer, Milton, Chatterton, Wordsworth, and Byron. And the letters show the kind of relationship, the interaction of minds, that can exist between the poet and the reader.

Keats is aware that the reader's enjoyment and understanding of a poem depend on his recognition of the experience in the poem. Writing to Reynolds on 3 May 1818, Keats refers to Wordsworth's poetry and observes: (Keats 1952: 140-1)

> In regard to his genius alone – we find what he says true as far as we have experienced and we can judge no further but by larger experience – for axioms in philosophy are not axioms until they are proved upon our pulses. We read fine things but never feel them to the full until we have gone the same steps as the Author.

He is referring to different kinds of experience. In the act of reading poetry, or even thinking about poetry, Keats sometimes became so excited that the experience of reading was physical as well as mental; he felt the truth of poems – not their rhythms but the truth of the experiences in the poems – being proved, quite literally, on his pulse. Experience is also our understanding of events in our own life and the lives of others, an understanding of ourselves and other selves; that is, experience is knowledge that has been transmuted by memory and imagination into understanding.

Mentally and figuratively we go "the same steps as the Author". If we have not or cannot go the same steps, we might still be able to apprehend the general experience in the poem and also enjoy the experience of the poem as a work of art. But we cannot have the sensation of the full meeting of minds that Keats refers to in his letter to Taylor in February 1818, when he says that the poem: (Keats 1952: 107) "should strike the Reader as a wording of his own highest thoughts, and appear almost a Remembrance". The "almost a Remembrance" experience has already been discussed in an earlier chapter, but the experience can bear this further interpretation. Readers and poets alike have experiences, perhaps large areas of experience, including the life of the mind, that are unresolved because they have not become part of our fully assimilated experience. We also have more coherent bodies of experience that have been assimilated but have never been transduced into words or even into fully conscious thought. Part of the assimilation process involves encoding the event for memory. As we follow the developing experience in a poem, we sometimes find – instantaneously, or gradually, or retrospectively – that the poet's words represent our own experience so closely that his words seem like a formulation of our own experience. The experience is ours but the words are the poet's. We cannot have thoughts that are exactly like Keats', or any other poet's, until the poet has done that particular bit of thinking for us. The poet's structured sequences of thought and feeling give shape to the reader's inchoate thoughts and feelings; the poet's words utter themselves in the reader's mind almost as if the words were emerging from the reader's memory and are "almost a Remembrance".

Coleridge's comment on that kind of mental process seems too deliberate and too negative. In Chapter XIV of *Biographia Literaria*, he recalls his contribution to *Lyrical Ballads*, and he states: (Coleridge 1956: 168-9)

it was agreed that my endeavours should be directed to persons and characters supernatural, or at least romantic; yet so as to transfer from our inward nature a human interest and a semblance of truth sufficient

> to procure for these shadows of imagination that willing suspension of
> disbelief for the moment, which constitutes poetic faith.

Perhaps Coleridge is merely assuming an authorial modesty in saying that his poems were merely "shadows of imagination". But whether his word, "willing", means a conscious act of will by the reader or merely the reader's unquestioning acceptance of the poem seems irrelevant; if the reader finds the experience in the poem to be imaginable and thus imaginatively true, then there is no disbelief to be suspended.

If the reader is to enjoy and understand a poem, then the working of the mind in the act of reading must have some features in common with the working of the poet's mind in the act of creating. Even so, the acts of reading and writing a poem are so different that one can give only partial agreement to Laura Riding's claim in her Introduction to the later editions of her *Collected Poems*: (Riding 1991: 406) "The reasons for which poems are read ought not to be very different from the reasons for which they are written". The main reason for writing a poem is to realize the creative impulse through the transforming power of the creative imagination, a process that can be demanding and occasionally disturbing because the poet has to extend the imagination in order to transduce unpredictable, sometimes intractable, nonconscious information into consciousness, and then transform the conscious information into a work of art. The main reasons for reading a poem are the pleasure of discovering truths of the human condition and thus truths about oneself, and the pleasure to be found in the poet's artistry and craft. The reader does not need a creative impulse or even a fully creative imagination in order to enjoy these features.

Wordsworth in his Preface to *Lyrical Ballads* repeatedly states that his main purpose in publishing poetry is to give pleasure; and, as the chapter, 'Emotion in Poetry', has shown, Wordsworth experiences pleasure when writing poems: "in describing any passions whatsoever, which are voluntarily described, the mind will, upon the whole, be in a state of enjoyment". Coleridge found composition an ordeal, but he, too, states that the reader's aim is pleasure. In chapter XIV of *Biographia Literaria* he writes: (Coleridge 1956: 173) "The reader should be carried forward, not merely or chiefly by the mechanical impulse of curiosity, or by a restless desire to arrive at the final solution; but by the pleasurable activity of mind excited by the attraction of the journey itself". Pleasure can be gained from a first reading of a poem, but the pleasures of recognition and understanding become possible only after several readings, because a well-made poem usually contains more than can be apprehended in a single reading: subject and theme, the particular experience in the poem, diction and its connotations, the presence of rhythm, rhyme and other musical effects, the ideational figures created by ideas and images, the nature of the poet's voice and vision, the overall structure of the poem, and the layers of meaning. Although we cannot apprehend all these things at once, we respond almost automatically to two vital components in a poem. Our minds are designed to detect the emotional and moral content in any account of human experience; and the language centres of our minds spontaneously decode writing and speech into meaning. In effect, we begin to interpret, and perhaps enjoy, a poem on a first reading, but we get a fuller pleasure and understanding only with the familiarity that comes after several readings.

Eliot discusses the question of readers in the *Idea of a Christian Society*. He states: (Eliot 1939: 38) "We write for our friends – most of whom are also writers – or for our pupils – most of whom are going to be writers". One of Eliot's pupils, John Betjeman, was later to be a British poet laureate. Eliot adds: "or we aim at a hypothetical popular audience which we do not know and which perhaps does not exist". At the time of writing, 1939, Eliot could not have known that his poetry and criticism would be widely read, that his verse drama, *Murder in the Cathedral*, first performed in 1935, would continue to attract audiences into the twenty-first century, or that his volume of light verse, *Old Possum's Book of Practical Cats*, also published in 1939, would be adapted as the musical, *Cats*.

For Spender the act of reading is a reciprocal sacrament. In an entry for January 1980 in his *Journals 1939-83* he says of reading: (Spender 1992: 399) "It is the passive, receptive side of civilization without which the active and creative would be meaningless. It is the immortal spirit of the dead realized within the bodies of the living. It is sacramental".

## The Critic as Reader

The general reader is likely to read poetry reviews in the press and perhaps in poetry magazines, but he or she is less likely to read the work of academic literary critics, some of whom pursue a kind of understanding that is divorced from the pleasure of poetry, and from the practice of it.

Academic jargon reflects academic orthodoxies, and a prevailing orthodoxy is intolerant of other thoughts and modes of thought. F. R. Leavis reflects an older and more open approach to criticism when he writes in 'Literary Criticism and Philosophy' in *The Common Pursuit*: (Leavis 1962: 212) "By the critic of poetry I understand the complete reader: the ideal critic is the ideal reader". The ideal critic could, perhaps, be a complete reader in the sense that he might be able to make a comprehensive, exhaustive analysis of a poem, but that kind of ability would not make him the ideal reader. The ideal critic is the creative critic whose concern is to liberate the meanings of the poem and at the same time to reveal the kinds of pleasure to be gained from the meanings and from the poem as a work of art.

Edwin Morgan states that the poet-critic is more likely to fulfil that role than the critic who is not a creative writer. In 'Creator and Critic: Jekyll and Hyde' in *Nothing Not Giving Messages* Morgan writes: (Morgan 1990: 237)

> it is a notable fact that most of our best critics have also been creative writers: Dryden, Johnson, Coleridge, Arnold, Eliot, Pound. And even below that rank of critics, Pope, Wordsworth, Shelley, Keats and Yeats have all contributed a great deal to both criticism and creative writing.

Morgan's case is persuasive, although we could question the inclusion of Pound, whose prescriptions and proscriptions are sometimes gratuitous and have a negative rather than a liberating effect. We could question, too, the omission of Edwin Muir, whose *The Structure of the Novel* in 1928, *Scott and Scotland* in 1936, *Essays on Literature and Society* in 1949 and *The Estate of Poetry* in 1962 contain much wisdom.

Morgan himself gives a unique account of the mental processes involved in reading, creating and re-creating a literary work. In 'The Translation of Poetry' in *Nothing Not Giving Messages* he writes: (Morgan 1990: 233)

> I can only assume that the brain has recorded a pattern of impulses which by their nature were only partly verbal in origin, and that in the process of organising the discrete impulses of the poem into an intelligible unit the brain transforms them into its own language, a language of

nervous or electrical energy; and that the poem the brain stores, the de-verbalized foreign poem, is in some way made accessible to the transla-tor, who proceeds to reverbalize it into his own tongue. Without trying to be mystical, I believe there does seem to be some sense (and it is a sense unlocked not even by the devoted critic – only by the translator, who is committed to an *action* in a way that the critic is not) in which the poem exists independently of the language of its composition.

A translator is, of course, both reader and writer, and some of the mental processes that Morgan attributes exclusively to the translator are expe-rienced by the reader, and others are experienced by the poet in the act of composition. Morgan's account is a rare attempt to understand the neurophysiological states that are involved in language generating and language processing; and despite his disclaimer, the process is mystical in that it reveals a mysterious dimension of mind.

If, as a preceding paragraph suggested, the ideal critic is one who reveals the meanings and the kinds of pleasure to be gained from a poem, then A. C. Bradley, I. A. Richards, F. R. Leavis and Lionel Trill-ing, none of them poets, are ideal critics. Trilling published a novel, *The Middle of the Journey*, in 1947, but he is essentially a critic. Through their understanding of the creative process and the mind of the creative writer, Bradley, Richards, Leavis, and Trilling are ideal mediators be-tween the creative writer and the reader, because they, as creative crit-ics, are also ideal readers.

## Poet and Reader

Received opinion states that the "I" of the poet corresponds with the "you" of the reader. Spender, for example, writes in 'Short History of Pers. Pron. 1st Sing. Nom.' in *The Struggle of the Modern*: (Spender 1963: 139-40) "for the 'I' is the connecting link between the poet him-self and the responsive personal consciousness of the reader. One can-not write 'I' in a poem without assuming a relationship with a *thou* who reads it". That is certainly the logical and common-sense relationship between the writer and the reader, but it does not represent the way in which we actually read a poem. In reading a poem, or a short story or a novel or a newspaper report, we usually adopt the narrative viewpoint, or the rhetorical viewpoint, of the writer; that is, the reader sees what the writer sees, and sees it in the writer's terms.

There are exceptions, of course: the reader might find the poet's voice or vision unconvincing, or the poem's subject or theme too trivial; but even on these occasions most readers, at least on a first reading, adopt the poet's rhetorical viewpoint. Indeed, on a first reading of a poem no other viewpoint is available to the honest reader. But in the act of reading, the reader is more than an observer; as we progressively decode the text, we are the agency that makes the text work. What Spender calls "the responsive personal consciousness of the reader" is, to the reader, not a "you" or a "thou" but an "I". When the reader identifies with the poet in these ways, the relationship is more than "I" and "you"; it is the "I" of the poet and the "I" of the reader.

Later in 'Short History of Pers. Pron. 1st Sing. Nom.' Spender partly modifies his view when he writes: (Spender 1963: 135) "When the writer and reader belong to a community which provides as it were a continuous context of values and beliefs enclosing them both within the same symbolic referents, then the 'I' is also 'we', and 'thou' and 'he'". Even this statement does not represent the actual relationship between the poet and the reader. Common values and beliefs can certainly create a bond, but one can read and enjoy Coleridge without accepting his belief in the supernatural, Hopkins without sharing his form of Roman Catholicism and Graves without sharing his faith in the White Goddess. The bond between poet and reader begins when the reader adopts the poet's rhetorical viewpoint, and that bond is strengthened if the poet's imagination as revealed in the poem activates the reader's imagination so that the act of reading is a minor re-enactment of the poet's act of creating. When the reader identifies with the poet to that extent, the relationship is, once again, the "I" of the poet and the "I" of the reader.

On some occasions, when the reader suspends his or her identity and imaginatively assumes the identity of the poet, then there can be a merging of identities in the mutual "I" of poet and reader. Wallace Stevens understands the relationship when he states in 'Adagia': (Stevens 1982: 158) "The poet seems to confer his identity on the reader". If the act of reading is a minor re-enactment of the poet's act of creating, then the reader's recognition of the experience in the poem completes the cycle of creativity and confirms the truth of that experience and the truth of the poem.

# Bibliography

Abercrombie, Lascelles 1926. *The Theory of Poetry.* London

Adams, Hazard (ed.) 1971. *Critical Theory since Plato.* San Diego, New York, Chicago

Aitchison, a, James 1988. *The Golden Harvester: the Vision of Edwin Muir.* Aberdeen

1990. *Second Nature.* Aberdeen

1998. *Brain Scans.* Edinburgh

Aitchison, b Jean. 1998. 'The Media are Ruining English' in *Language Myths.* Laurie Bauer and Peter Trudgill (eds). London

Aitken, Conrad 1966. 'Poetry and the Mind of Modern Man' in *Poets on Poetry.* (ed.) Howard Nemerov. New York and London

Ames, Lois and Sexton, Linda Gray (eds). 1977. *Anne Sexton: A self-portrait in Letters.* Boston

Aristotle 1955. *Poetics.* London

Arnold, Matthew 1903. *The Poetical Works of Matthew Arnold.* London and New York

1865. *Essays in Criticism.* London

1888. *Essays in Criticism.* Second Series. Leipzig

Atwood, Margaret 2002. *Negotiating with the Dead.* London

2005. *Curious Pursuits.* London

Auden, W. H. 1950. *Collected Shorter Poems 1930-1944.* London

1977. *Collected Longer Poems.* London

1963. *The Dyer's Hand.* London

1968. *Secondary Worlds.* London

Barry, Peter 2009. *Beginning Theory.* Manchester and New York

Barthes, Roland 1984. *Mythologies.* London

1988. 'The Death of the Author' in *Modern Criticism and Theory.* (ed.) David Lodge. London and New York

Bauer, Laurie and Trudgill, Peter (eds). 1998. *Language Myths.* London and New York

Berryman, John 1968. *Selected Poems 1938-1968.* London

Bishop, Elizabeth 1991. *Complete Poems.* London

Blake, William 1956. *The Poetical Works of William Blake.* (ed.) John Sampson. London and New York

Blonsky, Marshall (ed). 1986. *On Signs.* Oxford

Bodkin, Maud 1951. *Archetypal Patterns in Poetry: Psychological Studies of Imagination.* London and New York

Bold, Alan 1988. *MacDiarmid: A Critical Biography.* London

Bradley, A. C. 1909. *Oxford Lectures on Poetry.* London

Brooker, Peter with Selden, Raman and Widdowson, Peter 1997. *A Reader's Guide to Contemporary Literary Theory.* Hemel Hempstead

Brooks, Cleanth 1971. 'Irony as a Principle of Structure' in *Critical Theory Since Plato.* San Diego, New York, Chicago

Browning, Robert 1903. *The Poetical Works of Robert Browning.* London

Burns, Robert 1950. *The Poetical Works of Robert Burns.* (ed.) J. Logie Robertson. London and New York

Byron, George Gordon (Lord) s.d. *The Poetical Works of Lord Byron.* Edinburgh

Campbell, Roy 1959. *Collected Poems of Roy Campbell.* London

Caplan, David 1992. *Language: Structure, Processing and Disorders.* Massachusetts

Carney, Edward 1998. 'English Spelling Is Kattastroffik' in *Language Myths.* Laurie Bauer and Peter Trudgill (eds). London

Carruthers, Peter 1998. *Language, thought and consciousness: An essay in philosophical psychology.* Cambridge (U.K.)

Cavalli-Sforza, Luigi Luca 2000. *Genes, People and Languages.* London and New York

Chaucer, Geoffrey 1897. *The Canterbury Tales* in *The Student's Chaucer.* (ed.) Walter W. Skeat. Oxford

Chomsky, Noam 1976. *Reflections on Language.* s.l.
2006. *Language and Mind.* Cambridge (U.K.) and New York

Clare, John 1975. *John Clare: Selected Poems.* J. W. Tibble and Anne Tibble (eds). London and New York

Claxton, Guy 2005. *The Wayward Mind.* London

Coleridge, Samuel Taylor 1993. *Poems.* (ed.) John Beer. London
1956. *Biographia Literaria.* London and New York
1951. *Essays and Lectures on Shakespeare.* London and New York
2002. *Coleridge's Notebooks: A Selection.* (ed.) Seamus Perry. Oxford
1988. *Samuel Taylor Coleridge: Selected Letters.* (ed.) H. J. Jackson. Oxford and New York

Cruse, Alan 2004. *Meaning in Language: An Introduction to Semantics and Pragmatics.* Oxford and New York

Crystal, David 1998. *Language Play.* London and New York

2005. *How Language Works.* London and New York

cummings, e. e. 1960. *Selected Poems 1923-58.* London

Curtiss, S. 1977. *Genie: a psycholinguistic study of a modern-day wild child.* New York

Damasio, Antonio 1999. *The Feeling of What Happens.* London

　2003. *Looking for Spinoza.* London and New York

Darwin, Charles 1988. *The Origin of Species by Means of Natural Selection.* London

　1981. *The Descent of Man and Selection in Relation to Sex.* Princeton

　1998. *The Expression of the Emotions in Man and Animals.* London

Davie, Donald 1967. *Purity of Diction in English Verse.* London

Dawkins, Richard 1999. *Unweaving the Rainbow: Science, Delusion and the Appetite for Wonder.* London

　2006. *The God Delusion.* London

Day Lewis, C. 1954. *Collected Poems of C. Day Lewis.* London

　1944. *A Hope for Poetry.* Oxford

　1947. *The Poetic Image.* London

　1957. *The Poet's Way of Knowledge.* Cambridge (U.K.)

　1965. *The Lyric Impulse.* London

Day-Lewis, Sean 1980. *C. Day-Lewis: An English Literary Life.* London

Dennett, Daniel C. 1991. *Consciousness Explained.* London and New York

　1995. *Darwin's Dangerous Idea: Evolution and the Meanings of Life.* London and New York

　1996. *Kinds of Minds: Towards an Understanding of Consciousness.* London and New York

　2004. *Freedom Evolves.* London and New York

　2005. *Sweet Dreams: Philosophical Obstacles to a Science of Consciousness.* Cambridge (U.S.A.)

Dickinson, Emily 1982. *Collected Poems of Emily Dickinson.* Mabel Loomis Todd and T. W. Higginson (eds). New York

Donald, Merlin 2001. *A Mind So Rare: The Evolution of Human Consciousness.* New York and London

Donne, John 1957. *The Poems of John Donne.* (ed.) Sir Herbert Grierson. London and New York

Doolittle, Hilda (H. D.) 1980. *End to Torment: a Memoir of Ezra Pound by H. D.* Norman Holmes Pearson and Michael King (eds). Manchester

Dryden, John 1956. *The Poems of John Dryden.* (ed.) John Sargeaunt. London and New York

1950. *Dramatic Poesy and Other Essays*. London and New York

2009. *The State of Innocence and Fall of Man*. Google eBook

Dunbar, Robin 1996. *Grooming, Gossip and the Evolution of Language*. London

Dunn, Douglas 1981. in *Viewpoints*. London

Eagleton, Terry 2008. *Literary Theory: An Introduction*. Oxford and Cambridge (U.S.A.)

Eberhart, Richard 1960. *Collected Poems 1930-1960*. London

1966. 'How I Write Poetry' in *Poets on Poetry*. (ed.) Howard Nemerov. New York

Eliot, T. S. 1958. *Collected Poems 1909-1935*. London

1955. *Four Quartets*. London

1950. *The Sacred Wood: Essays on Poetry and Criticism*. London

1955. *T. S. Eliot: Selected Prose*. (ed.) John Hayward. London

1933. *The Use of Poetry and the Use of Criticism*. London

1939. *The Idea of a Christian Society*. London

1948. *Notes Towards the Definition of Culture*. London

1970. *For Lancelot Andrewes*. London

1935. *Murder in the Cathedral*. London

1942. *Old Possum's Book of Practical Cats*. London

1988. *The Letters of T. S. Eliot: Volume I 1898-1922*. (ed.) Valerie Eliot. London

Eliot, Valerie, (ed.) 1988. *The Letters of T. S. Eliot: Volume I 1898-1922*. London

Elmes, Simon 2005. *Talking for Britain: A Journey through the Nation's Dialects*. London

Emerson, Ralph Waldo s.d. *The Complete Prose Works of Ralph Waldo Emerson*. London

Empson, William 1984. *Seven Types of Ambiguity*. London

Flint, F. S. 1972 in Imagist *Poetry*. (ed.) Peter Jones, London

Forman, Maurice Buxton (ed.) 1952. *The Letters of John Keats*. London

Foster, Don 2000. *Author Unknown*. London and New York

Foucault, Michel 1988. 'What Is an Author?' in *Modern Criticism and Theory*. (ed.) David Lodge. London and New York

Frazer, James George 1950. *The Golden Bough: a Study of Magic and Religion*. London

Freud, Sigmund 1920. *A General Introduction to Psychoanalysis*. London

1971. 'Creative Writers and Day-Dreaming' in *Critical Theory since Plato*.

San Diego, New York, Chicago

1979. *The Freud/Jung Letters*. William McGuire and Alan McGlashan (eds). London

1937. *New Introductory Lectures on Psychoanalysis*. London

1961. *Civilization and its Discontents*. New York

1939. *Moses and Monotheism*. London

2005. *Sigmund Freud: The Unconscious*. (ed.) Mark Cousins. London and New York

Freund, Philip 1964. *Myths of Creation*. London

Frost, Robert 1951. *The Complete Poems of Robert Frost*. London

Frye, Northrop 1973. *The Anatomy of Criticism*. Princeton

Fuller, Roy 1985. *New and Collected Poems*. London

1971. *Owls and Artificers*. London

1973. *Professors and Gods: Last Oxford Lectures on Poetry*. London

Gardner, Howard 1985. *Frames of Mind: The Theory of Multiple Intelligences* s.l.

Gascoyne, David 1988. *Collected Poems 1988*. Oxford and New York

Gawain Poet *Sir Gawain and the Green Knight*. 1925. J. R. R. Tolkien and E. V. Gordon (eds). Oxford

Ginsberg, Allen 1985. *Collected Poems 1947-1980*. Harmondsworth

Glück, Louise 1986. in *Contemporary American Poetry*. (ed.) Helen Vendler London and Boston

Graves, Richard Perceval 1995. *Robert Graves and the White Goddess 1940-1985*. London

Graves, Robert 1975. *Collected Poems*. London

1948. *The White Goddess: A Historical Grammar of Poetic Myth*. London

1959. *The Crowning Privilege*. London

1967. *Poetic Craft and Principle*. London

2002. *Survey of Modernist Poetry*. with Laura Riding. Manchester

Gray, Thomas 1955. *Gray's Poems, Letters and Essays*. London and New York

Grieve, Christopher Murray see MacDiarmid, Hugh

Gunn, Thom 1993. *Collected Poems*. London and Boston

1981. in *Viewpoints*. London

Hardy, Thomas 1991. *The Complete Poems of Thomas Hardy*. (ed.) James Gibson. London

Harrison, Tony 1984. *Selected Poems*. Harmondsworth

Heaney, Seamus 1969. *Death of a Naturalist*. London

1981. in *Viewpoints* (ed.) John Haffenden

1991. *Seeing Things*. London and Boston

1998. *Opened Ground: Poems 1966-1996*. London

1988. *Government of the Tongue*. London

2002. *Finders Keepers: Selected Prose 1971-2001*. London

2008. *Stepping Stones: Interviews with Seamus Heaney*. (ed.) Dennis O'Driscoll. London

Herbert, George 1863. *The Poetical Works of George Herbert*. (ed.) Charles Cowden Clarke. Edinburgh and London

Hill, Geoffrey 1981. in *Viewpoints*. London

1985. *Collected Poems*. London

Hobsbaum, Philip 1996. *Metre, Rhythm and Verse Form*. London and New York

Hollander, John 1991. *Types of Shape*. New Haven and London

Hopkins, Gerard Manley 1967. *The Poems of Gerard Manley Hopkins*. W. H. Gardner and N. H. Mackenzie (eds). London and New York

Horace 1955. *The Art of Poetry* in *Aristotle's Poetics and Rhetoric*. London

Housman, A. E. 1955. *The Collected Poems of A. E. Housman*. London

1939. *The Name and Nature of Poetry*. Cambridge

1961. *A E Housman: Selected Prose*. (ed.) John Carter. Cambridge

Hughes, Ted 1957. *The Hawk in the Rain*. London

1989. *Wolfwatching*. London

1993. *Shakespeare and the Goddess of Supreme Being*. London

1994. *Winter Pollen*. (ed.) William Scammell. London and Boston

Huizinga, Johan 1970. *Homo Ludens: A Study of the Play Element in Culture*. London

Itard, Jean 1972. *The Wild Boy of Aveyron*. London

James, William 1983. *The Principles of Psychology*. Cambridge (U.S.A.)

1982 *The Varieties of Religious Experience*. New York

1975. *Pragmatism*. Cambridge (U.S.A.) and London

Jamison, Kay Redfield 1993. *Touched with Fire: Manic-Depressive Illness and the Artistic Temperament*. New York and London

Jarrell, Randall 1971. *Randall Jarrell: The Complete Poems*. London and Boston

Jones, Peter (ed.) 1972. *Imagist Poetry*. London

Jones, Steve 1993. *The Language of the Genes*. London

Jonson, Ben 1951. *Timber* or *Discoveries* in *The Great Critics: an Anthology of Criticism*. James Harry Smith and Edd Winfield Parks (eds). New York

Jung, C. G. 1971a. 'On the Relation of Analytical Psychology to Poetry' in *Critical Theory since Plato*. (ed.) Hazard Adams. San Diego, New York, Chicago

1946. *Psychological Types*. London and New York

1970. *Modern Man in Search of a Soul*. London

1964. *Answer to Job*. London

1971b. *Memories, Dreams, Reflections*. (ed.) Aniela Jaffé. London

Kant, Immanuel 1971. 'Of the Faculties of Mind that Constitute Genius' in *Critique of Judgment* in *Critical Theory Since Plato*. San Diego, New York, Chicago

Keats, John 1879. *The Poetical Works of John Keats*. London

1952. *The Letters of John Keats*. (ed.) Maurice Buxton Forman. London

1967. *Critics on Keats*. (ed.) Judith O'Neill. London

Keyes, Sidney 1945. *The Collected Poems of Sidney Keyes*. (ed.) Michael Meyer. London

La Drière, James Craig 1975. 'Prosody' in The Princeton Encyclopedia of Poetry and Poetics. (ed.) Alex Preminger. London

Lacan, Jacques 1986. 'Sign, Symbol, Imaginary' in *On Signs*. (ed.) Marshall Blonsky. Oxford

1988. 'The insistence of the letter in the unconscious' in *Modern Criticism and Theory*. (ed.) David Lodge. London and New York

Lamb, Charles s.d. *The Works of Charles Lamb*. (ed.) Charles Kent. London, Manchester and New York

Larkin, Philip 1988. *Collected Poems*. (ed.) Anthony Thwaite. London and Boston

1983. *Required Writing: Miscellaneous Pieces 1955-1982*. London and Boston

2001. *Further Requirement: Interviews, Broadcasts, Statements and Book Reviews*. (ed.) Anthony Thwaite. London

Lawrence, D. H. 1933. *Fantasia of the Unconscious*. London

Leavis, F. R. 1963. *New Bearings in English Poetry*. Harmondsworth

1978. *The Common Pursuit*. Harmondsworth

Lehrer, Jonah 2012. *Imagine: How Creativity Works*. Edinburgh

Lentricchia, Frank 1994. *Modernist Quartet*. Cambridge (U.K.)

Leonard, Tom 1984. *Intimate Voices*. Newcastle upon Tyne

Lerner, Laurence 1960. *The Truest Poetry*. London

Levertov, Denise 1992. *New & Selected Essays*. New York

Levitin, Daniel 2007. *This Is Your Brain on Music*. London

Lewis-Williams, David 2004. *The Mind in the Cave: Consciousness and the Origins of Art.* London

Lockhart, John Gibson 1967. in *Critics on Keats.* (ed.) Judith O'Neill. London

Lodge, David, (ed.) 1988. *Modern Criticism and Theory.* London and New York

Lowell, Robert 1970. *Notebook.* London

Malson, Lucien 1972. *Wolf Children.* London

McCully, C. B. 1994. (ed.) *The Poet's Voice and Craft.* Manchester

MacDiarmid, Hugh 1985. *The Complete Poems of Hugh MacDiarmid.* Michael Grieve and W. R. Aitken (eds). Harmondsworth and New York

McGlashan, Alan and McGuire, William (eds). 1979. *The Freud/Jung Letters.* London

McGuire, William and McGlashan, Alan (eds). 1979. *The Freud/Jung Letters.* London

MacLeish, Archibald 1935. *Poems.* London

MacNeice, Louis 1966. *The Collected Poems of Louis MacNeice.* (ed.) E. R. Dodds. London

Martin, Graham Dunstan 1975. *Language, Truth and Poetry.* Edinburgh

Marvell, Andrew 1901. *The Poems of Andrew Marvell.* (ed.) G. A. Aitken. London

Mascaró, Juan 1965. (ed.) *The Upanishads.* Harmondsworth

Middlebrook, Diane Wood 1991. *Anne Sexton: A Biography.* London

Miller, Karl 1970 (ed.) *Memoirs of a Modern Scotland.* London

Milton, John 1862. *The Poetical Works of John Milton.* London

Moore, Marianne 1985. *Marianne Moore: Complete Poems.* London

Morgan, Edwin 1968. *The Second Life.* Edinburgh

1984. *Sonnets from Scotland.* Glasgow

1990. *Nothing Not Giving Messages.* Edinburgh

Morris, William 1876. *Story of Sigmund the Volsung and the Fall of the Niblungs.* London

Muir, Edwin 1928. *The Structure of the Novel.* London

1982. *Scott and Scotland.* Edinburgh

1954. *An Autobiography.* London;

1956. *One Foot in Eden.* London;

1991. *The Complete Poems of Edwin Muir.* (ed.) Peter Butter. Aberdeen

1962. *The Estate of Poetry.* London

1966. *Essays on Literature and Society.* London

Nemerov, Howard 1966. 'Attentiveness and Obedience' in *Poets on*

*Poetry.* (ed.) Howard Nemerov. New York

Nye, Robert 1989. *A Collection of Poems 1955-1988.* London

   1995. *Collected Poems.* London

   2012. *An Almost Dancer.* London

   1996. (ed.) *A Selection of the Poems of Laura Riding.* New York

O'Driscoll, Dennis, (ed.) 2008. *Stepping Stones: Interviews with Seamus Heaney.* London

Olson, Charles 1966. 'Projective Verse' in *Modern Poets on Modern Poetry.* s.l.

Owen, Wilfred 1960. *The Poems of Wilfred Owen.* (ed.) Edmund Blunden. London

Parks, Edd Winfield and Smith, James Harry (eds). 1951. *The Great Critics.* New York

Pater, Walter 1907. *The Renaissance.* London

Peacock, Thomas Love 1951. *The Four Ages of Poetry* in *The Great Critics.* James Harry Smith and Edd Winfield Parks (eds). New York

Persinger, Michael 2009. *Skeptiko.* http://www.skeptiko.com

Pinker, Steven 1994. *The Language Instinct.* London and New York

   1998. *How the Mind Works.* London

   1999. *Words and Rules: The Ingredients of Language.* London

   2008. *The Stuff of Thought.* London and New York

   2011. *The Better Angels of Our Nature.* London and New York

Plath, Aurelia Schober 1975. (ed.) *Sylvia Plath: Letters Home – Correspondence 1950-1963.* London

Plath, Sylvia 1965. *Ariel.* London

   1972. *The Colossus.* London

   1971a. *Winter Trees.* London

   1971b. *Crossing the Water.* London

Plato 2001. *Ion* in *Selected Dialogues of Plato.* (ed.) Hayden Pelliccia. New York

   1956. *The Republic.* (ed.) H. D. P. Lee. Harmondsworth and Baltimore

Poe, Edgar Allan 1858. 'The Poetic Principle' in *The Poetical Works of Edgar Allan Poe.* London

   1997. *Eureka: A Prose Poem.* New York

Pope, Alexander 1930. *The Poetical Works of Alexander Pope.* (ed.) Adolphus William Ward. London

Pound, Ezra 1959. *Ezra Pound: Selected Poems.* (ed.) T. S. Eliot. London

   1951. *A B C of Reading.* London

1953. *The Translations of Ezra Pound*. London

1966. 'Credo' in *Modern Poets on Modern Poetry*. s.l.

Preminger, Alex 1979. (ed.) *Princeton Encyclopedia of Poetry and Poetics*. London and Princeton

Putter, Ad 1996. *An Introduction to the Gawain-Poet*. London and New York

Raine, Kathleen 1973. *Autobiographies*. London

Ralegh, Walter 1972. *A Choice of Sir Walter Ralegh's Verse*. (ed.) Robert Nye. London

Ramachandran, V. S. 1998. *Phantoms in the Brain*. London

2009. 'The Artful Brain' BBC Reith Lectures 2003

Ransom, John Crowe 1970. *John Crowe Ransom: Selected Poems*. London

Ratey, John 2001. *A User's Guide to the Brain*. London

Reid, Alastair 1970. 'Borderlines', in *Memoirs of a Modern Scotland*. (ed.) Karl Miller. London

Rich, Adrienne 1967. *Selected Poems* London

Richards, I. A. 1925. *Principles of Literary Criticism*. London and New York

1960. *Practical Criticism*. London

1951. *Science and Poetry* in The Great Critics. James Harry Smith and Edd Winfield Parks (eds). New York

1962. *Coleridge on Imagination*. London

1977. *Complementarities: Uncollected Essays*. (ed.) John Paul Russo. Manchester

Riding, Laura 1991. *The Poems of Laura Riding*. Manchester

1996. *A Selection of the Poems of Laura Riding*. (ed.) Robert Nye, New York

2002 with Graves, Robert. *A Survey of Modernist Poetry*. Manchester

Rimbaud, Arthur 1973. *A Season in Hell* and *The Illuminations*. London and Oxford

Roethke, Theodore 1968. *Collected Poems of Theodore Roethke*. London and Boston

Ryle, Gilbert 1990. *The Concept of Mind*. London

Sacks, Oliver 2011. *Musicophilia: Tales of Music and the Brain*. London

Scott, Walter 1897. *The Poetical Works of Sir Walter Scott*. London and New York

Selden, Raman, Widdowson, Peter and Brooker, Peter (eds). 1997. *A Reader's Guide to Contemporary Literary Theory*. Hemel Hempstead

Sexton, Anne 1981 *The Complete Poems: Anne Sexton*. Boston

Sexton, Linda Gray and Ames, Lois (eds). 1977. *Anne Sexton: A self-portrait in Letters*. Boston

Seymour-Smith, Martin 1982. *Robert Graves: His Life and Work*. New York

Shakespeare, William 1986. *The Sonnets and a Lover's Complaint*. (ed.) John
　　Kerrigan. London and New York

Shelley, Percy Bysshe 1945. *The Complete Poetical Works of Percy Bysshe
　　Shelley*. (ed.) Thomas Hutchinson. London New York

　　1956. *A Defence of Poetry* in *English Critical Essays: Nineteenth Century*.
　　(ed.) Edmund D. Jones. London

Sidney, Philip 1979. *Sir Philip Sidney: Selected Poems*. (ed.) Katherine
　　Duncan-Jones. Oxford

　　1947. *An Apology for Poetry*. (ed.) J. Churton Collins. London

Sitwell, Edith 1982. *Collected Poems*. London

　　1943. *A Poet's Notebook*. London

　　1998. *Selected Letters of Edith Sitwell*. (ed.) Richard Greene. London

Smart, Christopher 1984. in *The New Oxford Book of Eighteenth-Century
　　Verse*. (ed.) Roger Lonsdale. Oxford and New York

Smith, Iain Crichton 1981. in *Viewpoints*. London

Smith, James Harry and Edd Winfield Parks (eds). 1951. *The Great Critics:
　　an Anthology of Criticism*. New York

Spark, Muriel 2004. *All the Poems*. Manchester

Spender, Stephen 1955a. *Collected Poems*. London

　　1953. *The Creative Element*. London

　　1955b. *The Making of a Poem*. London

　　1963. *The Struggle of the Modern*. London

　　1974. *Love-Hate Relations: A Study of Anglo-American Sensibili
　　ties*. London

　　1975. *Eliot*. London

　　1992. *Journals 1939-83*. London

Spenser, Edmund 1952. *The Poetical Works of Edmund Spenser*. J. C.
　　Smith and E. De Selincourt (eds). London

Stevens, Wallace 1965. *Selected Poems*. London

　　1971. 'The Noble Rider and the Sound of Words' in *Critical Theory Since
　　Plato*. San Diego, New York, Chicago

　　1982. *Opus Posthumous*. New York

Storr, Anthony 1960. *The Integrity of the Personality*. Harmondsworth

　　1976. *The Dynamics of Creation*. Harmondsworth

　　1986. *Jung*. London

　　1992. *Music and the Mind*. London

Swift, Jonathan 1967. *Swift: Poetical Works.* (ed.) Herbert Davis. London and New York

Swinburne, Algernon Charles 1884. *Tristram of Lyonesse.* London

Szirtes, George 1986. *The Photographer in Winter.* London
1988. *Metro.* Oxford and New York

Tennyson, Alfred 1881. *The Works of Alfred Tennyson.* London

Thomas, Dylan *Dylan Thomas: Collected Poems 1934-1952.* London
1966. 'Notes on the Art of Poetry' in *Modern Poets on Modern Poetry.* (ed.) James Scully. s.l.

Thomas, R. S. 1955 'Cynddylan on a Tractor' in *Song at the Year's Turning.* London

Todorov, Tzvetan 1981. *Introduction to Poetics.* Brighton

Traherne, Thomas 1966. *Thomas Traherne: Poems, Centuries and Three Thanksgivings.* (ed.) Anne Ridler. London and New York

Trilling, Lionel 1970. *The Liberal Imagination.* Harmondsworth

Trudgill, Peter and Bauer, Laurie (eds). 1998 *Language Myths.* London and New York

Tusa, John (ed.) 2004. *On Creativity.* London

Vendler, Helen (ed.) 1986.*Contemporary American Poetry.* London

Wain, John 1977. *Professing Poetry.* London

Walcott, Derek 1986. *Derek Walcott: Collected Poems 1948-1984.* New York
1988. *The Arkansas Testament.* New York and London

Whitman, Walt 1987. *Walt Whitman: The Complete Poems.* (ed.) Francis Murphy. Harmondsworth and New York

Widdowson, Peter, Selden, Raman, and Brooker, Peter (eds). 1997. *A Reader's Guide to Contemporary Literary Theory.* Hemel Hempstead

Wilbur, Richard 1989. *New and Collected Poems: 1930-1960.* London and Boston
1966 'On My Own Work' in *Poets on Poetry.* (ed.) Howard Nemerov. New York and London

Williams, William Carlos 1988. *The Collected Poems of William Carlos Williams.* A. Walton Litz and Christopher MacGowan (eds). London
1969. *Selected Essays.* New York
1966 'A New Measure' in *Modern Poets on Modern Poetry* (ed.) James Scully s.l.

Winfield, Edd (ed.) 1951. *The Great Critics: an Anthology of Criticism.* New York

Winston, Robert 2003. *The Human Mind.* London

Wittgenstein, Ludwig 1974. *Tractatus Logico-Philosophicus.* London

    1972. *Philosophical Investigations.* Oxford

Woolf, Virginia 1942. *The Death of the Moth.* London

Wordsworth, William 1956. *The Poetical Works of Wordsworth.* (ed.) Ernest
    De Selincourt. London and New York

    1984. *The Letters of William Wordsworth.* (ed.) Alan G. Hill. Oxford and
    New York

    1925. *Wordsworth's Literary Criticism.* (ed.) Nowell C. Smith. London

Yeats, W. B. 1961. *The Collected Poems of W. B. Yeats.* London

    1971. 'The Symbolism of Poetry' in *Critical Theory since Plato.* San
    Diego, New York, Chicago

    1964. *Letters on Poetry from W. B. Yeats to Dorothy Wellesley.* Oxford and
    New York

    1972. *W. B. Yeats Memoirs: Autobiography and Journal.* (ed.) Denis
    Donoghue. London

    1970. *The Ten Principal Upanishads* (with Shree Purohit Swami). London

# Index of Names

# Index of Topics